Dudley Lev

The Methodists in Ireland

A SHORT HISTORY

the columba press

First published in 2001 by
the columba press
55A Spruce Avenue, Stillorgan Industrial Park,
Blackrock, Co Dublin

Cover by Bill Bolger
The cover picture is *Wesley Preaching under a Tree in Ireland* by Maria
Spilsbury (1777-1820). The figures in the crowd include members of the
artists's family and people associated with the Tighe Estate at Rosanna
near Ashford in Co Wicklow. It was painted c. 1815.
Reproduced by permission of the Managing Trustees of Wesley's
Chapel, City Road, London.

Origination by The Columba Press
Printed in Ireland by Colour Books Ltd, Dublin

ISBN 1 85607 335 1

Contents

Acknowledgements   7

Foreword   8

PART I: INTRODUCTION

1. The Historic Background   12
2. The Wesleys   16
3. The Methodist Contribution   22

PART II: THE CONNEXIONS

4. In Wesley's Time   26
5. After Wesley   46
6. Methodism Divided   63
7. The Methodist Church in Ireland   81
8. Under Two Jurisdictions   104
9. Structures   125
10. Smaller Connexions   134

PART III: PREACHERS AND PEOPLE

11. The Life of the Preachers   144
12. Circuit Life   163

PART IV: SOCIAL CONCERNS

13. Education   180
14. Poverty and Suffering   201
15. Manners and Morals   216

PART V: IRISH METHODISTS OVERSEAS

16. Emigrants and Missionaries   230

PART VI: CONCLUSION

17. And so on …   248

Appendix   253
Sources and Notes   259
Select Bibliography   265
Index   268

Acknowledgements

The idea that I should write this book was first mooted many years ago, and it would be quite impossible to adequately thank all those who have assisted and encouraged me. I hope I will be forgiven if I name only a representative few.

First I must express my warm thanks to Risteard Ó Glaisne who continued to encourage me through the years as I changed my mind about its shape and and purpose. I am grateful to the Wesley Historical Society, and the Old Dublin Society who provided me with the opportunity of publishing papers exploring various aspects of the subject, and to those whose reactions obliged me to justify or revise my conclusions. At one time or another I have been greatly assisted by Charles Benson of Trinity College Library, Maire Kennedy of the Gilbert Library and Gerard Whelan-Horring of the Royal Dublin Society Library. The staffs of the National Library, and the Registry of Deeds in Dublin, and of several County Libraries also deserve my thanks. My main resource has been the invaluable collection of the Wesley Historical Society. There I am most grateful to Marion Kelly and Robin Roddie.

My thanks are also due to the Rev Dr William Marshall of the Church of Ireland Theological College, and to Basil McIvor for their willing assistance with my somewhat off-beat questions.

I must express my particular thanks to Edmund Mawhinney for his Foreword, and to Robin Roddie, David Bolton and Seán O Boyle, who from different perspectives read my first drafts, and made most helpful suggestions and comments. I have incorporated most, but not all. For the final judgements in this book and for its weaknesses I must take full responsibility.

Foreword

The publication of this short history of the Methodists in Ireland is both welcome and timely. There is a need to inform a new generation, Methodists among them, of the story of this denomination which, although comparatively small, has had a significant impact on Irish society. However, older Methodists and many from the wider community will find this account both interesting and informative,

The Rev Charles H. Crookshank's *History of Methodism* in three volumes was regarded as the standard work of the history of Methodism in Ireland. The record ended in 1859. The Rev R. Lee Cole who, like the present author, was President of the Irish Branch of the Wesley Historical Society at the time, brought the story to 1960 in his *History of Methodism In Ireland – One Methodist Church.* Earlier, in 1931, a number of contributors presented a series of papers on such themes as Missions, Education, Social Service, Theology, Rural Life and Political Changes, which were published under the title *Irish Methodism in the Twentieth Century.* In 1964 Mr Fred Jeffery wrote his book, *Irish Methodism: An Historical Account of its Tradition, Theology and Influences.* These and others have enhanced our knowledge of the story of the people who are the followers of John Wesley

The story of the origin of the Church and its subsequent history is crowded with incident and is rich in the characters who helped to shape its story. Like all Churches, Methodism has its faults and has made mistakes, and we are made aware of them in these pages. It is a Church, however, which has always sought to combine a deep perception of spiritual religion with a concern for social issues, which continues in the witness of the

Church today. Sometimes that concern has heen expressed in an adventurous application of gospel values to daily life. Methodism has also tried to express a true catholic spirit, claiming to be 'the friends of all and the enemies of none'. The position of the Church in this respect was clearly set out in a statement adopted by the Annual Conference on the matter of Inter-Church Activity. 'It does not imply that each participating Church accepts all that the others believe. It does not imply that they are actively attempting to "sink differences" and reach a "common denominator". It does imply that each accepts the sincerity and contribution of the others, that all believe that God has a purpose and will for his Church, that each is trying sincerely to discover and do that will, and that each denomination is part of the Body of Christ.' Methodism has an important part to play in the universal Church of Christ. Irish Methodism may not be numerically large, but it is part of a Methodist family in 90 countries in the world, and the contribution of Irish Methodism to the World Church has been significant.

The publication of this book will provide a useful resource in the task of informing members of the Methodist Church of the history of their own denomination from its roots in England and formation in Dublin in 1745. However, the book is clearly intended for a much wider readership among those who belong to other Christian traditions and none, and will provide interesting information as to who Methodists are and what they have done. These pages contain many interesting facts and insights, remind us of the record of those who have served in previous generations, and relates the contribution of Methodism to social and community life in Ireland

Recent years have witnessed a welcome growth in relationships and inter-church co-operation among churches in Ireland. In an atmosphere of increasing ecumenical contact, many are involved in a new learning experience as they meet in church and community groups and undertake study courses. In such contacts there is a growing interest in the need to be better informed about the history, customs and practices of the various religious

traditions. In religious education courses in schools young people are learning about other churches. Those undertaking such
studies frequently ask for information about the Methodist
Church. I believe that the record and inspiration in the pages of
this very readable and interesting account of Methodism in
Ireland will prove to be a valuable resource and contribute to increased mutual understanding and respect.

Rev Dudley Levistone Cooney has provided us with an informative and interesting book. He has a wide knowledge of
Methodism in Ireland, having worked in several areas of the
country. His interest and enthusiasm for history are infectious,
as any who have listened to his lectures and talks on historical
topics, or read his contributions in historical journals, can confirm. As a convinced Methodist who has a deep interest in history
and who wants to share that with others, it has been his wish for
some time to write the record as we have it in these pages, and
we are in his debt. After earlier disappointment, I am very
pleased that this work is now being published and made available to a wider readership.

I welcome this book. It deserves to be widely read.

Edmund T. I. Mawhinney
Secretary of the Methodist Church in Ireland

PART I

Introduction

CHAPTER 1

The Historic Background

The Methodist Church, which at the time of writing numbers over seventy million adherents throughout the world,[1] owes its origin to the work of the Rev John Wesley in England during the second half of the eighteenth century.

There were two significant features of life in England at the time which contributed to Wesley's success. The first was the aftermath of the religious conflict of the previous century – the Cromwellian wars. These had not only divided the English nation, they had divided communities, and even families. The settlement of the English church after the Reformation was intended to ensure that this sort of internecine conflict would never happen again. It was the Age of Enlightenment in Europe, and from the Enlightenment the English church learned its strategy. It accepted the traditional sources of Christian orthodoxy, the Bible and tradition, but was also very strongly influenced by reason. This was the opposite to feeling and emotion and was at the very heart of Enlightenment philosophy.

The antithesis of reason was enthusiasm, and this became one of the major fears of the English church at the time. It could inflame people to fanaticism, and plunge the country again into religious strife. That could all be avoided if people would only be reasonable about their faith. The fear of enthusiasm lay behind much of the opposition to Methodism in its early years. However, the trouble with reasonable religion was that it could, and did, degenerate into a general philosophy, where all that was required was reasonable decency, and the spiritualities of the church were neglected.

That the Church of England was at a spiritually low ebb during most of the eighteenth century is beyond doubt, with Deists prominent among its leaders, absenteeism rife among its parochial clergy, and its parish system failing to meet the vast social changes taking place. That, however, must not be thought to be the whole picture. The spirituality of the church was kept alive in places where there were conscientious bishops and godly rectors. The pity was that there were not more of them. However, there were lay people prepared to take initiatives which they hoped would balance the neglect.

The late years of the seventeenth century and the first half of the eighteenth saw the rise of the religious societies, not as alternatives to the church, but as organised bodies of people within it. Some of these were directed to specific objects, and have survived to the present day. Such were the Society for the Propagation of Christian Knowledge (SPCK) founded in 1698, and the Society for the Propagation of the Gospel in Foreign Parts (SPG) founded in 1701. The former is still an important publishing house, and the latter in 1965 joined with the Universities Mission to Central Africa to form the United Society for the Propagation of the Gospel (USPG). The majority of the societies, however, were of more personal concern, and shorter lived.

These were groups of men and women, some quite large and more quite small in number, who met regularly to foster their own spirituality by Bible study, prayer, and sermons. The usual factors of fading enthusiasm, migration and death of members, and internal disputes certainly contributed to their decline, but probably more significant was that in the latter half of the century many of those who might have formed such societies were being recruited into the Methodist organisation.

In religious terms John Wesley was working at a period when some people were becoming increasingly aware of the need to revive a real and practical religion in England, and were willing to do something about it. It has sometimes been suggested that the evangelical revival of the eighteenth century was created by Wesley. It was not. He emerged as the most permanently significant leader of it, but he did not originate it.

The other factor which assisted Wesley was the immense social upheaval of the period. Much has been written about the agricultural revolution, and more about the industrial revolution, but it is not easy to separate their effects. On the one hand the improvement of agricultural methods, replacing the old rundale fields by enclosed farms, the rotation of crops, the careful breeding of livestock, and the development of new machines, made it possible to increase food production, and therefore feed a larger population. On the other hand it reduced the number of people holding land, and created a new class, the agricultural labourer. But there was not now enough agricultural work to employ those who would have worked on the land, and those who could not find employment were driven to seek it in the growing industrial towns.

The invention of power spinning by Sir Richard Arkwright, the spinning jenny by James Hargreaves, and the spinning mule by Samuel Crompton in the 1760s and 1770s made possible the development of the spinning mill, and the village weaver with his loom in one room of his cottage gave way to the mill hand in the burgeoning industrial cities of the north of England. Josiah Wedgwood was doing something similar to the making of pottery as he developed his china factories in the midlands. These developments demanded power and communication, so that coal mines, iron foundries, canal and road building prospered. It was all of these which created the new class of industrial labourer.

The vast increase in population in industrial areas placed an enormous strain on the parish system, geared as it was to smaller agricultural communities. The labourers became, to use a modern term, unchurched. They did not have the manners or the fine clothes to make them acceptable to the fashionable church goers. It was the realisation of this which made the Methodist preachers go to them. What has come to be called 'field preaching' in Methodism, actually took place in market squares, on village greens, in friendly barns, or at crossroads, as well as in fields. In short, Wesley and his preachers would address any crowd, wherever it might be gathered.

Many of these labouring people responded with enthusiasm to the message that God was concerned about them, and that there was a place for them in his mercy. In its English origins Methodism was essentially a working class movement. And that is somewhat surprising when you consider who Wesley was.

CHAPTER 2

The Wesleys

In the year 1662 the re-establishment of the Church of England was effected by the Act of Uniformity, which required all of the clergy to affirm their 'unfeigned consent and assent' to everything contained in the Book of Common Prayer. Two thousand clergy refused to do so, and in what came to be called the Great Ejectment were obliged to leave their parishes. Among them were one John Wesley, who was vicar of Winterborne Whitechurch, and Dr Samuel Annesley, who was vicar of St Giles, Cripplegate in London. Both embarked on the difficult and dangerous career of dissenting ministers. Wesley died after a few years, but Annesley lived to become one of the leaders of dissent in the city

Wesley had a son, Samuel, born in the year of his ejectment, and Annesley's 25th child was a daughter, Susanna. Both children inherited something of the independence of mind which marked their fathers, but in their case it led them back into the Church of England. Samuel was ordained to the priesthood in 1689, and within a year had married Susanna Annesley. Through the patronage of the Marquess of Normanby he was appointed to the living of South Ormsby in Lincolnshire, and his patron even went so far as to recommend him for an Irish bishopric. This proposal came to nothing thanks to the opposition of John Tillotson, the Archbishop of Canterbury, and in 1697 Samuel Wesley moved to the rectory in Epworth, where he was to spend the rest of his life. Epworth was the one small town in the Isle of Axholme, still isolated in the North Lincolnshire fens in those years before drainage schemes made the area somewhat more accessible.

Samuel and Susanna Wesley had nineteen children, of whom ten grew to adulthood, three sons and seven daughters. All three of the sons were to become priests of the Church of England. The fourteenth child was the second surviving son, who was given the name John after his grandfather, and after two elder brothers neither of whom had survived birth for more than twelve months. This John was born in 1703.[1] The seventeenth child was also a son, and was given the name Charles, which had not been used in the family before. He was born towards the end of 1707. The education of the girls and the early education of the boys was very largely conducted by their mother, with some lessons in Latin and Greek from their father. This was certainly because no one else in the village was sufficiently qualified to do so, and the Wesleys were too poor to employ a tutor. Samuel was so incapable of managing his very small income as to spend some time in a debtor's prison. However, they did manage to afford the visits of a dancing master to the rectory, chiefly for the purpose of teaching the children deportment.

Samuel Wesley was not a popular rector, striving to correct the laxity of his parishioners with a stern discipline which they resented, and more than once his property was set on fire. In 1709 it was the rectory itself which was torched, and on this occasion the six year old John was only rescued from the blaze at the very last minute. This led Susanna to the conviction that God had a special purpose for the boy, and she devoted more time and care to his spiritual formation than to that of any of the other children.

In 1714 the erstwhile Marquess of Normanby, now advanced to the dignity of Duke of Buckingham, nominated John to a place in the Charterhouse School, where he seems to have had a satisfactory but undistinguished career. His quite remarkable physical stamina, which lasted throughout his long life, may have been developed by his practice throughout his time in Charterhouse of running around the college garden three times every morning. From Charterhouse he went to Christ Church College, Oxford on an exhibition worth £20 a year. His elder brother had been there before, and Charles would follow after. He took his bachelor's degree in 1725, and in the September of the same year was ordained a deacon. At the end of the year a vacancy arose for a fellowship of Lincoln College, Oxford, and after some uncertainty he was unanimously elected. He was ordained to the priesthood in the September of 1728.

He was given some years leave of absence to serve as his father's curate at Wroot, a neighbouring parish which had recently been added to Epworth, and on his return to take up the duties of his fellowship found that his brother Charles, by now at Christ Church, had formed a small society with some other undergraduates. Meeting in each other's rooms, they studied the Bible and other Christian books. John joined the group, and by seniority and personal charisma, became its leader. Throughout the years of its existence it remained a small society, but it contained in its membership several, such as George Whitfield and Benjamin Ingham, who were to become leaders of the evangelical revival, and John Gambold, who was to become the first English bishop of the Moravian Church. Another member was William Morgan of Dublin, whose father was the Second Remembrancer of the Court of Exchequer in Ireland.

The group began to give expression to their reading by a careful observance of the rules of the church regarding feasts and fasts, and to practise the works of charity, notably the visitation of those who were in prison. Their activities soon attracted the notice of other, unsympathetic undergraduates, who gave them derisive nicknames – Bible Moths, The Holy Club, Methodists. This last title was a jest at the expense of their methodical approach to Christian devotion and charity. It suggested that they relied more on method than on faith. They and their followers later took up the name with some pride, and Methodists today use the title 'The Holy Club' to identify that original group, which was the forerunner rather than the origin of modern Methodism. In the early years the term Methodist was more widely applied than it is at present, and included the followers of George Whitefield, the group which later came to be called the Countess of Huntingdon's Connexion,[2] and the Welsh Calvinistic Methodists who arose from the work of Howell Harris. Each of these, derived from the Holy Club, ultimately chose different spheres and styles of work.

In 1732 General James Oglethorpe obtained a charter to found the colony of Georgia in America. The original colonists included poor people from England, and a number of Moravians from Germany who were seeking a place where they could freely practise their religion. Having failed to increase the numbers and influence of the Holy Club as he would have wished, John Wesley thought that in the new colony, free from the inhibiting traditions of Europe, an ideal Christian community might be developed. Accordingly, in 1735 he accepted Oglethorpe's invitation to go there as chaplain. With him he brought his brother Charles and Benjamin Ingham, both now also ordained, and Charles Delamotte. The experiment was a failure simply because most of the colonists were in Georgia no different from what they had been in England, and in 1738 the disillusioned Wesleys were back in London.

The ship in which they had sailed to America, the *Simmonds* had been caught in a severe storm in mid-Atlantic, and John Wesley had been deeply impressed by the calm behaviour of a group of Moravians on board, not even the children of whom had betrayed any sign of being afraid of death. His own faith was not as confident as that. Through the years in Georgia and on his return to London he maintained contact with Moravian groups, seeking that confidence, and on 24 May in 1738 went, somewhat unwillingly, to one of their meetings, probably that in Nettleton Court off Aldersgate Street. There he had a religious experience which gave him the assurance of salvation which he sought. The event has been called his evangelical conversion, though it was certainly not the sort of first commitment to which evangelical Christians normally apply the word conversion. Whatever it may be called, it revitalised his faith. In his *Journal* he gives as extended account of that day, and the crisis is thus described:

> In the evening I went very unwillingly to a society in Aldersgate Street, where one was reading Luther's preface to the Epistle to the Romans. About a quarter before nine, while he was describing the change which God works in the heart through faith in Christ, I felt my heart strangely warmed. I felt I did trust in Christ, Christ alone for salvation, and an assurance was given me that he had taken away *my* sins, even *mine*, and saved *me* from the law of sin and death.[3]

His brother Charles had had a similar experience three days previously. For the next twelve months John sought a direction for his life, travelling in August to Herrnhut, the Moravian community in Germany, to meet its leader Count Zinzendorf.

Meanwhile George Whitefield, who had been a member of the Holy Club at Oxford, and who had since developed a considerable reputation as an evangelist, was working in the west of England. Never willing to stay too long in one place, he wanted to move on from Bristol, and invited John Wesley to go there and continue the work which he had begun. Wesley arrived on 31 March 1739, and Whitefield left two days later. Within that period he had convinced Wesley by the evidence of what was happening of the value of field preaching. In somewhat quaint language Wesley writes in his *Journal* on Monday 2 April:

> At four in the afternoon I submitted to 'be more vile', and proclaimed in the highways the glad tidings of salvation, speaking from a little eminence in a ground adjoining to the city, to about three thousand people.

Wesley had found his direction. From a dual base of societies in London and Bristol, he began the preaching tours and organisation which gathered Methodist societies throughout England and Ireland, and parts of Wales and Scotland. A strain of quietism was developing among the English Moravians, teaching that the individual should do nothing, not even worship, until moved by God to do it. Wesley was unable to accept this, being convinced that people should positively seek God by attending worship, and engaging in study with Christian groups. It was this which led him to break company with the Moravians.

What sort of a man was Wesley? Physically he was short, being less that five feet six inches in height, and he was lean, but muscular. The most prominent features of his face were an aquiline nose and piercing blue eyes. He wore his hair long and without powder, regarding wigs and powder alike as unnecessary expense. He had a commanding presence. His published sermons make very dry reading, but those who recorded their impressions of his preaching suggest that he had a well modulated voice, and garnished his addresses with stories which made them attractive and compelling.

Religious reformers are often expected to be rather forbidding, but there is ample evidence that Wesley was not. Many people sought and valued his friendship. In 1748, on the occasion of his second visit to Athlone, the Methodists there rode out along the road to meet him. But they were forestalled by a small number of barefooted boys, aged about twelve, who ran ahead of them, determined that they should be the first with their welcome. Twelve year old boys don't do that unless there is something very pleasant about the person they are meeting.

CHAPTER 3

The Methodist Contribution

What did the Methodists offer that held such an appeal for so many people? In essence nothing new. The Methodists held, and still hold, the catholic christian faith expressed in the Nicene Creed, and accept the principal teaching of the Protestant reformers. Wesley inherited the three Anglican sources of authority, scripture, tradition and reason, but to these he added a fourth, experience. He constantly sought to relate Christian doctrine to the lives which people were living. To Wesley scripture was always central, but tradition contributes to its interpretation, and Christian doctrine must always be reasonable and relevant to the present human situation as experienced.

At the immediate impact of this we have already hinted. The Wesleys were convinced that the redeeming love of God was for every person. Charles Wesley was probably the most prolific hymn writer there has been, enabling the Methodists to sing their faith, and to learn it by singing. The word 'all' sounds like a clarion call though many of his hymns, as for instance:

> O for a trumpet voice
> On all the world to call,
> To bid their hearts rejoice
> In him who died for all!
> For all my Lord was crucified,
> For all, for all my Saviour died.[1]

To the working classes of eighteenth-century England, with whom the church had largely lost contact, and who had no vote in the government of the country, the Methodist preachers delivered the liberating idea that each individual was important to God, who offered to him or to her the gift of salvation in Christ.

In that conviction they found a new personal worth. Charles enabled them to sing about that too:

> My God, I am thine;
> What a comfort divine,
> What a blessing to know that my Jesus is mine!
> In the heavenly Lamb
> Thrice happy I am,
> And my heart it doth dance at the sound of his name.[2]

That gift having been accepted, Wesley believed that God by his Holy Spirit began the process of making the person holy, and much of the Methodist organisation was geared to the development of that holiness, as we shall later see. Again Charles puts the idea into verse:

> What is our calling's glorious hope
> But inward holiness?
> For this to Jesus I look up,
> I calmly wait for this.
> I wait, till he shall make me clean,
> Shall life and power impart,
> Give me the faith that casts out sin
> And purifies the heart.[3]

However, Wesley believed that holiness was not only personal, but also social, and needed to be expressed in terms of compassion and service to the needy members of the community. We shall examine the outworking of that in the Irish context, but for the moment we hear Charles once more:

> Help us to help each other, Lord,
> Each other's cross to bear,
> Let each his friendly aid afford,
> And feel his brother's care.[4]

Finally, because few clergy were prepared to work with him, Wesley evolved a system, basically simple in its elements, which allowed the plain people to manage the affairs of the Methodist societies. This has always made great use of lay leadership, and it is interesting to observe that in nineteenth-century England many Methodists brought the organisational skills which they had learned in Methodist meetings to the development of the early trade unions.

Methodism has been very free of heresy trials. There is no formal statement of faith which a member or minister is required to sign at any stage, but ministers are regularly required to affirm that they believe and preach 'our doctrines'. The basis of these doctrines is the Bible, interpreted along the lines set out in Wesley's standard sermons, and his *Notes on the New Testament*. While that has held the church to essentials, it has allowed a measure of difference in interpretation.[5]

PART II

The Connexions

CHAPTER 4

In Wesley's Time

The Ireland to which Methodism first came, Ireland of the eighteenth century, was a very different country from Wesley's England. It underwent no agricultural revolution, and the division of the countryside into a pattern of farms and fields similar to that developing in England had to wait until after the Great Irish Famine in the middle of the nineteenth century. It did not experience an industrial revolution either, and the nearest approach to the industrial centres of the north and midlands of England were the much smaller linen towns of Ulster. At first glance, therefore, it is somewhat surprising that a movement which appealed so strongly to the English working classes should have done as well as it did in Ireland, with so different a social structure.

That social structure had been created by two major conflicts in the previous century. Contemporary with the Cromwellian wars in England, there had been a similar series of conflicts in Ireland when five different parties, each with its own army, sought to control the country, moving in and out of uneasy alliances with each other as fortune smiled or otherwise. Three of these parties were internal – the Gaelic Irish, the Old English Catholics descended from settlers of previous centuries, and the King's party. Two were external, the Scots and the English Parliamentarians. It was these last who won the day, as they had done in England. The victorious Cromwell settled some of the arrears of pay due to the Parliamentarian officers, and the debts due to those who had financed his campaigns by giving them grants of land in Ireland. The previous landlords had their property confiscated for opposition to the Parliamentarians. In many cases their smaller tenants were left undisturbed, though in others English tenants were brought in. The peasants were also undisturbed, being needed to work the land.

In 1689 William III came to the throne in what has sometimes been called by English historians 'the Glorious Bloodless Revolution'. The name is justified by the fact that no blood was shed in England; it was shed in Ireland at Derry, Aughrim, Enniskillen, the Boyne, Newtownbutler, Athlone and Limerick. Again there were officers and financial supporters to be rewarded, and again there were grants of Irish estates. Between the two settlements, Cromwellian and Williamite, about half of the land in Ireland changed ownership. The new owners were Protestants, their descendants being known in later years as the Protestant Ascendancy. They were a community under constant threat.

Looking back from the vantage point of the twenty-first century, we are apt to think of the endurance of this as inevitable, but it was by no means so. The Jacobite risings in Scotland in 1715 and 1745 were the more outstanding evidences of the constant possibility that the Hanoverian kings and the new government in London could be overthrown. Such remained a very real fear in the new establishment until the death of the Old Pretender in 1766 altered the European political climate. The new Irish landlords lived in the additional fear that the dispossessed would rise to reclaim their estates, and for this reason demanded, and imposed, laws designed to maintain political power in their own hands. Remembered chiefly for the disadvantages they imposed on Roman Catholics, they also operated against Dissenters, such as Presbyterians, Quakers and Baptists. The new landlords for the same reason demanded and received the protection of a garrison of between 12,000 and 15,000 troops in barracks throughout the country, drawn from the British regiments.

In 1744 John Wesley called a Conference in London of those few clergy and lay preachers then working with him and this became an annual event, evolving into the governing body of the church. The Conference agenda was formulated in a series of questions to be answered in what was then, because of small numbers, quite informal debate. In the Minutes of the 1746 Conference there are the following question and answer:

> What is a sufficient call of Providence to a new place? Suppose to Edinburgh or Dublin?
>
> A. 1. An invitation from someone that is worthy; from a serious man fearing God, who has a house to receive us.
>
> 2. A probability of doing more good by going thither than by staying longer where we are.

The question indicates that already, within seven years of his commencing work, Wesley was interested in extending it beyond the bounds of England. The answer exemplifies his policy of going nowhere that he could not be assured of a base from which to work, and of willingness to abandon effort that is proving to be fruitless. They are the counterpart of his advice to his preachers, 'Go not to those who need you, but to those who need you most.'

What Wesley did not know was that a Methodist society was already meeting in Dublin.

The British regiments which formed the garrison in Ireland recruited their junior officers from the working classes – the classes which responded most enthusiastically to the Methodist preachers. When these men were posted to Ireland they sought for a Methodist society to give them the support they needed to nourish their own spirituality, and where there was none they sought to establish one. The likelihood is that they first looked to their fellow officers, but they were happy to welcome anyone from the locality who was sympathetic. It was in this way that the first Irish Methodist society came into being in Dublin. In later years officers similarly placed founded or strengthened Methodist societies in places as widely scattered as Galway, Newry, Belturbet, Nenagh, Limerick, Carrickfergus, Arklow, Cashel, Cahir, Mullingar, Charlemont, Carlow and Kilkenny.

The name of the man who formed the first Methodist society in Dublin, and the particular barracks in which it met have, unhappily, not been remembered, but the leadership quite quickly passed into the hands of one Benjamin La Trobe.[1] La Trobe was a Baptist, and had the advantage of having studied at Glasgow, intending to become a Baptist pastor. One of the members of the society was a local merchant named Antisel Tayler, who had spent some time in London, where he had heard John Cennick preaching. Cennick had been one of Wesley's preachers, but had left to join the Moravian church. Tayler persuaded the society to invite Cennick to Dublin in 1746, and under Cennick's influence the society became the original Moravian congregation in Ireland with La Trobe as its pastor. It met in Skinners' Alley.[2]

What happened next is not quite clear. It is possible that one of the other members of the society wrote to Wesley, but no letter survives. In any case Thomas Williams, one of Wesley's preachers arrived in the city early in 1747. He began preaching at Oxmantown Green, and soon formed another Methodist society, drawing some of the members from Skinners' Alley. Williams then wrote to Wesley urging him to come to Dublin in person, and this he did in the August of the same year.

It was on Sunday, 9 August 1747 that John Wesley paid his first visit to Dublin, landing at George's Quay in time to attend morning service in one of the Church of Ireland parish churches, of which he heard the bell ringing. He does not specify the church in his *Journal*, but St Mark's was not then finished, and it was more likely to have been St Andrew's. After the service he met his host and hostess, William and Anne Lunell.[3] Of Huguenot extraction, Lunell was a woollen merchant and banker in Francis Street. It was possibly his friendship which opened the way for Wesley to preach that afternoon in St Mary's church, where the curate was also a Huguenot, Moses Roquier. Roquier was friendly, but the Archbishop of Dublin, Charles Cobbe was not. He was not willing that a field preacher should speak from the pulpits of his diocese. On the Tuesday Wesley rode to Donabate, where Cobbe was building Newbridge House, and spent two or three hours with the archbishop.

Neither persuaded the other. Though four archbishops successively followed Cobbe in office during Wesley's lifetime, he was
never again permitted to occupy a pulpit in the diocese. On the
other hand, of course, Cobbe did not persuade Wesley to go
away. The Dean of St Patrick's, William Cradock, in 1789 treated
him, by then aged and greatly esteemed, with some respect, and
invited him to assist in the administration of Holy Communion,
but not to preach.

For Wesley's meetings Williams had obtained the use of a
former Lutheran chapel on Great Marlborough Street. The building accommodated about four hundred people, and Wesley
estimated that nearly two thousand could stand in the spacious
forecourt. He remained in the city for two weeks, preaching in
the chapel daily, and meeting the society. This numbered nearly
two hundred and eighty members, which was no mean achievement for the short time that Williams had been there. Wesley left
the city on 24 August and returned to England. John Trembath
remained in charge of the work in the city.

Within a couple of weeks a riotous mob attacked the chapel,
tore the wooden wainscotting from the walls, and piled it and
the timber furniture in the forecourt, setting fire to the lot. A
number of the Methodists sustained some injury, and the
women were terrified. Trembath wrote anxiously to Wesley,
'No one is fit to be a preacher here who is not ready to die at any
moment.' Poor Mr Trembath had panicked. In fact there had
long been a fierce rivalry between the butchers' apprentices of
the Ormond Market and the weaver's apprentices of the
Coombe, and this periodically broke out into violence. On this
particular occasion the rioters found the novel amusement of
attacking a group only recently come to the city. It is not at all
certain that there was any animosity to the Methodists in the incident, and the next time the apprentices rioted they found other
prey. We hear no more of such violence against Methodists in
Dublin.

The incident, however, had two positive consequences for
the Methodist work. One was that the letter from Trembath

sufficiently alarmed John Wesley as to persuade him to send his brother Charles to Dublin without delay. Charles came, and is generally credited with calming the frightened society. In fact the members, having more experience of the apprentices, may have calmed without him, but his presence in Dublin from the September of 1747 to the March of 1748, when John returned, was a very considerable strength to the society in the city, and saw the expansion of the work into the Irish midlands. Without his presence that expansion might have been very much slower.

The second consequence was that the owner of the chapel, Mrs Agnes Felster, gave notice to the Methodists to leave, and Wesley was convinced of the need to acquire a freehold premises for their use. That was not so easily achieved, and there was pressure to get an alternative to Marlborough Street without delay. A weaver's shed in Cork Street was leased and adapted, but that was rather far out of town. The chapel in Skinners' Alley which the Moravians were using belonged to the Baptists, whose trustee was Samuel Edwards. Williams appears to have suggested to Edwards that it was worth twice the rent which the Moravians were paying, and that the Methodists would pay the higher figure. When the Moravian lease expired, therefore, Edwards offered it to Wesley. After a lengthy, and somewhat unseemly dispute, the Moravians moved to a premises on what came to be Lower Kevin Street, where they remained happily for more than two hundred years. The Methodists moved into Skinners' Alley, where they remained only until they built a chapel of their own.[4]

During the time that Cennick was preaching there, in one of his occasional emotional outbursts he alluded to 'the Babe wrapped in swaddling clouts'. This phrase was misunderstood by one of his hearers who was probably not as familiar with the Christmas story as he might have been. He dubbed the congregation in Skinners' Alley 'Swaddlers'. The nickname was transferred to the Methodists when they acquired the use of the premises, and travelled to various parts of Ireland. It was even known in the Isle of Man.[5]

The first panic over, Mrs Felster appears to have relented, and the Methodists had further use of the Marlborough Street premises off and on for quite a number of years. The search for a freehold premises was unsuccessful, and in 1752 Wesley compromised by taking a 99 year lease on a site in Whitefriar Street, where the first Methodist chapel in Ireland was built. Subsequent leases of adjoining property enlarged the site to house eventually a widows' almshouse, schools for boys and girls, a bookroom, and residences for two preachers.

In March of 1748 Charles Wesley was set free by the arrival of his brother John in Dublin once more, and returned to England. In August he returned to Ireland for a second, and in the event final, visit to this country, remaining here until October of the same year. After that he gradually withdrew from much of the active Methodist work, settling happily in Bristol. His major contribution to the Methodist cause was his writing of over six and a half thousand hymns, many of which remain in use today. They were noted not only for their remarkable variety of metre, but also for the degree to which they are filled with Biblical allusion. They enabled the Methodist people to sing their doctrine, and singing is the most readily memorable form of repetition.

John continued to come to Ireland, at first annually, and then generally at intervals of two years until 1789, twenty-one visits, in the course of which he spent a total of about five and a half years in this country. His first visit, in 1747, had been confined to Dublin. In 1748 he visited the societies that had been formed in some of the midland towns, and in 1749 he entered Munster for the first time, preaching at Cork, Bandon, Limerick and other places. In 1748 we have the first record of his preaching in Connacht, at Aughrim in Co Galway, but it was his tour of 1756 which first included much of the province, including Galway city, Castlebar, and Tuam. In 1785 he was to lay the foundation stone of a new Methodist chapel in Castlebar, the only building in Ireland for which he performed this service. The building remains, though not in Methodist use. 1756 was also the year in which he paid his first visit to Ulster, preaching at Newry,

Lisburn, Belfast, and other towns.

Wesley in Ireland was not a pioneer; he went where Methodist work had already been commenced by others. We have noted the pioneering work of the army officers in various places. A small amount of pioneering work was done by Methodist families who moved from one town to another in pursuit of their craft or trade, and if there was no Methodist society in the place to which they went, commenced meetings. For the most part pioneering was the work of the preachers. In some places these were invited by a local landlord, who offered them the hospitality of his house, but more often they entered a village or town, found a convenient open space, and preached to whoever would gather to listen, hoping that someone would then offer their house as a base for further development. The hope was frequently fulfilled.

Wesley's work was that of oversight, discipline and encouragment. His coming to any particular town excited more interest that that of the regular preachers, and to accommodate the crowds the largest available building was secured for the occasion. We find him referring in one place or another to the court house, the market house, or the assembly rooms. In the smaller towns the one building served all three purposes, with a simple rearrangement of the furniture. If such a venue was refused, then a convenient place out of doors was found. The market place, an old ring fort, a field, or a friendly barn could be pressed into service. Quite large crowds could be attracted by curiosity to the first meeting in any place, and Wesley's comments are sometimes amusingly perceptive. His first sermon in Dublin was addressed to 'as gay and senseless a congregation as ever I saw'. Once at Aughrim he addressed 'a serious but sleepy congregation'. At Tyrrellspass he spoke to 'a heap of fine, gay [i.e. frivolous] people'. At Cork 'a person hugely daubed with gold thrust violently in'. In Belfast he was heard by a congregation the poorer of whom were attentive, while the rich 'cared for none of these things'. His favourite epithet for an inattentive congregation was 'wild as asses colts untamed', which he used in several places. Their curiosity satisfied, the idle did not return, and his comments on the later gatherings in each place are generally more positive.

We have noted that the attack on the Lutheran chapel in Marlborough Street was probably not an expression of opposition to Methodist work; the attitude of Archbishop Cobbe was more serious. Much of the opposition to Methodists in Ireland was expressed in the form of hostile sermons mostly preached by Church of Ireland clergy, and pamphlets from the same source. Replies had to be made to these, and it is possible that the only people who derived any benefit from the exchange were the printers. George L. Fleury, a curate in the city of Waterford and later Archdeacon of Waterford, published one such attack, describing the Methodists as 'grievous wolves'. In later years he ruefully admitted 'I was a greenhorn then'.

Behind these attacks lay, as we have noted, a certain fear of enthusiasm which might disturb the peace of church and community. There was certainly a resentment of the fact that the mere presence of the Methodists reflected adversely on the zeal or effectiveness of the clergy, and while Wesley never faltered in his affection for and loyalty to the Established Church, not all of his preachers were as tactful. Even Wesley, it must be admitted, while constantly proclaiming his affection for all things Anglican, was quite prepared to bend its rules to suit what he saw as the spiritual needs of the people. In addition to these considerations, there was the fear in the powers that were that a new uncontrolled movement might upset the political balance. That is what made the attitude of the magistrates more serious.

There was generally less anti-Methodist violence in Ireland than in England, and much of what violence there was at the time was incited by a few men in each case, obviously infected by the then widespread fondness for faction fighting. Too often they found encouragement rather than rebuke from the magistrates taking the attitude that the Methodist preachers had started it by preaching out of doors. There were instances where magistrates actively encouraged anti-Methodist violence. Occasionally the hostility of the magistrates descended to the level of farce. When Thomas Walsh went to Clonakilty in 1752, the local magistrate, who was also the local Church of Ireland clergyman, ordered him to cease, and when he declined had him put in prison. A sympathetic crowd gathered outside, and Walsh preached to them through the grated window.

In 1798 Adam Averell arrived to preach in Cloughjordan, and was told that if he did not go away he would be brought before the magistrate. It did not suit the magistrate to hold a court until the following day, and Averell preached that evening and the following morning. Eventually appearing before the magistrate he was ordered to leave the town within twenty-four hours. Bowing to the bench Averell assured him that he did not need as long, as his business required him to leave within the hour!

In 1773 Wesley wrote to his brother Charles:

I have been in two mobs since I came into Ireland, one in the South and one in the North. The Protestant mob was far the worst. But I am still in an *whole skin*. Dum vivimus vivamus.[6]

The Catholic riot in the south was at Waterford on 25 April. He had been preaching on the Bowling Green in the evening, and was just finishing when some trouble makers knocked down several of the people who had been listening. However, a group of gentlemen rushed into the midst of the fray, identifying the ringleader, seized him and handed him over to the constable. Deprived of their leader, the mob soon dispersed.

On 24 May he encountered a Protestant mob at Enniskillen, where some workmen were repairing the bridge by which he entered the town. One of the horses drawing his chaise had cast a shoe, and so he went ahead with only two companions, and was treated to coarse abuse as he rode the length of the main street. The presence of some soldiers restrained the mob from anything worse. When his chaise came it was pelted with stones from one end of the town to the other, severely damaging the vehicle, and it is amazing that the coachman was not hit by any of the missiles.

John Smith, who had pioneered Methodist work in the

Enniskillen area some eight years before, was the subject of several threats and attacks before in 1774 he was waylaid at Aughentain near Clogher while on the way to a meeting at Charlemont. The bailiff of one of the local estates attacked him with a pitchfork, and mauled him so badly that he had difficulty in getting back onto his horse, and it is a matter of amazement that he was able to reach his destination. He died a few days later, the first Irish Methodist martyr. On the day after the Enniskillen riot Wesley heard from John McBurney himself the story of an attack on a house in which he was preaching at Brookeborough, and recorded it in his *Journal.* The account of the attack on McBurney himself is quite horrific. He never quite recovered from his injuries, and lingered in poor health for several years, dying in 1779.[7]

The most sustained persecution endured by Irish Methodists, however, occurred in Cork over a period of fourteen months in 1749 and 1750. It was incited by a ballad monger named Nicholas Butler, who paraded through the city dressed in gown and bands to caricature a preacher, and carrying a Bible in one hand and a sheaf of ballads in the other. Mobs attacked Methodist houses and shops, and refusal of the Mayor of Cork to put any restraint on Butler's activities only encouraged further attacks. The Mayor took the attitude that it was the fault of the Methodists for bringing preachers to the city. The depositions which the Methodists laid before the Grand Jury are transcribed in Wesley's *Journal* under dates 20 July 1749 and 14 April 1750. Property and trade were severely damaged, and people were injured. It is astonishing that none were killed. Butler was using the catch cry 'Five pounds for a Swaddler's head!' The Grand Jury refused to accept the depositions, and charged all the Methodist preachers then in Ireland with disturbing the peace, requesting that they all be transported. Happily the Assize Judge was better advised, and treated the charges with disdain. But neither that nor the attempts of friends to seek assistance from Parliament put an end to the sufferings of the Cork Methodists. Only when the army took an interest, and offered a measure of protection to the preachers did the persecution subside.

The motive behind Butler's commencement of the riots was probably no more than an attempt to gain attention. His persistence and the growth of violence were certainly symptoms of the intoxication of power. Far more deplorable in the episode was the stance adopted by two successive mayors of Cork, and by the members of the Grand Jury, all of whom, of course, were members of the Established Church, and therefore highly sensitive to anything which might prove to be a threat to the *status quo*. That the army took so long to act was due to nothing more than the chance of who happened to be commanding officer at the time.

In the course of his twenty-one visits to Ireland, Wesley visited every county in the country except Kerry and Roscommon. He may actually have entered Roscommon but there is no record of his ever having preached there. How many people he influenced it is not possible to estimate, for the majority of those who heard him were not Methodists and never became Methodists. However, through his work and that of his preachers, especially the latter, in the forty-two years from 1747 to 1789 the membership of Irish Methodist societies rose to just over 14,000. One factor in their success was the sheer novelty of men preaching in the open air. That at least was sufficient to attract a crowd. More important was the fact that it was a religious age. Religious awakening was happening throughout Britain and Ireland, across Europe, and in America. Even those who did not go to church believed in God, and talked about him.

On Wednesday 29 June 1785 Wesley, accompanied by twelve or fourteen friends, travelled from Dublin to Prosperous in a fly boat on the Grand Canal. His is the earliest surviving account of such an expedition. He thought it a most elegant way of travelling, though the shorthand diary from which he later wrote his *Journal,* tells us that he could not complete the whole of the outward journey sitting quietly in the boat. The party left Dublin at seven in the morning, and at eleven Wesley got out of the boat and walked on the towpath until noon before again getting on board for the rest of the journey. They reached Prosperous at a quarter past two. On that journey Wesley estimated that there were between fifty and sixty passengers, and on the return journey next day even more. When they discovered his presence among them, members of both groups invited him to give them a sermon, which he did, and was heard with appreciation. He was, of course, then eighty-two years old and widely respected.

It is hard to imagine passengers on a modern car ferry asking any clergyman among them, however distinguished, to give them a sermon. That is not the temper of our age; it was the temper of Wesley's. Incidentally, it is interesting to note that the distance from Dublin to Prosperous is about thirty miles. That the journey was accomplished in seven and a quarter hours gives an average speed of just over four and a half miles per hour – a normal brisk walking pace. Allowing for the delays at locks, the speed of the boat at any given time must have been even higher. That at eighty-two Wesley could keep up with the boat for an hour says much for the stamina first developed around the garden at Charterhouse more than seventy years before.

The audience on board the fly boat listened to Wesley with appreciation; none of them became Methodists. That would have been true of many of his hearers. It would also have been true of some of those who assisted his work. There were, however, those among the landed gentry in Ireland, such as the Gayers of Derriaghy, the Handys of Coolalough, the Wades of Aughrim, the Boyles of Kirlish Lodge, the Tighes of Rosanna, and the Slackes of Annadale, who were prepared to allow their houses to be used as the base of Methodist work in their neighbourhood.

In 1775 Wesley arrived at Derriaghy suffering from a fever, and lay there semi-conscious for several days. His friends almost despaired of his life, and as the crisis of the fever approached some of them gathered in the drawingroom to pray for his recovery. One was moved to pray that Wesley's life would be spared as was that of King Hezekiah. Suddenly Henrietta Gayer rose from her knees with the comment 'The prayer is granted!' The Bible, in the second Book of Kings, chapter 20, tells of Hezekiah's serious illness, and of his life being extended for fifteen years. Wesley recovered from the fever at Derriaghy, and lived for another fifteen years and nine months.

The families we have named, and others ,provided hospitality for the preachers, and more attended Methodist meetings but not all became members of the societies. They believed that Methodism was good for their tenants; it made them better people, encouraging church-going and industry. They did not necessarily see it as good for themselves, and the Methodism they encouraged was a society within the Established Church. When, a quarter of a century after Wesley's death, the Irish Methodists became a separate denomination, they withdrew their support, or even became hostile. In some cases their present descendants have been astonished to learn that their ancestors had entertained Wesley, the memory having been quite banished from the family.

Most of the gentry, if they came from curiosity to hear Wesley, did no more. To say to the Almighty 'have mercy upon us miserable sinners' in the course of divine worship was all very well. That was the way in which the liturgy required people to address him. However, they did not care to be told that they were sinners in a tone which implied reality.

In the country areas it was from the tenants that the majority of the Methodist members were recruited, and in the towns and cities it was generally the craftspeople and shopkeepers, with a few gentlefolk. Not many membership lists survive from those early days, but those which do reveal few names of old Irish origin. In the course of his 1747 visit to Dublin Wesley stayed at home one Saturday and spoke to all that came. He remarked, 'I found scarce any Irish among them.' He wrote to Ebenezer Blackwell, 'Indeed, all I converse with are only English transplanted to another soil; and they are much mended by the removal, having left all their roughness and surliness behind them'. This was a first impression, but it was not altogether unrepresentative of what was to be the Methodist experience through all of Wesley's time. Members continued to be recruited from the ranks of the more recently arrived English, Scottish, Welsh, French Huguenot, or German families.

Hempton and Hill have shown that the greatest concentration of Methodists in Ireland is to be found in the 'Linen triangle of Ulster' just south of Lough Neagh, and the 'Lough Erne rectangle', which is mainly Co Fermanagh.[8] These were areas where English settlement was strong. Apart from the conurbations of Dublin and Belfast that pattern holds good throughout the country. There was a vigorous Methodist community in West Cork, which was planted in the Elizabethan period, another in North Tipperary, where the Cromwellian settlement created the village of Cloughjordan and developed Borrisokane, and a third in central Limerick where German refugees were settled in 1709. Elsewhere in the rural areas Methodists have tended to be sparse. In the last fifty years they have virtually disappeared from Connacht and the north of Leinster.

The central Limerick community which embraced Methodism with enthusiasm was that of the Irish Palatines, whose parents had come from the Rhenish Palatinate in the west of Germany at a time when war and a severe winter had destroyed the economy there. They were settled on the Southwell estate, establishing the villages of Courtmatrix, Killeheen and Ballingrane. Their most important contribution to Methodist history is something we must examine later.

The failure to make much impression on the Irish people may be explained by political and cultural factors. Wesley and the majority of the early preachers were English, and they were encouraging the members of the Methodist societies to support the Established Church in England and in Ireland. The Irish Catholics may have wondered at them, but they probably regarded their message as directed to their own kind. Again, the preachers were speaking English. Though most understood enough English to deal with their English-speaking neighbours, the first language of many Irish Catholics was Irish, and in that language they customarily thought. The cultural barrier of language was one which Wesley possibly never appreciated.

It was from Dublin in 1749 that he addressed his celebrated *Letter to a Roman Catholic*. In this he irenically advances all those beliefs which he holds dear, and recognises that Catholics hold, and which are the essence of Christian faith. These were the doctrines of the historic creeds and basic moral teaching. He asks to differ on other points, pleading that the difference of opinion may not be seen as barring friendship or tolerance. In recent years his argument has been hailed by at least one commentator as expressing an ecumenism two centuries ahead of its time.

In 1780 he would appear to be taking an opposite view. The Catholic Relief Act of 1778 had provoked Protestant opposition, and in January 1780 Wesley was persuaded to write to the *Public Advertiser* citing the maxim of the Council of Constance, 'No faith is to be kept with heretics', and arguing from this that none could rely on the loyalty of Catholics to a Protestant government. In fact it was not a change of mind; on the first occasion Wesley was talking about religion, and on the second about politics. A Dublin Capuchin, the Rev Arthur O'Leary replied, and a public correspondence ensued. Boswell reckoned that O'Leary got the better of the argument. In one sense he certainly did, for Wesley's Irish friends persuaded Wesley to stay out of Ireland until the matter was forgotten – a period of five years. Later the two men met at breakfast in Cork, and Wesley was pleasantly surprised by the priest.

There were Irish Catholics who joined the Methodist societies, but they were comparatively few. Fewer still became preachers, but two who did had very distinguished careers. The first of these was Thomas Walsh, who was born in Co Limerick. At the age of eight he was sent to school to learn English, having spoken nothing but Irish until then. He later learned Latin from one of his older brothers. Of deeply religious and introspective temperament, his youth was greatly troubled with doubt, and at the age of eighteen he left the church of his birth and joined the Church of Ireland. In the following year he heard the Robert Swindells and Thomas Williams preaching in Limerick, and this led him to form a Methodist society in Pallaskenry, where he was then living and teaching a school of his own. Before long Wesley called him to the work of a preacher. In his enormous enthusiasm he neglected his own well being in the interests of the work. Wesley recognised the brilliance of his mind, saying that he was one of the best biblical scholars he ever knew, but instead of leaving him in Ireland, where his ability to preach in his native Irish would have been a valuable asset, brought him for some years to London. Walsh's refusal to spare himself undermined his health, and he died at Dublin before he was twenty-nine years old. His burial place in the graveyard known as the Cabbage Garden was never marked.[9]

Where the second, John Bredin, was born nobody knows, but he was sufficiently well educated to conduct a school near Cootehill in Co Cavan. The quality of his teaching was destroyed by his fondness for whiskey, and so great was his addiction that when his money was exhausted, he sold his clothes to buy more. Travelling near Cootehill in 1766 John Smith, later to be martyred, found poor Bredin lying in the ditch by the roadside, where he had been all night, totally drunk, and only half clothed. Smith's concern so impressed the poor man that Bredin followed him for several days. His life was changed, and he joined the Methodist society spending much of his time in good works, and doing some preaching in the locality. In 1769 Wesley called him into work as what was then called a travelling preacher, and is now called a minister. For the next twelve years he served in England and Scotland as well as in Ireland. In 1781 his health obliged him to withdraw from official work, but he continued to give whatever help he could in whichever circuit he was living. In Coleraine he made the acquaintance of Adam Clarke, whom he introduced to Wesley, helping to start that remarkable polymath on his distinguished career. Bredin died in 1819 at the age of eighty-two, and is buried in Lambeg churchyard.[10]

In the July of 1756, during his first tour of Ulster, Wesley caused some surprise at Carrickfergus by going to the Sunday morning service in the Church of Ireland. After dinner he was asked if he would go to the Presbyterian meeting, and caused even greater surprise by saying that he never went to such. He comments:

> He [the enquirer] seemed as much astonished as the old Scot at Newcastle, who left us because we were mere Church of England men. We are so, although we condemn none who have been brought up in another way.[11]

In a sense this incident encapsulates Wesley's attitude to all other denominations. He was a priest of the Church of England, and as such expected to attend the services of the Established Church wherever possible. He did not expect to attend those of other denominations; he felt he had no business there.

In and after 1778, when he needed larger premises for his meetings in Ulster, he was happy to make use of Presbyterian premises. They were, quite simply, the largest available in the locality. This he did at Cootehill, Kilrea, Coleraine, Lisburn, Newry (twice), Ballymena, Antrim, Belfast (twice), Rathfriland, Newtownards and Portaferry. His use of the Meeting House at Rathfriland in 1787 represented a change of attitude on the part of his hosts. In 1760 the Presbyterian minister there had written the local Catholic priest warning him to keep his people away from Wesley.[12] Having strongly criticised the Presbyterian Seceders in 1767, he was surprised to be offered the use of their Meeting House at Armagh in 1787, when rain prevented his preaching in the avenue, as he was wont to do when visiting the city.

That small numbers of Presbyterians joined the Methodist societies is probable, though difficult to establish, but it is significant that Methodist societies are sparse in those areas of Ulster where Presbyterianism is strongest.

Among the early supporters of Methodism in Ireland were several members of the Religious Society of Friends or Quakers, then quite strong in the Irish midlands. During his first provincial tour in 1748, Wesley records baptizing seven of them at Aughrim in Co Galway.[13] In that Quakers did not administer the sacraments Wesley viewed their Christian practise as lacking, and was supplying the deficiency. There was no Quaker meeting in Aughrim, and those in question may have been under the oversight of the Ballymurray Meeting in Co Roscommon. Their remoteness from the Meeting may have made them that much more open to outside influence. It may well have been this, and other similar actions on the part of Wesley, which led the Quakers soon to withdraw their support from him.

In 1749 Wesley's hearers in Edenderry were largely Quakers, but he also reported that John Curtis, a Quaker from Bristol, had been counselling them against Methodism. The Quaker archives have no record of a visit by Curtis at the time, but in the February of that year the Edenderry Monthly Meeting had sent for copies of pamphlets by Curtis and William Fisher. Curtis's *Epistle of Love and Advice to Friends of the Kingdom of Ireland* is a general exhortation to the reader to be loyal to Quaker principles. In 1773 Wesley was refused the use of the Quaker Meeting House in Enniscorthy.[14]

The denomination on which the coming of the Methodist had the greatest effect was the Church of Ireland. Given the fact that Wesley saw his societies as an agency within the Established Church, that is hardly surprising. We have already noted the political reasons why his work was viewed with suspicion by some of the Establishment, religious and secular, and the measure of support which he received from some of the gentry. There were several clergy who gave him support too, welcoming him when he came to their parishes. In the main two things, closely related, impressed them. The first was the rise in numbers attending the services in the parish churches. The second was the increase in the number of regular communicants. The Methodist experience was not only a preaching revival, but also a sacramental revival. We will note at a later point the reasons why this did not continue, but Wesley himself was a frequent communicant, and encouraged his people to be the same.

It was this sort of thing which persuaded the Rev Moore Booker of Delvin to encourage Methodist work in his parish.

Booker even went so far as to defy his diocesan, Henry Maule, Bishop of Meath. When Maule endeavoured to dissuade Booker from supporting Wesley's preachers, the valiant rector wrote him two letters asserting reasons for his actions, and subsequently published them. The Rev Richard Lloyd of Rathcormac was not quite so indomitable. He welcomed Wesley to his parish, and undertook one journey with him, introducing him to the Lloyds of Gloster near Birr. When Lloyd's diocesan, George Berkeley of Cloyne, sent a message to him ordering him to desist, Lloyd protested, but complied. The Rev James Creighton of Swanlinbar seems to have escaped much diocesan censure, and did short Methodist preaching tours in neighbouring counties until 1783, when he resigned his curacy, and went to London to work with Wesley at the City Road chapel.

CHAPTER 5

After Wesley

John Wesley paid his last visit to Ireland in 1789. He died in the March of 1791 within three months short of his eighty-eighth birthday. Throughout his life he had never ceased to protest his loyalty to the Church of England, and by implication to its sister church in Ireland. Nevertheless certain actions during his later years had made the separation of the Methodist societies from that church inevitable.

The first of these was his ordination of Methodist preachers in 1784. Methodism had been introduced into America in 1766, and by 1784 there were about 15,000 members in the Methodist societies there. None of the Methodist preachers there were ordained, and it was useless to urge the members to go to the Church of England, even had there been such a church near them, which was not always the case. Wesley therefore asked the Bishop of London to ordain a man for America, and was met with a firm refusal. Convinced by his reading of Stillingfleet's book *Irenicum* and one or two other works that bishops and priests were of the same order, Wesley discussed the matter with some of his preachers. Then on 1 September 1784, assisted by Thomas Coke, a Welshman, and James Creighton, an Irishman, both of whom were Anglican priests, he ordained two men deacons. On the following day he ordained the same two men 'presbyters', and Coke 'superintendent'. The three men then left for America where among Coke's first actions were to ordain the leading preacher in America, Francis Asbury, deacon, elder and superintendent on successive days. The ordination of the same man as deacon and priest on successive days was not unknown in eighteenth century English practice.

In the August of 1785 he ordained three more, this time for work in Scotland. Here he argued that the Methodists had no connection with the Church of Scotland, which was Presbyterian. Thus in one way or another he justified his action on the fact that the Church of England writ did not run in either. Having ordained several others for work outside England, Wesley in 1788 took the next step, and ordained Alexander Mather for work in England. His great concern always was the continuity of the work to which God had called him, and if the bishops would not ordain men for that, he either ordained them himself, or permitted the work to lapse. When in 1789 he ordained three more preachers for work in England one of them was an Irishman, Henry Moore, who was his principal assistant in London. It was his ordination of these men, be their work wherever, which made it inevitable that the Methodist societies should become a separate church.

However, in the meantime another problem had vexed the Methodists in Dublin. In 1788, when Dr Thomas Coke arrived in Dublin to preside on Wesley's behalf over the Conference, he learned that many members of the society there were going on Sundays to Dissenting meetings. Methodist meetings were held at a different hour in order that the people might attend worship in the Church of Ireland, and to go elsewhere was regarded as unacceptable. To prevent it Coke arranged that on three Sundays out of four there should be a service in the Whitefriar Street chapel at the same time as the Dissenting meetings, but also, of course, at the same time as the church services. The Church of Ireland Prayer Book was to be used in Whitefriar Street, and on the fourth Sunday the people were to be encouraged to go to St Patrick's Cathedral or to their local parish church for Holy Communion.

It was the conflict with the Church of Ireland times which incensed some of the more influential members of the Dublin society, on the grounds that it meant separation from the church. An appeal was made to Wesley who at first overruled the arrangement. Later he did make the concession, and indeed abridged the Prayer Book for use in Dublin, or in any Methodist chapels in England or in Ireland where services were held at the same time as those in the church.

When Coke arrived in America in 1784 with Wesley's instruction to ordain Asbury, the latter declined to accept ordination without the consent of the other preachers there. They met at Christmas in Baltimore, Maryland, and agreed that Asbury should be ordained as their superintendent. It was, in effect a declaration of independence from Wesley's authority, and they went on to organise themselves as the Methodist Episcopal Church, with Asbury and Coke as bishops. Wesley was annoyed at the use of the title 'bishop', preferring the term 'superintendent'. However, it is hard to escape the conclusion that it had been his intention when ordaining Coke that the latter should organise a church in America. The event is historic as the first occasion on which a Methodist body claimed to be a church.

Wesley has been compared to an oarsman who has to row in one direction while looking in the other. He constantly protested his loyalty to the Established Church, but his actions in ordaining preachers, and in permitting Methodists to meet for worship at the same time as the parish church services, were separatist in effect. The Methodist societies in England and in Ireland would have formally separated from the church earlier than they did had it not been for the strength of Wesley's autocratic hold on their actions, and to some extent on their thinking.

After Wesley's death in 1791 the British Conference was almost immediately presented with the question of what to do about the sacraments. There was a strong demand that they be administered by the preachers in the chapels, and that people who had lost any real connection with the Church of England should not be asked to attend its services. The debate came to a climax in 1795 and was resolved by a committee which recommended a Plan of Pacification, allowing the administration of the sacraments in those chapels where the trustees were agreeable. This is generally taken as the recognition by the British

Conference that the Methodist societies were no longer part of the Church of England. The Plan of Pacification did not apply to Ireland, and the Irish societies continued to cling to the Church of Ireland for another twenty years.

The first major crisis with which the Irish Methodists had to deal after Wesley's death was thrust upon them by political events. The Society of United Irishmen had been formed under the influence of ideas developed in the French Revolution. One of their leaders, Theobald Wolfe Tone expressed their ideal as the replacement of the names of Catholic, Protestant and Dissenter with the common name of Irishman. The Society planned a simultaneous rising throughout the country, supported by a force from France, to overthrow the government in 1798, and had this happened as planned it might very possibly have succeeded. However, the arrest and imprisonment of the Dublin leaders on the eve of the rising stifled any action in the city, and the four rural areas where risings did take place failed to co-ordinate their action. Kildare was the first to rise, Wexford followed, then came Antrim and Down, and finally the landing of the French force at Killala initiated a rising in Mayo. The time lapse in each case enabled the government forces to suppress each in turn.

The Dublin leadership of the United Irishmen was predominantly Church of Ireland. That in Wexford was mainly Catholic, but two Church of Ireland landlords were prominent there. While several Catholic priests were involved in the Wexford leadership, their bishop and the large majority of priests in the diocese supported the government. In Antrim and Down the leadership was largely Presbyterian. In fact, of the four main churches in Ireland today, only the Methodists could be said to be consistently on the side of the government. A few did join the insurgents, but they played no leading role among them.

Crookshank tells of a leading Methodist in Dublin whose suspicions were aroused by the urgency with which his brother, a United Irishman, pressed him to take his family out of the city.

He reported the matter to the authorities, thereby alerting them to the fact that some trouble was being planned.[1] There is no reason to doubt this story, except in one particular: the man was telling the authorities nothing that they did not already know. Informers had infiltrated the councils of the United Irishmen for quite some time.

In the areas where there was fighting, the Methodists shared the sufferings of the population, and stories are told in several places of quite extraordinary escapes from death or personal injury.[2] The most dramatic concerns a Methodist local preacher at Wexford. The insurgents seized control of the town and imprisoned a large number of government supporters. They began to take groups of these to the bridge over the Slaney, where they hoisted them on the points of pikes, and threw them into the river to drown. In one group the Methodist was actually next in line to be piked when the parish priest, Fr John Currin, returned to town, learned what was going on, and hurried to the bridge. There he succeeded in persuading the insurgents to stop the slaughter. The local preacher who had so narrow an escape is differently identified in two versions of the story. In one he is named as George Taylor, and in the other as William Gurley. The balance of probability is that it was Taylor.

After their defeat in Wexford, a group of the insurgents made their way across country through Laois, then Queen's County, and did some damage at Tentower, the home of the Methodist evangelist, the Rev Adam Averell, who was away at the time. They attacked the nearby town of Castlecomer, where several houses were set alight. The Methodist society was meeting in an upper room in one house, and the members were exceptionally fortunate to escape without injury.

John Galt, a local preacher at Coleraine in Co Antrim, enjoyed considerable respect from the authorities in the town. The circuit preacher, travelling about his business in the area, was seized by some soldiers who found in his saddlebag a notebook with some entries which they could not understand against local towns and villages. They concluded that he was a spy, and that the entries were coded details of the military forces in the area. The man protested his innocence, and the book was brought to Galt for his comment. Galt was able to explain that the combinations of letters and numbers were simply references to the biblical texts from which the man had preached in the towns in question, and he was duly set at liberty again.

There were probably five influences at work in forming the Methodist attitude to the rising. The first was Wesley's profound respect for the principle of law and order. If magistrates were unjust, he saw that as a problem with the particular magistrates, and not with the system. Redress, when needed, was always to be sought by process of law and not by violence. The second was that Methodism had not been politicised. Unlike the other three churches it had never been in a position in any country to participate in or influence government. The third was that it had no radical wing. It was the radicals in the Church of Ireland and the Presbyterian Church who provided leaders for the rising, but the Methodist societies were essentially conservative and religious. The fourth was that the inspiration of the United Irishmen came from the French Revolution, which had not only abolished the monarchy; it had sought to abolish religion from France. Methodists were deeply suspicious of anything that came from such a source. Finally there was the influence of the gentry who, if they encouraged their tenants to be Methodists, also encouraged them to be law abiding.

One of the measures which the government took in an attempt to quell the rising was to ban any gathering of more than five men other than the army. In the thirty-two Methodist circuits there were then fifty-two active preachers, twenty-four active preachers on trial, five supernumerary preachers, and five preachers on the list of reserve, a total of eighty-six. In the region of sixty of these could be expected to attend the Conference at Dublin in July. By then the conflict in Kildare, Wexford and Antrim and Down was over, and nobody could have known that the French would land at Killala in the following month, but everyone must have been aware that the country had not been pacified, and further outbreaks were a possibility.

As usual Dr Thomas Coke came to Ireland to preside over the meetings of the Conference, and sought permission for it to assemble, notwithstanding the ban. The Lord Lieutenant, appointed in the middle of June, was Charles, Marquess Cornwallis, and the Chief Secretary Robert, Viscount Castlereagh. Castlereagh's Secretary was Alexander Knox, whose father, also Alexander Knox, had been a member of the Methodist society in Londonderry. John Wesley had stayed with the elder Knox on one of his visits to that city. The younger Knox was never a Methodist, believing that the Church of Ireland catered adequately for his spiritual needs, but he remained sympathetic, and in 1802, when the Rev John Walker, chaplain at the Bethesda Chapel in Dublin, published an attack on the Methodists, Knox published a reply. Now, in 1798 it was Knox who persuaded Castlereagh to advise the Lord Lieutenant to exempt the Methodist Conference from the ban. It duly met on 13 July. The exemption given reflected the degree to which the Methodists had been successful in convincing the authorities that they posed no threat to the peace of the community.

Naturally one of the principal topics of discussion was the rising. As usual, Coke had made a short tour of Ireland in the days before the Conference, and from the preachers who gathered he heard more of the sufferings of the people, and the destruction of property. As an evangelical Coke was convinced that the only way to ensure that such did not happen again was to convert people to evangelical Christianity, and he asked what the Conference would do about it. The Conference could make no suggestion. However, it returned to the subject in 1799, and set apart three general missionaries.

The idea that the political ills of this country could be resolved by a religious campaign may have been somewhat naïve, but it obliged the Conference to think again about the reasons for its existence, and to reconsider its policy for the future. The outcome was a major renewal of Methodist work in this country. The proposal was that a number of ministers should be set apart from circuit work to tour the country, either together or singly, preaching and exhorting wherever they could find an opening. They were required to keep journals of all that they did, and all of the Methodist chapels were to be available for their use. They were not to form any new circuits, but to feed converts into the existing circuits which the Conference might then reorganise if growing numbers demanded it. Possibly more significant was the fact that the Conference at last recognised the significance of the Irish language; the missionaries were required to be so fluent as to be capable of preaching in it. It was thought that three would be sufficient for the start. Fears about the cost of the enterprise were allayed when Coke offered support from England. The general missionaries were, and continued to be, funded by the Wesleyan Methodist Missionary Society in England.

Immediately two names came to mind: Charles Graham and James McQuigg. Graham's family had come to Ireland from Scotland in the 1690s and settled at Drumahair in Co Sligo. Finding no Presbyterian church in the vicinity, they conformed to the Church of Ireland. Charles was born in 1750, and his parents, though devout, seem to have over-indulged their son, who grew into a careless and irreligious youth. A friend brought him to hear a Methodist preacher in Sligo, and this led to his conversion. From about the age of twenty he became a Methodist and a local preacher, preaching with marked effect in Sligo and the area around it. Eventually, in 1790, he was received by Conference as a travelling preacher, and sent immediately to Kerry. That a newly accepted preacher should be sent to pioneer work in a county may seem strange, but he had behind him the twenty years experience as a local preacher. His new work was so effective that he is known in Methodist circles as the Apostle of Kerry.[3]

Of McQuigg's birth and ancestry nothing is now known, though the name is an old Irish one, originally Ó Cuaig, and associated with north Ulster. He was received as a preacher on trial by the Conference of 1789, and served on circuits in Munster, Leinster and Connacht before his appointment to the

General Mission.[4] Both he and Graham were, as the Conference required for this particular work, fluent Irish speakers. The problem was that they were the only two preachers sufficiently fluent, and the Conference wanted three. Then somebody suggested Gideon Ouseley.

The Ouseleys had been a Northamptonshire family, but had suffered severe losses supporting the Royalist cause during the Cromwellian period. Thus impoverished, some of the family realised that it was cheaper to live in Ireland, and so crossed the Irish Sea. One member settled in Dunmore, Co Galway, and it was there in 1762 that Gideon Ouseley was born. Unusually for a family of their background, the Ouseleys allowed Gideon in his childhood to roam freely in and out of the cabins of the local peasants, and from this the child not only acquired fluency in the Irish language, but also a great familiarity with Irish music and folklore. Having some intention of making a Church of Ireland clergyman out of the boy, his father ensured that he got an appropriate education. However, this intention was not to be fulfilled. He became a wild young man, his wildness not tamed by an early marriage. On one occasion in Dunmore he met some friends who had just returned from a wildfowling expedition, and in the ensuing drunken frolic a fowling piece was discharged. The shot peppered the right side of Gideon's face and neck. He recovered from the injury, but his right eye was destroyed, and for the rest of his life he wore a black patch over the scar. It gave him a half sinister, half comical appearance.

Not long after that, in 1791 a detachment of the Royal Irish Dragoons was sent to Dunmore. Their Quartermaster, Sergeant Robinet, and some of the other soldiers were Methodists, and also immediately engaged a room in Mrs Kennedy's inn in the town for their meetings. That soldiers should go to an inn to pray was soon the talk of the town, and the more sceptical refused to believe that that was really what they were doing. Ouseley determined to find the truth. On his first visit to the meetings, surely enough, a couple of hymns were sung, Robinet gave a short reading from the Bible followed by a sermon, and there were prayers. Ouseley reckoned that this was a cloak to lull the suspicions of the newcomer, and determined to return until he got at the truth. After several visits he was convinced that Robinet and his colleagues were genuine, and more than that, he began to be alarmed about his own religious indiffer- ence. The end of the story was that he became a Methodist him- self. For some years he worked as a local preacher in an around Dunmore before moving, in 1797, first to Ballymote and then to Sligo, where he conducted a school for boys in the Methodist chapel.

This was the man who was suggested as the third general missionary. Of course, he could not be consulted, as communic- ation between Dublin and Sligo required several days, and so the appointment could not be regarded as regular. A footnote was added to the list of preachers' stations in the Minutes of Conference:

> Gideon Ouseley is not hereby received into the regular trav- elling Connexion, but is to have the allowance of a travelling Preacher for himself and his wife while he is employed in this Mission.

He remains the only Irish Methodist preacher to have been ex- empted from the normal rules of admission. His achievements proved him worthy of it.[5]

Graham worked as a general missionary until 1807, when he returned to circuit work. McQuigg was obliged by ill health to relinquish the mission work in 1801, and after a year's recuper- ation returned to circuit. Ouseley remained in the mission work for the rest of his life. With the retirements of the first three, others were found to replace them, and more than a hundred preachers engaged in this ministry during a period of fifty years.

The most tragic of them was James McQuigg. As we have noted, he returned to circuit work in 1802 and in 1814 was stat- ioned as the second preacher at Boyle in Co Roscommon. There a woman accused him of making improper advances to her, and the Conference of 1815 examined the charge. McQuigg stoutly denied it, but the Conference took the view that a Methodist preacher must be above suspicion, and McQuigg was expelled. His gifts as an Irish scholar were later put to good use by the British and Foreign Bible Society, for whom he revised and edited Irish translations of the Old and New Testaments. After his death, the woman who made the accusation in 1815, herself nearing death, admitted that the charge had been a fabrication and McQuigg was finally vindicated.

The story is worth telling for more than one reason, but one is the fact that it illustrates the attitude of the Irish preachers at the time, strict to the point of harshness. It is normal to presume that the accused is innocent until proved guilty, but McQuigg appears to have been presumed guilty until he proved his innocence. That in the circumstances was no easier to prove than guilt. It is very likely that his colleagues were seeking to safeguard the reputation of Methodist societies at a time when opponents were happy enough to seize on the least pretext to attack them. The occasional appearance of such attacks may well have given them a sense of insecurity, but the fact remains that in the interests of the general reputation they were willing to sacrifice that of the individual. In later years the Conference would have been more compassionate.

As the man brought in from outside the Conference, Ouseley might have been regarded as the junior of the three missionaries, but he soon established himself as the most effective of them, and the greatest innovator, so that he is the best remembered. One of his methods was highly original. He would ride to a fair, and stop his horse at the edge of the crowd. Still in the saddle, he would begin to sing. The crowd would quickly recognise the tunes as being some that they would sing themselves wherever they gathered for a convivial evening, but with something a little odd about them. Before long they would realise that the oddity lay in the unfamiliar words being sung. Ouseley wrote Christian hymns to suit the tunes, some of them translations of hymns by Charles Wesley. When a large enough crowd had gathered around him, Ouseley, still on horseback, would begin to preach.

The other preachers on the mission adopted Ouseley's methods to some degree, and their habit of preaching from horseback earned them the nickname 'The Cavalry Preachers'. The name had nothing whatever to do with any cavalry regiment. The fact that they wore the customary black hats of the period earned them the less often used nickname, 'The Black Cap Preachers'. Their immediate success was remarkable. In three years the membership of the Methodist societies rose by 10,473 from 16,227 to 26,700. Not all of this, of course, was due to the activity of the missionaries; there was the natural increase of Methodist families, and there continued to be those who joined because they were influenced by the work of the circuit preachers, or the behaviour of existing members. The rise of 64.54% in three years is none the less surprising. There was, inevitably, a reaction, and the two years from 1803 to 1805 saw a loss of 3,746, which the Conference wisely saw as a consolidation, and indeed from then on there was generally a greater gain than loss.

Not all of these new recruits came through the missionaries preaching in Irish. Where it was more appropriate they preached in English, and influenced the English-speaking members of the community. How many of the Irish-speaking Catholics were included among the new members it is impossible to say with any precision, as the only statistic recorded at the time was the present membership in the circuits, and their total. It has been generally held among students of Irish Methodist history that they constituted a significant number, but Hempton has queried this. He has argued that Methodist propagandists in the nineteenth century made much of the few Catholic converts there were.[6] There are, however, two other considerations to be taken into account.

The Minutes of the Wesleyan Methodist Conference in Ireland did not begin to record the number of 'emigrations' – that is, members leaving Ireland to live in Britain, America, or elsewhere – until 1831, in which year they were 4.13% of the membership (1027 from 22,470). The Primitive Wesleyans, whose separation from the main body of Irish Methodists lasted from 1816 to 1878, never recorded emigrations at all. It has been suggested that the rise in emigration figures to significant proportions was related to the conversion of Catholics. The incidence of Irish names among the early leaders of American Methodism would confirm this. Jeffery has suggested that Catholics who were converted by the Black Cap preachers 'found it easier to enjoy their new-found religious liberty if they left Ireland'.[7] While that is fair comment, it is also true that those who are quickest to see a spiritual advantage in changing their religion are likely to be the quickest to see an economic advantage in moving to a new country.

Hempton has set this particular aspect of Methodist history in its context by drawing attention to the other agencies working for the conversion of Irish Catholics in the first quarter of the nineteenth century.[8] While the evangelical desire to promote true religion cannot be justly questioned, he argues that the fact that some of the agencies involved originated in England, or were funded from there, gave sectarian and cultural overtones to the movement as a whole. Not all of the consequences, therefore, have been what the protagonists would have wished.

The dispute which was to rend Irish Methodists in two first appeared in 1795. An increasing number of members had no real connection with the Church of Ireland, and were not willing to go to the parish churches for Holy Communion, so that they were being deprived of it. News of the agitation in England for the administration of sacraments in Methodist chapels had undoubtedly reached some of the Irish circuits. The Plan of Pacification by which the problem was solved there had not been devised when the Irish Conference met, as it always did, shortly before its British counterpart. The Lisburn circuit requested that the Conference permit the administration of the sacraments. The Conference refused the request, on the ground that administration would have broken the last link with the church. In spite of this ruling Joseph Sutcliffe, who had been sent from England to Cork, and John McFarland administered the sacrament in that city, and David Gordon did the same in

Lisburn. All three were responding to local demand. For their breach of discipline all three were put back on trial by the Conference in 1796. Sutcliffe returned to England, and in fact his name never appears in the list of stations in the Irish Minutes

The refusal of the Conference to sanction administration, and its discipline of their preacher for yielding to the demands of the members, further annoyed the leaders of the Lisburn circuit, and in 1798 they submitted two petitions. One was again for the sacraments; the other was for lay representation in the Conference, then entirely composed of preachers. The Conference viewed the request for lay representation as 'founded on the principles of Jacobinism', and thirty-two leaders of the Lisburn circuit were expelled. Jacobinism, the philosophy of the more extreme party in the French Revolution, was a convenient name with which to attack any group that threatened the *status quo*. The unwisely strong terms in which the Conference reacted alienated two hundred members, and gave an opening to the Methodist New Connexion, an English secession, to open work in Ireland.

There the matter appeared to rest for the next fourteen years. It reopened in 1812 with a circular letter addressed by the Belfast leaders to those of other circuits. They not only drew attention once more to the fact that many members had no connection with the Church of Ireland, but pointed out that some of their members were Presbyterians, and both Church of Ireland clergy and Presbyterian ministers were unwilling to give Communion to any of their people who were attending Methodist meetings. The agitation grew, and by 1814 the Conference was obliged to face the issue.

When it met on 1 July Thomas Coke was absent. He had been unable to travel to Ireland to preside over its sessions, and the Rev Adam Averell was appointed to preside. Averell was opposed to any change. After discussion a vote was taken, and the proposal for administration of the sacraments was passed by a majority of ten. It was too small a margin to settle the issue. On the following day the minority requested that the operation of this decision might be deferred for a year. That placed the President in a difficult position, particularly as he supported the minority view. He allowed the point to be discussed, and in an attempt at reconciliation the Conference voted for the deferral. Unfortunately the second vote was seen as a sign of weakness or indecision by the advocates of change, and the pressure continued to mount, with pamphlets being published on either side making the dispute a very public matter.

In 1815 the Conference had Walter Griffith as President. Again the issue was warmly debated, but this time the result was a firm refusal of change. However, in an attempt to meet the difficulties of those who wanted the Holy Communion administered in the Methodist chapels, the Conference requested that the Rev Adam Averell might do so in as many places as possible.

Averell was a native of Tyrone, whose education had been funded by two relatives, John Averell, Dean of Armagh and later Bishop of Limerick, and the bishop's nephew Francis Andrews, Provost of Trinity College, Dublin. The intention was that Adam should be ordained in the Church of Ireland and receive a parish through the patronage of his sponsors, but both died before he had completed his studies. He was ordained deacon, but never took priest's orders. He married a Miss Gregory, heiress of Tentower in Laois, and served as curate in the neighbouring parish of Aghaboe. A chance meeting with John Wesley in Dublin convinced him of the value of Methodism, and he resigned his curacy to devote himself to the conduct of Methodist meetings in the area near Tentower, and to periodic evangelistic tours in various other counties. Though his name was recorded as one of the preachers at Mountrath, he was never under the same direction as other preachers. He worked as he pleased, and was never paid an allowance by the Methodists, always living on the income of his wife's estate.[9] As a deacon he was not authorised to celebrate the Holy Communion, but did so on occasion at Methodist quarterly meetings. This gave rise to criticism among members of the Church of Ireland, and received adverse comment in the correspondence of the younger Alexander Knox with Henry Jebb, Bishop of Limerick.

In the light of this, the suggestion by the Conference in 1815 seems curiously inept. It would have done as much to alienate the Church of Ireland as administration by the preachers. There was a further objection to it. It would have been a physical impossibility for one man to get around the Methodist societies throughout the country with any frequency, and the infrequent visits that would have been possible would have satisfied nobody. In fact Averell seems to have made no attempt at it.

During the following year eight preachers breached the regulation. Samuel Steele broke ranks at Armagh, and with his colleague Robert Cranston administered the Communion to the society there. George Stephenson followed his example at Belfast and Thomas Johnston at Newry before the end of the year. In the new year, Thomas Kerr and James Johnston administered at Strabane. Coleraine divided on the issue and the preachers appointed there, Alexander Sturgeon and Edward Cobain, refused to administer. Matthew Lanktree and William Hamilton administered to those who wished it. Lanktree was then the Chairman of the Belfast District. This was one of the ten Districts into which Irish Methodism was divided for administration, and the one to which Coleraine belonged. Hamilton was the second preacher on the Londonderry and Antrim Mission, whose area partly overlapped that of the circuit.

The Conference in 1816 was obliged to discipline these preachers, but the penalty was reasonably mild. All were barred for one year from serving as Secretary of the Conference, Representative to the British Conference or Chairman of District. Kerr, Hamilton and Johnston, deemed to have been under less pressure in the matter, were further barred for the same period from serving as superintendent of circuit. Having dealt with past misdemeanours, the Conference turned to the future. The demand for the sacraments was as strong as ever, and the Conference yielded to the inevitable. There was still a note of caution in that administration was permitted, but only in those circuits which the conference named – Sligo, Newry,

Armagh, Tanderagee, Belfast, Carrickfergus, Strabane and Coleraine. But the defences had been finally breached, and the permission soon became general.

It was, as its opponents had argued, the admission that the Methodist societies were no longer an evangelistic movement within the Established Church. It was a recognition that they had become a separate denomination. Those who favoured the old tradition of receiving the sacraments in the Established Church moved swiftly. They convened a conference at Clones on 2 October. There they began the process of establishing an alternative Methodist connexion. Irish Methodism had split in two.

CHAPTER 6

Methodism Divided

Those who summoned the Clones Conference asked circuits to send to it those accredited local preachers whom they believed to be fit to serve as travelling preachers, and nineteen such were duly received as preachers, and stationed in some of the twenty-one circuits which requested them. The effect of this action was to establish a rival Methodist connexion, but the members of the Conference would have warmly repudiated the suggestion. They argued that in continuing the sacramental practise of Wesley's time, they were his true heirs, and had preserved continuity. They claimed that the Conference in Dublin had departed from Wesley's design, and were therefore not true Methodists. On the basis of that argument, they claimed all the Methodist property in Ireland.

A meeting of officials of the circuits in the north of Ireland – the Newry, Belfast, Londonderry, Enniskillen and Clones Districts – was convened at Dungannon, and established a committee of thirteen prominent laymen to resist these claims. Subsequently eight more names were added to what came to be called the Dungannon Committee. The Chairman was Thomas Shillington of Portadown, and the Secretary Alexander Wilkinson of Newry. The test case was that of the Londonderry chapel, where the preacher appointed by the Dublin Conference, John Dinnen, had been excluded. The Dungannon Committee supported Dinnen in taking action for recovery. The case was heard in Chancery, and judgement was duly given that the Dublin Conference had followed the lead given by John Wesley in taking actions without reference to the authority of the Established Church. It therefore was deemed to be in continuity with his work, and Mr Dinnen was entitled to the full use of the premises.

The Dungannon Committee gave further advice and support in other cases, resisting attempts of the 'Clones society' as it was then unofficially called, to gain possession of other places. The judgement of the Master of the Rolls in one of these cases in 1819 was regarded as final, bringing an eventual end to the dispute in so far as property was concerned. The great majority of the chapels thereafter remained in the undisputed possession of the original society, but where deeds were defective, or had never been executed, some were lost to the Clones supporters.

In the January of 1818 those who supported the Clones society appointed representatives to a meeting in Dublin to draft a constitution for them. This met in a house in South Great George's Street in Dublin, which they had acquired to serve as a headquarters. It met on three successive days, 5, 6 and 7 January. On the 5th the first twenty-one articles of the constitution were agreed, apparently unanimously, and on the 6th three more were added and matters of finance were agreed. On the third day the provision of a Bookroom was discussed. A meeting at Clones on 21 January added six more articles to the constitution. The composition of the Dublin meeting is interesting.[1]

The Chairman was the Rev Adam Averell. Originally opposed to the change, he had accepted the decision of the Conference in 1816, and had gone so far as to visit a number of places urging the societies to do the same. However, he had since reverted to his first opinion, and had given his support to the succession. Of the nineteen men stationed as preachers by the Clones Conference in 1816 only one was present, George M. West, who had been put into the Londonderry chapel to the exclusion of John Dinnen before the Chancery Court decision. Nehemiah Price had been one of Wesley's travelling preachers, but had withdrawn in 1790, after which date little is known about his activity. There was one representative from each of ten circuits – Celbridge, Londonderry, Newry, Oldcastle (Co Meath), Monasterevan, Ross & Waterford, Cavan, Aughrim, Athlone and Enniskillen. John Handy of Aughrim sat with the committee 'by permission', presumably because of the important role the Handy family of Coolalough and Aughrim had played thoroughout the preceding seventy years in the development of Irish Methodist work. Dublin city gave twenty members to the committee. The dominance of Dublin in the membership is not surprising; democracy was not then fashionable. What is interesting is that not all of them were major businessmen; some were in quite humble trade, and one was the sexton of St Patrick's Cathedral. What is probably more significant, only Averell and West were what would today be called ministers. This was very much a lay committee, and its secretary, John Curry, was a Dublin timber merchant.

The constitution agreed in Dublin in January was presented to a Conference which met in Dublin in July. With its acceptance the new body became the Primitive Wesleyan Methodist Society. The name enshrined two basic principles: it adhered to what it believed to be Wesley's original plan, and it was a religious society within the Church of Ireland. It promptly elected the Rev Adam Averell as its President, and continued to do so for the rest of his life, appointing an assistant to do his duties when he became enfeebled by age. His wife had died in 1813, so that he had lost the estate in Tentower and had moved to Clones. He continued to work without any stipend, and when, in later years, the Primitive Wesleyan Conference gave him a carriage to assist his travels, they had great difficulty in persuading him to accept the gift.

The main body of British Methodists had by now come to be known as the Wesleyan Methodists, and the same name was now applied to the main body of Irish Methodists. The nature of their relationship is something we will discuss later. One of the English branches adopted the name Primitive Methodists, and for some time worked in Belfast and some other parts of Ulster. There were thus in Ireland three separate Methodist bodies – Wesleyan, Primitive Wesleyan and Primitive – the similarity of whose names has remained a snare for the unwary.

The ostensible reason for the secession of the Primitive Wesleyans was, as the name indicates, to preserve the original

plan of Wesley's Methodist societies, but reality in human affairs is rarely simple, and a number of other motives may be dis-
cerned. Certainly the maintenance of the old tradition was one
of them, and it would be quite wrong to suppose that there was
anything false about the way in which it was put forward. The
other motives were in the background of the debate.

The dominant question in Irish politics at the time was
Catholic emancipation. When the kingdoms of Great Britain and
Ireland were united by the Act of Union, which took effect in
1801, there was a suggestion that, with a substantial Protestant
majority in the population of the United Kingdom, it might be
possible to extend the franchise to Catholics, but George III
voiced determined opposition, regarding that as a breach of his
coronation oath. Catholics, however, continued to press for the
vote, and the king could not live for ever. In fact he died in 1820.
In 1808 Daniel O'Connell had emerged as the leader of the campaign in Ireland, and in 1813 the House of Commons in
Westminster accepted the principle of Catholic emancipation,
but with certain safeguards. Its proposals, however, were defeated by the House of Lords until 1829, when emancipation
was granted. There was among the Primitive Wesleyans a certain fear that separation from the Church of Ireland would in
some way weaken its position as the Established Church at a
time when this was seen to be under threat.

The move for secession arose in Clones, actually in Co
Monaghan but on the border of Co Fermanagh, and it was in the
Fermanagh area that the Primitive Wesleyans were always to
find their greatest strength. In that area there was a strain of radical thought, which indeed was reflected elsewhere to a greater
or lesser degree. This is the significance of the composition of the
committee which drafted the constitution. It was, as we have observed, an almost completely lay body. The Wesleyan
Conference was made up entirely of travelling preachers. The
Primitive Wesleyan Conference added to their travelling
preachers one representative from each circuit. In effect they
were demanding a voice in their own government.

The two most important leaders of the Primitive Wesleyans in Dublin were not at the meeting of the constitutional committee, adopting the role of elder statesmen in the background. Arthur Keene had been a dominant figure in Dublin Methodism for many years. His marriage to Isabella Martin in 1775 was the only marriage John Wesley is known to have performed in this country. Isabella's father was a hatter, whose success in trade enabled him to acquire considerable property in the city and in the provinces. The inheritance of this enabled Arthur to retire from business as a goldsmith, and live the life of a gentleman in the Charlemont Street house which had belonged to his father-in-law. At the beginning of 1818 he may have been in poor health, as he died before the end of the year.[2]

Bennett Dugdale was the largest and most important bookseller in Dublin, having commenced business on the north side of the Liffey in Capel Street. He later moved to a more prestigious location in Dame Street, and after some years, ceased to live over the shop and established his residence just off the fashionable Mountjoy Square. His memorial in St George's Church gave him the title 'Esq'. When the Primitive Wesleyans acquired the building in South Great George's Street it was his name that headed the list of trustees. When they built behind this a chapel which was to serve as their headquarters for sixty years, it was he who laid the foundation stone. It was his money that supported their principal premises on the north side of the city, Wesley Chapel, and before his death he became its proprietor. He died in 1824.[3]

If neither Arthur Keene not Bennett Dugdale shared in the constitutional drafting, both of Keene's sons, Martin and James did, and Martin was married to Dugdale's eldest daughter. Like his father-in-law he made his career in printing and bookselling, having a business premises in College Green, a town house in Lower Leeson Street, and a country residence at Ballinteer. Men of that calibre would not have been wholly insensible to the social advantages of the link with the Church of Ireland.

This was, as we have observed, the point at which several of

the provincial gentry withdrew their support. The Methodist society in Aughrim, in Co Galway, had been encouraged by the
Wade family, and the chapel had been built by John Handy. This
was one of the chapels which passed into the possession of the
Primitive Wesleyans. The Wesleyans acquired a nearby barn belonging to a farmer named Seale and adapted it to use as a
chapel and school. When Seale's lease next came due for renewal,
he was evicted and the barn was seized by the landlord and
given to the local Church of Ireland, which used it as a school for
many years. Not all families were so actively hostile; others con-
tented themselves with a simple withdrawal.[4]

The immediate effect of the secession was to be seen in the
numbers of members. In 1813 the Methodist societies in Ireland
recorded 28,770 members, which number had risen in 1814 to
29,388. By 1816 the agitation had cost the societies more than 800
members, and the figure had dropped to 28,542. In the next two
years losses were reported of 7,511 and 1,979 respectively, bringing the total down to 19,052. Between 1818 and 1821 the
Conference was pleased to note a drift back, either of those who
had gone to the Primitive Wesleyans, or of those who had just
stopped attending, together with some new members. Membership rose to 23,538 in 1821. After that it settled for eleven years at
a figure between 22,039 and 22,899.

The first year in which the Primitive Wesleyans were able to
count their membership was 1818, when they reported a figure
of 8,095, which was rather less than the 9,490 members lost by
the Wesleyans. The drift back which the Wesleyans reported between 1818 and 1821 was not reflected in losses among the
Primitive Wesleyans, whose membership rose to 13,563.
Membership remained a little below this figure for the next
eleven years. The total of the two was in the region 37,000, which
indicates a gain in total Methodist membership in the country of
about 8,000 since 1814.

That membership should then have remained static for
eleven years has been attributed to the amount of energy ex-
pended on the establishment of new structures, and, particularly,

new buildings. It was now necessary to have two buildings in many places to house the two societies. The greater prosperity of the people was creating a demand for better buildings, and there was certainly a degree of rivalry in the size and dignity of the buildings. Classic examples of the buildings of this period are to be found in Bandon, Birr and Brookeborough, all three built by the Wesleyans. They were rectangular, gable-fronted buildings with restrained decoration, and usually with internal porches and sufficient height to accommodate a gallery if such should later be required.

The numbers in the Primitive Wesleyan circuits in 1818 were:

Enniskillen	1,767	Newtownstewart	364
Charlemont	1,069	Londonderry	189
Cavan	904	Oldcastle	164
Clones	638	Limerick	160
Downpatrick	537	Roscrea	104
Dublin	507	Wicklow	100
Ballyshannon	500	Castlebar	84
Newry	480	Waterford	71
Longford	457		

This pattern of membership was to remain, with the greatest strength in Fermanagh, Tyrone, Monaghan and Cavan, where the number of Primitive Wesleyan gains from the Wesleyans obliged the latter to amalgamate some of their circuits.

The division did take a certain amount of tension out of the individual societies. People now had a choice of Methodism as a church with all the services which a church could be expected to provide, or Methodism as a society within the church. The Wesleyans, however, in separating from the Church of Ireland lost a certain variety of worship, and were thereby impoverished.

The Irish people were no strangers to famine in the eighteenth and nineteenth centuries. The peculiar system of land tenure in the country had resulted in large numbers of very poor people depending on the potato for sustenance. These were the landless agricultural labourers, and those whose land was only a fraction of an acre. They were fortunate in that the potato was a very nourishing vegetable, and the favoured lumper potato was prolific. If the crop failed, as it did in one part of the country or another from time to time, it was these people at the bottom of the social scale who were threatened with starvation. Happily, it was generally the case that wherever the crop failed in one year, it produced a good harvest in the next. In 1840 the occurrence of such a famine had been followed in 1841 by the announcement of a decline of 641 in Primitive Wesleyan membership. This was attributed to emigration, but emigration at so exceptionally high a level may have been prompted by the shortage of food.

In 1842 a hitherto unknown form of potato blight appeared on the eastern coastal States of America, and was carried to Britain and north western Europe by 1844. In 1845 it appeared in parts of Ireland. The cause was only later identified as a fungus, *phytophthera infestans.* For the moment the people suffered, and hoped that the next crop would be a good one. The Peel administration took steps to relieve the famine in the worst hit areas. It was in 1846 that disaster struck. The crop was a total failure. To complicate matters the Peel administration had fallen, and Lord John Russell, who followed him, was committed to a policy of allowing market forces to take their course. In addition conflicting reports from various parts of Ireland confused the official understanding of the situation.

Starvation did not cause fever, but it weakened the resistance to fevers which were already endemic in a community which, of course, had no knowledge of hygiene as we now understand it. The fevers were liable to infect those who were not actually starving as well as those who were. Between the starvation and the fever epidemics, in an age with much less scientific understanding, people found religious explanations of the calamity, and it began to be thought that Ireland was doomed under the judgement of God. People began to flee overseas, many to America, but others to Australia.

Generally speaking the Methodist people belonged to those strata of society which were not dependent on the potato, and therefore less likely to starve.[5] The exception to that was in the Fermanagh area, where, as we have noted, Methodist membership penetrated into the whole of society to a degree it did not elsewhere. It is impossible to calculate the number of Methodists who died of starvation; the statistics are simply not available. What are still extant are the minute books of the Portadown Wesleyan circuit quarterly meeting, and these record a number of families who were given gifts of food and money by the circuit in the famine years, and for quite a long time afterwards. This explains why so few Methodists had recourse to the workhouse there; their fellow Methodists were giving them the means of survival.

At the far end of the country, James H. Swanton was a Wesleyan miller at Skibbereen, where the population was in dire straits. He was importing grain for his mill from ports in the west of England and in Wales. As the ships returned empty for a fresh cargo, he offered free passage to any of the starving in the area who wished to take it. The local workhouse doctor, Daniel O'Donovan, used relief funds to supply them with 'seastock' – presumably rations for the voyage. There is a horrendous account of one protracted voyage by one of Swanton's ships, the *Wanderer*, which took a full six weeks to get from Baltimore in Cork to Newport in what is now Gwent. So great were their sufferings that one woman and her three children died on arrival. Blame was attached to the captain of the vessel, but the unfortunate passengers had nothing but praise for Swanton. The authorities took a different view. They were furious with both Swanton and O'Donovan for 'shovelling paupers' into England and Wales. The Welsh people in Newport seem to have been very compassionate, giving the poor refugees what help they could.

Where Methodist deaths were related to the famine, they were usually from typhoid fever which the good people had contracted from contact with the infected victims whose hunger they were attempting to relieve. Four preachers died in this way. William Gunne was a Primitive Wesleyan working at Dundalk on the Newry mission. The other three were Wesleyans: William

Richey at Youghal, William Starkey at Bandon, and Fossey Tackaberry at Sligo.

Neither Wesleyans nor Primitive Wesleyans were exempt from the panic which led so many to emigrate. It has been estimated that out of a total population in Ireland of approximately eight millions, nearly one million people died, and a further million emigrated. That was a total loss of one quarter of the population of the country. Methodist figures more or less reflect the same proportion. In the four years from 1846 to 1850 Wesleyan membership declined from 27,926 to 21,107, a loss of 24.42%. In the same years the Primitive Wesleyan loss was even greater, as numbers fell from 14,372 to 10,420, a decline of 27.50%.

The effect was most severe in Co Fermanagh and the areas bordering it. Here 15% of the Wesleyan membership was to be found, and here 28.22% of the loss was experienced. The Clones circuit lost no fewer than 43.60% of its members. The Primitive Wesleyan presence in the area was even stronger, being 39.58% of its total. Here the loss was 51.17% of the total for their Society. The decline in Wesleyan membership continued until 1855. There is a suggestion behind these figures that the Primitive Wesleyan membership in this part of the country included more people on lower incomes than did the Wesleyan. The Primitive Wesleyan Minutes of 1847 add a curious footnote to the membership returns:

> N.B. With regard to the diminution of our numbers, when we consider the losses sustained by death and emigration, and how many of our poorer members were obliged to take refuge in the workhouses, together with those who are prevented from attending the means of grace for want of clothing, we feel cause of great thankfulness that our Society has been preserved in such a state of prosperity.

Strange prosperity! In fact the Primitive Wesleyans had a flair for putting the best face on things. In 1754 they reported a loss of 1,693 members, or 16.80%. No explanation of this decrease was offered, but they commented:

> We have been cheered in hearing that upon several of our

stations there are marked indications of a revival of the Lord's work. The statements of some of the brethren have been intensely interesting and delightful, and we are led to look forward to the year on which we are entering as one of great prosperity.

The anticipation was about six years premature.

Revival came to Ulster in 1859. It was very largely a Presbyterian phenomenon, though it affected all of the Protestant churches to some degree or other. It was not the first revival in Ulster, or indeed in Ireland. The word recurs like a leitmotif in the third volume of Crookshank's *History of Methodism in Ireland,* where it usually refers to a significant increase in fervour in a circuit following the appointment of a new minister, as the travelling preachers were now beginning to be called. This would be accompanied by a larger than usual increase in the membership. Sometimes the experience would spread to neighbouring circuits. What was remarkable about the '59 revival in Ulster was its magnitude. It was the most remarkable religious experience that the area had ever witnessed.

As the story is most often told, the origin lay with a small group of young Presbyterians at Kells, near Connor in Co Antrim. That, however, does less than justice to the sort of experience we have just mentioned in Methodist circuits, which were found in other denominations as well. This sort of thing prepared the way for revival by creating an expectancy. It must also be remembered that at the same time similar phenomena were occurring in America.[6] Crookshank gives a Methodist prelude to the story.

William G. Campbell had been appointed a general missionary in 1851. The G in his name stood for Graham; he was a nephew of Charles Graham, one of the original Cavalry Preachers. Anxious to improve his Irish, he sought the help of John Feely, who was then in the Antrim circuit. Feely agreed to give the necessary instruction, but demanded a 'fee' – Campbell should preach at a series of special services in Antrim. Campbell very gladly did so, and one of those who made a Christian commitment as a result was a young man named James McQuilkin. It was McQuilkin who, returning to his native Connor, started the prayer meeting in the Presbyterian church at Kells from which the revival began.

The impact of the revival was felt most strongly in Antrim, Londonderry, Tyrone, Armagh and Down, but Monaghan, Cavan, Fermanagh and Donegal were also affected. In towns, villages and country areas there was great religious excitement, as individuals were first convinced of their sinfulness to the point of deep despair, and then transformed into joy by the realisation of salvation. When the revival was at its height the American Methodist evangelists Walter and Phoebe Palmer visited Ulster. It was she who began the practice of asking converts to go to the front, which was both an expression of commitment and a witness to others of what was happening.

The immediate effect on the membership of Methodist societies was dramatic. The Wesleyan membership rose in one year from 19,727 to 22,860, a rise of 15.9%. The Primitive Wesleyan increase was even more spectacular, from 9,979 to 15,341, a rise of 53.7%. Bringing people in was one thing, but keeping them was another, and the new members were quite quickly lost as the early enthusiasm abated. The Wesleyans reported a further increase in 1861, but the Primitive Wesleyans obscured their loss by failing to total the members in the several circuits. By 1865 the Primitive Wesleyan numbers had dropped to the level they were at before the revival, but it was not until two years later that the Wesleyan numbers did so.

The most lasting effect of the revival was in the way it was seen by later generations, who failed to take into account the speed of the decline which followed it. The word acquired a much more limited meaning. No longer would it be used as it had been used in the Methodist circuits in the years before. Revival was not now to be regarded as a local event; it was only revival if it affected a large area. For a hundred years the people of Ulster, Methodists among them, thought of '59 as 'the glory days', and it is not without significance that Crookshank, writing between 1885 and 1888, chose to end his account of Methodism with the revival, rather than with the reunion of Irish Methodism twenty years later.

At the beginning of the nineteenth century the Church of Ireland had four archbishops and eighteen bishops, and this establishment was maintained by a tithe, the payment of which was deeply resented by those who did not subscribe to its beliefs or wish to avail of its services. It was unique in being an established church whose members formed only a minority of the population. The first move to remedy this anomaly came in 1833 when a Whig administration introduced a bill in parliament to reduce two of the archbishops to the rank of bishops, and to 'suppress' ten of the bishoprics. In fact what this achieved was to amalgamate ten dioceses with others when the bishops in office at the time died, or were moved elsewhere. Almost immediately Waterford & Lismore was attached to Cashel & Emly, and the process was completed in 1854 when Elfin was joined to Kilmore & Ardagh. At the same time the revenues of the bishops were reduced to reasonable proportions.

An unexpected consequence of the Act was a protest in Oxford by John Keble, who was joined by John Henry Newman and Edward Pusey in leading what later came to be called the Tractarian Movement. When the writer of one of the tracts was identified as Pusey, contemporaries referred to the group as 'the Puseyites'. The Primitive Wesleyans saw in the Tractarian Movement a serious threat to its evangelical support. In 1842 its Conference, in the pastoral address to the members of the society, said that 'the prevalence of dangerous error in the Established Church has caused us serious grief', and went on to deplore the fact that rites and ceremonies should be regarded as of more importance than faith. It returned to the subject in the following year, saying:

We more deeply lament, as a greater evil, not only the continued existence, but the rapid spread of the pernicious errors, commonly called Puseyism, in the Church of England.

The Primitive Wesleyans, of course, saw this as a threat to their future, not so much in terms of the possibility of Puseyism spreading to Ireland, as in altering the mind of the Church of England to the detriment of evangelicalism. For many years they had been receiving financial support from sympathetic people in England and Scotland, and may have feared a decline in evangelical numbers there that would have reduced such support. They reacted in the same way in 1845 when the government helped to fund the college for the training of Catholic priests at Maynooth. A year later they welcomed the formation of the Evangelical Alliance.

The ultimate threats to the future of the Primitive Wesleyan Society, however, were neither the Puseyites nor the priests trained at Maynooth. One was internal. Since the remarkable boost in 1860 following the '59 Revival numbers had continuously declined. The loss was running at more than one thousand each year. With a membership in 1863 of 11,769 that sort of loss could not be sustained for very long. The other threat was disestablishment.

It was in 1868 that Gladstone made the first move at Westminster towards the introduction of a bill to disestablish the Church of Ireland, but the matter had been under discussion for some time before that. One of the provisions of the Disestablishment Act was that the government would continue to fund the stipends of clergy who were in parishes on the operative date – 1 January 1871. In anticipation of that the Church of Ireland was anxious to have every parish filled, so that the subvention would be maximised. An obvious source of candidates to fill the vacancies was the Primitive Wesleyan Society, and approaches were made to several of the preachers to be ordained and installed as rectors. Some refused; others accepted.

Between 1863 and 1870 thirty-two Primitive Wesleyan ministers 'ceased to travel'. This was the phrase used in the minutes of their Conference to describe what was a withdrawal from the ministry – a resignation. Of the thirty-two, one was said to be 'for reasons of health only'. In the other cases no reason is given, but by 1871 ten of them were curates in Church of Ireland parishes. The remaining twenty-two may well have been discouraged by the steadily declining numbers.

The disestablishment of the Church of Ireland called in question the very existence of the Primitive Wesleyan Society. It had come into being for the precise purpose of maintaining Methodist societies as an evangelical group within the Established Church, but from the beginning of 1871 there was to be no Established Church. What was to happen to the Primitive Wesleyans?

It would seem that the first thing which happened was an invitation from the Wesleyan Conference, which always met a few weeks earlier than theirs, to reunite. The Primitive Wesleyan Minutes of Conference in 1869 contain the question:

> What is our opinion respecting the proposal of the Wesleyan Conference for an amalgamation of the Wesleyans and Primitive Wesleyans in this country?

Their opinion was that the whole membership should be canvassed by means of discussion in each circuit and mission. That revealed a degree of division, and some representatives of the Conference met some representatives of the Church of Ireland to discuss the terms on which they might be integrated in to the parochial system. In an odd turn of phrase, the latter were described as 'several gentlemen of the Irish Church' when the outcome of this meeting was reported to the Conference in 1870. The phrase reflected the unofficial nature of the consultation. However, two things followed from it. One was the appointment of official representatives of the Church of Ireland General Synod to meet with official representatives of the Conference, and take the matter further. The other was the realisation that the Primitive Wesleyan Constitution left them no room for manoeuvre; they were obliged by it to remain a religious society, and prevented by it from administering the sacraments. During the next year they sought and obtained a private Act of Parliament to vary these terms, allowing them to negotiate union with another church, and their preachers to administer Baptism and Holy Communion.

The official representatives of Synod and Conference met on several occasions. The difficulties on both sides proved to be insuperable. On the one hand, the Church of Ireland looked with disfavour on the administration of the sacraments by preachers whom they regarded as laymen, and were not willing to accept the stationing of these men by a Conference over which the bishops would have no control. On the other hand, the Primitive Wesleyans were, as we have already observed, concerned about the apparent growth of ritualism in the Anglican Church, particularly in England, and were not prepared to abandon their own existence as an organised body. Here it is fair to comment that the Church of Ireland had damaged its own cause by the speed with which it ordained some Primitive Wesleyan preachers, so weakening the church party in the Conference. As late as 1872 the Conference was still declaring itself open to any proposals which the Church of Ireland might make, but none came. In the end the Church of Ireland lost several thousands of evangelicals from its membership as the Primitive Wesleyans turned elsewhere.

The obvious group to which to turn was the Wesleyans, and in 1874 the two Methodist Conferences appointed representatives to a negotiating committee. A year later the Primitive Wesleyan Conference, representing by far the smaller group, was insisting that union should be on a 'basis of equality'. By 1876 only two issues were admitted to be presenting difficulty, the matter of lay representation, and the uncertainty as to how many would enter the union 'cordially'. The Conferences of 1877 finally approved the terms on which the union could take place. The principal provisions were:

> That the terms Wesleyan and Primitive Wesleyan would cease to be used, and the new body be called The Methodist Church in Ireland.

> That all ministers in full connexion with either of the Conferences would be regarded as being in full connexion with the Methodist Church in Ireland.

That in the first year Wesleyans and Primitive Wesleyans should each provisionally arrange the stations of their own ministers.

That former Primitive Wesleyans should be proportionately represented on the Stationing Committee which recommended where ministers should serve each year.

That the Primitive Wesleyans would contribute a sum of £10,000 to the Wesleyan Auxiliary Fund, in recognition of which Primitive Wesleyan Supernumerary [retired] ministers and ministers' widows should receive the same allowances as their Wesleyan counterparts.

That if and when it became necessary to sell what had been a Primitive Wesleyan premises, the proceeds should be put into the fund which provided such allowances.

That the Primitive Wesleyan Book Room would be wound up.

That the Wesleyans would not require it as a condition that a certain number of the Primitive Wesleyan members would become members of the united body.

The matter of lay representation had been resolved already, as the Wesleyans had altered their constitution to admit lay representatives to their Conference, the numbers of ministers and laymen being equal. It was in 1877 that the change became effective, the number being seventy-two of each. At that time it was unthinkable that women should be admitted. Other problems were regarded as less significant, and remained to be resolved by the united church.

In 1878 the two Conferences met simultaneously in Dublin, the Wesleyan in the Methodist Centenary church on St Stephen's Green, and the Primitive Wesleyan in their church on South Great George's Street. Resolutions for union were formally proposed and passed, and the members of the Primitive Wesleyan Conference then left to walk together to the Centenary church. On arrival they entered the church where the Wesleyans awaited them, and as the Rev John Ker, President of the Primitive Wesleyan Conference, mounted the platform to be welcomed by the Rev Dr W. Burt Pope, President of the Wesleyan Conference, their warm handshake was seen as a symbol of the union.

The Methodist Church in Ireland was a reality, though in fact the term did not come into general use until somewhat later.

The terms of the agreement were faithfully observed. For some years there was the business of rationalising circuits, and deciding which of two premises should be used in one or other town. What is somewhat surprising is the speed with which this was achieved, and the sale of redundant buildings actually began in the following year. The determining factors would appear to have been size and imposing situation. When one notes that after a similar reunion of Methodist churches in England in 1932 local rationalisation of premises had not taken place thirty years later, the achievement of the Irish Methodists would indicate a considerable measure of goodwill.

It was, in theory, to be a union of equals; but it wasn't quite so. The Primitive Wesleyans brought into the union 60 active and retired ministers, 9 ministers on probation, and 6,650 members (the smallest membership they had ever recorded). The Wesleyans brought 167 active and retired ministers, 29 ministers on probation, and 19,950 members. History, it has been said, is written by the victors. In 1886 and 1888 Charles H. Crookshank published the second and third volumes of his *History of Methodism in Ireland*. He had been a Wesleyan, but to his lasting credit it must be said that he was scrupulously fair in giving adequate treatment to the Primitive Wesleyans. It is wholly regrettable that nobody at the time thought to take proper care of the Primitive Wesleyan records. It was only by chance that the manuscript minutes of their conferences, damaged by damp, came to light in the 1980s in the loft of a stable at Clones.

CHAPTER 7

The Methodist Church in Ireland

The euphoria of the 1859 revival remained with the evangelical churches in Ulster long after the converts. Indeed, in Ulster Presbyterianism it was to be found fully a century later. With it, in so far as the Methodists were concerned, went a confidence that they had not felt before, and which if anything was enhanced by the reunion of Wesleyans and Primitive Wesleyans twenty years later. The tone of the church in the last two decades of the nineteenth century was confident to the point of arrogance. Crookshank's *History of Methodism in Ireland*, published within ten years of the reunion is couched in language which suggests that it was the Methodists who were the most faithful advocates of Christian truth in the country. However, the wisdom of hindsight suggests that both the Church of Ireland and the Methodists lost something important to themselves by their separation.

An evangelical revival in the Church of Ireland during the first half of the nineteenth century has been attributed to the Rev Peter Roe, who was first curate and then rector of St Mary's, Kilkenny. Roe visited Dublin in 1800 and 1802. During the former visit he was impressed by Mr Cooper, the Countess of Huntingdon's preacher in the city, and during the latter met Arthur Keene, Bennett Dugdale, and 'Mr D'Olier', probably Isaac, all of whom were later to be prominent in the Primitive Wesleyan Society. Roe was not favourably impressed by every aspect of Methodism, but his views were evidently influenced by these and by others. He wrote:

> ... since I came here I have met Quakers, Moravians, Methodists and Episcopalians, who really love God. May

81

they also love each other; strengthen each other's hands; and
exert themselves to the utmost of their power to oppose sin
and Satan, and to erect that glorious kingdom of the Lord
Jesus.[1]

It is not to be supposed that all of the members of the Primitive
Wesleyan congregations in the 1860s were as faithful in attending the Church of Ireland services as their ideals would have
suggested, but the failure of the negotiations with the Church of
Ireland ensured that they never did, and that they eventually became enfolded in the Methodist flock. The loss of nearly seven
thousand evangelicals impoverished the theological spectrum
of the Church of Ireland.

The Methodist losses included an impoverishment of worship. When the early Methodists went to their own preaching
meeting at five o'clock in the morning it left them free to attend
the Church of Ireland morning services at whatever hour these
were held. Wesley's intention was to increase the loyalty of his
people to the Church of Ireland, but this was not simply because
it was the church established by law. It was his conviction that
the church's forms of worship and discipline were ideal when
properly used. Whenever Methodist societies demanded that
their meetings should be at the same time as the parish services,
he reluctantly allowed it, but on condition that the Prayer Book
forms were used. He went so far as to make an abridgement of
the Prayer Book for that purpose. This was not sentimentality,
but an attempt to ensure that the Methodists continued to have a
balanced diet of worship and preaching. With the separation
from the Church of Ireland the Irish Wesleyans lost that balance
in 1816, and the Primitive Wesleyans in 1870.

As a church the Irish Methodists felt the need to behave like
one, and it is in these years that we observe the most dramatic
change in the architecture of Methodist buildings. In the early
days many Methodist preaching houses were much like cottages
without the internal partitions, but this was more a matter of
economy than of choice. Where money was available, and as it
became available, better premises were erected, but these fol-

lowed a rectangular plan with gable ends, and an elevated pulpit at one end. They were lofty to allow for a gallery at the back, and sometimes at the sides. In some cases those galleries were never built. Classic examples still in use are to be found at Bandon, and at Brookeborough. Somewhat later, but in the same style with the addition of pillars and a portico are those at Thomas Street in Portadown and Darling Street in Enniskillen. These were usually called chapels, a usage which survives in the name of the Chapel Fund with gives grants for the repair of any Methodist place of worship.

With its growing self-consciousness the Methodist Church began to feel the need to look like a church, and in buildings of the late nineteenth and early twentieth centuries Victorian Gothic begins to make an appearance. Towers, spires, or at least pinnacles decorate the exterior. The major change in the interior is the introduction of a choir box behind the pulpit, possibly with a pipe organ behind it. In a few cases the pulpit moves to the side and the communion table is given the central position against the end wall. Notable examples of this would be at Clontarf, and Dun Laoghaire, which are both still in use. The most outstanding example was Carlisle Memorial Church in Belfast, now no longer in use. The University Road church, also in Belfast, built in 1864, is interesting for its Italianate style,

In both Portstewart and Portrush the churches are named Adam Clarke Memorial churches. Clarke was actually born near Maghera, but had moved by 1779 to Portstewart. There he came under the influence of the Methodist preacher, Thomas Barber. Immediately after his conversion he began to preach in the vicinity, but such was his success in this that in 1782 he was invited to England by John Wesley, and appointed to the Bradford upon Avon circuit. Most of his life thereafter was spent in England, but he never forgot the scenes of his boyhood. He later endowed six schools in the Coleraine area. He was a man of considerable scholarship, mastering Persian, Hebrew and Greek, and writing a greatly valued six-volume commentary on the Bible. He warmly advocated the printing of the Bible in Irish. He

was asked to help decipher the Rosetta Stone, and in 1808 oversaw the organisation of the British state papers. He died in 1832.
A bell, originally cast in 1681, was given by Tzar Alexander I to
the British Ambassador in Russia, who in turn gave it to the
Duke of Newcastle. The Duke gave it Dr Clarke. Clarke presented
it to Portrush for one of the schools. The Portstewart church was
opened in 1861. That in Portrush was opened in 1887, and was
distinguished by a steeple which now houses Dr Clarke's
'Russian Bell'.[2]

Not only did Methodism feel the need to look like a church, it
also felt the need to behave like one. In the Church of Ireland
and in the Presbyterian Church, the two largest reformed
churches in Ireland, it was usual for one minister to be responsible for one church, and the urban Methodists began to think in
these terms too. Methodist preachers had generally looked after
several chapels, but now the larger cities began to witness that
singular anomaly, the circuit with only one society. There the
minister could lead the services every Sunday, with the conse-
quent undervaluing of the local preacher. Happily, enough of
concern for the church as a whole remained in these circuits for
them to continue to make a significant contribution to Irish
Methodism as a whole.

The natural consequence of this was the development of
ministerial dominance. The Primitive Wesleyans had demanded
as a condition of reunion that Conference should no longer be an
assembly of ministers only, and the point had been conceded by
the Wesleyans. Membership of the church's governing body
would henceforward be ministerial and lay in equal numbers,
and most of its committees would have the same balance.
Ministerial dominance was more subtle, and it was not so much
assumed by the ministers as imposed on them by the laity. The
feeling began to grow that the word had not been properly
preached if it had not been preached by a minister, and numbers
notably declined on those Sundays, progressively fewer, when
local preachers occupied the pulpits. Again families did not
think they had been pastorally visited unless they had been

visited by the minister, and the role of the class leader diminished. Originally the leader was reponsible for the pastoral oversight of a small number of members who were his or her 'class', meeting regularly for fellowship and instruction. The leader's role now declined to the point where in many circuits it became a matter of literature distribution.

The official aspect of this was seen in the assumption that every committee, council and institution was required to have a minister at its head. A notable exception to this was Methodist College in Belfast, which had lay headmasters from 1873. Gurteen College, however, did not have its first lay principal until 1963, and Wesley College waited until 1972. The idea that a layman might preside over a board or committee was accepted in 1971, but no lay person was elected to the Conference secretariat until 2000.

With so much happening some of the leaders of the church saw a need for a publication which would spread the news, so that more people would be informed of events, and there would be a permanent record of the times. The first people to put this into practice were a Dublin solicitor and a young minister. The man of law was Theodore Cronhelm, and the young prophet William Crook. Inspired by the revival, in the October of 1859 they published the first issue of *The Irish Evangelist*. This paper continued to appear every month for twenty-four years, with Crook – later Dr William Crook – as the sole or chief editor. It never made a profit, and its principal problem was its lack of capital.

For some time suggestions were made that it should become a weekly paper, but any decision was pre-empted by the action of a group in Belfast which began the publication of a weekly paper in 1883. When, by 1884, it was evident that this was securely established *The Irish Evangelist* ceased independent publication and threw in its lot with the new paper.

The initiative for this weekly publication was taken by a Belfast Methodist, I. S. Allen, who was a printer by trade. He was joined by the Rev Dr John Donald as editor, and the first issue of *The Irish Christian Advocate* appeared in November 1883. With the accession of *The Irish Evangelist* in the following year a private company was formed, and the name of the paper was shortened to *The Christian Advocate*. In 1885 Dr Donald retired from the editorial chair, and the Rev Henry Evans was given permission by the Conference to leave circuit work and become the fulltime editor. His skill gave the paper a measure of literary merit, but it failed to generate the necessary finances, and Evans returned to circuit in 1888.

The new editor was the Rev Richard Cole, who undertook the work in addition to that of his circuit ministry. He remained editor for thirty-five years. Mr Cole was no stranger to journalism, having contributed leading articles to *The Belfast Telegraph*, and Methodist notes to *The Northern Whig* and *The Irish Times*. His work earned the commendation of a London weekly, *The Christian Age*, which applauded *The Christian Advocate* for its 'able treatment of current topics and its masterly leaders on subjects of vital importance to the moral and social welfare of Ireland'.

Under Mr Cole's guidance the paper survived the difficulties of the war years 1914-1918, and afterwards. In 1923, however, he laid down his pen, and the paper was sold to a new board of younger ministers and laymen, who formed the Irish Methodist Publishing Company. These, giving service on a voluntary basis, reverted to the original name of *The Irish Christian Advocate*, and developed in Belfast a very successful bookshop under the name Epworth House. Much of the credit for this must be given to the Rev Dr William Northridge who served for many years as editor. The manager of the bookshop was Trevor Roycroft.

The life of both paper and bookshop came to an abrupt end on 20 October 1971 when the building was destroyed by a bomb planted by the IRA.[3]

The last quarter of the nineteenth century saw the peak of American revivalist influence in Britain and Ireland. The earliest of these to come to this country was a Methodist, Lorenzo Dow, who came in 1806 and again in 1809, when his style divided opinion in Methodist circles. His preaching was strongly emotional, but it may well have been his appearance which perturbed the Conference rather more. He has been thus described:

> Pale, thin and somewhat consumptive looking, dressed in the plainest attire, often threadbare, his feet covered with what seemed sandals rather than shoes, and in later years wearing a long beard, and hair loosely hanging about his shoulders, his whole appearance was such as to excite the greatest interest and curiosity. Then the suddenness and promptitude of his advent in a town or village, at the very hour and minute he had appointed; the boldness with which he would attack the ruling vices of the place, which he seemed to know almost intuitively; together with the biting sarcasm and strong mother wit that pervaded his addresses, all served to invest his appearance in any vicinity, with an air of singular and romantic interest.[4]

Some of the older Methodist preachers welcomed him, but the Conference was wary of allowing somebody to travel through the country apparently with its sanction, but really outside its control. It discouraged his reception by Methodist circuits. Whatever impression he made at the time, Dow had little permanent effect on Irish Methodism, his memory surviving more as a curiosity than anything else.

During the 1859 revival the American Methodist evangelists Walter and Phoebe Palmer came to Belfast, and conducted very successful meetings in the Donegall Square church. This, however, was a small part of the great revival which was then in progress. The evangelists who made the greatest impact were the preacher Dwight Moody and his accompanying singer Ira Sankey, who visited Belfast and Dublin 1874, and returned to Dublin in 1883. Their much longer campaigns in England also had some effect here, through the press reports. In 1904 Reuben Torrey visited Belfast. A number of English evangelists who were following their example visited Ireland at one time or another between 1883 and 1904.

The more lasting effects of these late nineteenth century evangelists were twofold.[5] One was their emphasis on total abstinence, and the other was their hymn singing. None of them made any significant impact on people outside the churches. Those they influenced were all people from the middle classes who had an existing church connection, not always peripheral. But to be successful they had to count converts, and one of the ways of doing so was to convert people to total abstinence, even from a position of temperance. Their addresses abound with cases of men saved from drunkenness. It is from this period that total abstinence becomes a very strong feature of evangelical religion, to the point where some questioned the Christianity of those who drank alcohol at all.

Wesley was not a total abstainer, and did not require his people to be such, though he did discourage the drinking of whiskey and gin. In the days when one could be 'drunk for a penny, and dead drunk for tuppence' he recognised that addiction to spirits could make people unemployable, reduce them to poverty, and bring misery to their families. He did not have the same objection to wine or ale. Some Methodists and other Protestants signed the pledge to abstain from alcohol during the campaigns of Fr Theobald Mathew in the south and west of Ireland during the 1840s, but it was the American revivalists who made such total abstinence a criterion of evangelical religion. Their argument was accepted by the evangelicals of all churches, but Methodism was so predominantly evangelical that total abstinence has been seen as a Methodist characteristic.

Singing played a significant role in creating the right atmosphere for the evangelistic appeal, and each of these evangelists produced a book of songs for use during the mission. By far the greatest of these was Ira D. Sankey's *Sacred Songs and Solos*, compiled for Dwight L. Moody's missions. Beginning as a very small collection of under twenty pieces, it eventually expanded to 750. It has often been said that Moody was weak on theology, and strong on sentiment. Sankey's book reflects this, dwelling on the themes of rescue to the beleaguered, relief to the suffering, and the homecoming of the wanderer. A typical example comes from the pen of Fanny Crosby van Alstyne, who published under her maiden name, her married name, and several pseudonyms:

O my Saviour, love me,
Make me all thine own;
Leave me not to wander
In this world alone.

Sankey's hymn book never replaced the *Methodist Hymn Book* in the Sunday services of Irish Methodism, but it did have some use in the smaller meetings in some places, and it had a great influence in the homes of the Methodist people. In the days when there were no cinemas, no radio and no television people made their own entertainment, and gathering to sing around the parlour piano was a feature of most middle class homes. On Sundays in evangelical homes it was hymns which were sung, and the book most often used was Sankey's. That brought about a subtle change in Methodist piety. They had learned their theology by singing the hymns of Charles Wesley, but now theology began to give way to sentiment.

It is interesting to note that the Billy Graham campaigns in England in the 1960s also produced a hymn book. Again the missioner's impact on the people was transient, but *Mission Praise* has passed through several editions since. Only some of Sankey's hymns found their way into later Methodist hymnals, and so into the Sunday services, but *Mission Praise* has come into use in the church alongside the official book, *Hymns and Psalms.*

In the 1890s Belfast and Dublin Methodists were turning their minds to new forms of social service, and in 1892 in each city a forum was created for the purpose. The Belfast Methodist Council was formed in May, and had a short life. The Dublin Methodist Council was formed in October and continued to do interesting and useful work until the 1960s. The primary intention of the Councils was to bring together members of all the circuits in the particular city to consider matters of social concern, and even to propose the sort of action which the church should take in relation to them, but the Dublin Council expanded its brief to include a wide variety of subjects. Experts were invited to speak on religious, ethical and social welfare matters.

On a practical level the Dublin Council undertook or initiated a number of projects. In 1907 it arranged an event to celebrate the bicentenary of the birth of Charles Wesley, and in 1938 it marked the bicentenary of John Wesley's Aldersgate experience. In connection with the latter it commissioned a brass plate which was installed on a wall in St Mary's Church, Mary Street, to commemorate the fact that Wesley had preached his first sermon in Ireland there. Looking to the future rather than to the past, it encouraged the foundation of the Epworth Club.

It was the minister of the Centenary church, the Rev James D. Lamont who in 1898 actually brought the club into being. He and others in the Council had recognised the difficulties experienced by young men from the rural areas who came to the city seeking work. One of the greatest difficulties was in finding somewhere to live. A house on the west side of St Stephen's Green, No 110, was acquired, and most of the rooms let to such young man at a reasonable rent. A reading room was also provided, to which other young men living in the city were also welcomed. For several years the Epworth Club gave a much appreciated service to young men, and it was eventually difficulties in finance and staffing which brought it to a close.[6]

Longer lasting was the publication by the Council of the *Dublin Methodist Year Book* which appeared annually for nearly fifty years from 1904 to 1952. The last issue recorded the constitution and membership of the Council, officers of young people's organisations in the circuits, important dates in the Methodist year, ministers and officials of the circuits and of local institutions, officers and teachers in Sunday Schools, and organists and members of church choirs. In that year the price was one shilling and sixpence.

The greatest service, however, which the Council did, and from which the city still benefits was to suggest a plan for the establishment of a city mission in Dublin.

The concept of city missions arose in London as a response to the anonymous publication in 1883 of a book entitled *The Bitter Cry of Outcast London*. This came just at the time when two committees appointed by the Wesleyan Conference were reporting on the social needs of the city and the problem of redundant churches respectively. The Conference of 1885 was moved by a consideration of all three to establish the London Wesleyan Methodist Mission. This was to open halls in various parts of the city where the need was greatest, and attract the poorer people. The idea rapidly spread to provincial cities.

It was immediately recognised that such people would not go to churches, so the buildings, many of them quite quickly purpose built, were called halls. There were no pews, the assembled people being seated in theatrical style tip-up seats. Instead of pulpits there were platforms which accommodated preacher, choir and musical items. Contemporary advertising techniques were used to draw people to the services. There were, in fact, three programmes running in parallel. The first was the worship programme of religious services and meetings. The second was the 'cultural' programme of concerts, lectures and recreation. The third was the social relief programme, which provided meals, and whatever other things people needed to help them on the way to being self supporting.[7]

The first Irish venture along these lines was in Belfast, where in 1889 the Rev Crawford Johnson established the Belfast Central Mission. 'Established' may not be quite the right word, for the mission had no proper home for its first six years. It was first located in the Sandy Row Methodist church, but that was too small, and for a while a tent was used. Then the mission moved to a circus hall. Finally, in 1895 it acquired a permanent location in its own Grosvenor Hall, between Grosvenor Road and Fingall Street. This building in the event only served for thirty-two years, when it was demolished and new one with the same name built on the site.[8]

The Methodists of Dublin saw the need for a mission in their city, and it was the Dublin Methodist Council which suggested a solution. The South Great George's Street chapel, which had served the Primitive Wesleyans as their headquarters since it was built in 1820, had not been sold, but its congregation had scattered and the building was falling into disrepair. The suggestion was that this should be renovated, and suitably altered to serve as a mission. In 1893, with quite remarkable speed, the building was made ready, re-named George's Hall, and commenced work. The first superintendent here was the Rev William Crawford. Changing social conditions in the city led to the abandonment of George's Hall in 1961 and the relocation of the Mission in the Abbey Street Methodist Church, which had also been suitably redeveloped.[9]

A year later it was the turn of the Londonderry Methodists to redevelop a Primitive Wesleyan chapel in that city. This was on the east side of the Foyle, and was reopened under the name Clooney Hall. The pioneer minister in this Mission was the Rev P. Ernest Donovan.[10]

Finally for this period, a fourth city mission was opened, also in Belfast where the Rev William Maguire was in 1896 appointed minister of Frederick Street church in the northern part of the city. He saw the need for a second mission in the city to cater for the needs of the poor people living in that end. Against some opposition he succeeded in persuading the Conference to designate Frederick Street, and a few other adjacent areas 'The North Belfast Mission', and this they did in 1898. However the Mission only remained there for seven years as the lease of the premises was running out. In 1905 the Salem chapel of the Methodist New Connexion on the corner of York Street and Great George's Street was acquired, and to it, now called The People's Hall, the Mission duly moved. It remained for nearly seventy years. In 1974 it followed population movement to the new Rathcoole Estate just outside the city to the north-east. This was part of the borough of Newtownabbey, and in 1986 the Misson was re-named the Newtownabbey Mission.[11]

The work of none of these missions was long confined to the halls which were their headquarters. Premises were acquired in other parts of the cities, in rural locations, or by the seaside. These were occupied as hostels for the homeless, sheltered housing for the elderly, holiday homes providing holidays for people who could never afford to pay for such, and in one case an orphanage. Work was undertaken in promoting the health of children, rehabilitating ex-prisoners, and helping those who for any reason could not cope with the pressures of normal living. As time went by and local authorities undertook programmes of slum clearance, one mission or another would sponsor new churches in the housing developments to which their people had been moved. Their reputation for effective social relief and support was so great that they commanded the sympathy of a wide variety of people outside their own denomination, and financial contributions came from all sorts of people of every Christian persuasion and of none.

The approach of a new century prompted the Conference in 1899 to announce a Twentieth Century Fund to be subscribed by 1901. To administer this the Rev James D. Lamont was released from circuit work to act as General Secretary. He was supported by four secretaries, the Rev George R. Wedgwood of Dublin, the Rev William R. Budd of Bangor, John B. McCutcheon of Belfast and Alexander M. Fullerton of Dublin. Five treasurers were appointed: the Rev Dr William Nicholas, President and Theological Professor of Methodist College, the Rev Joseph W. R. Campbell, General Secretary of the Home Mission Fund, Robert Booth JP of Dalkey, Frank Megarry JP of Belfast, and John H. Thompson of Cork.

The target of the fund was set at 52,000 guineas, or £54,600. Assuming that the administration expenses would be £4,600, the Conference hoped eventually to disburse £50,000 in grants. The proposed allocation included £15,000 to the Home Mission Fund, of which £5,000 was to be spent on the general mission, the Special Evangelistic Agency, colportage, and open-air preaching, and the other £10,000 on the support of small Methodist churches in rural areas. The Chapel Fund was to receive £25,000 to be used in giving grants towards the purchase of sites, and the building of new churches. £3,500 was allocated to the General Education Fund, to provide grants for small schools, and some assistance in the cost of theological training. The orphanages were to have £3,500, part of which would be used to assist in the establishment of a new home. The Supernumerary Ministers' Fund, which provided pensions for retired ministers and their widows, was to have £1,000 to be added to its capital. £2,000 was to be given to Foreign Missions. In light of the fact that the church normally gave only a little less to Foreign Missions than it did to Home Missions, this last may seem out of balance, but it was probably regarded as a token gift. The main purpose of the fund was to strengthen the church in this country, and increase its effectiveness.

In 1900 the Conference called for a week of special missions to held simultaneously in every circuit throughout the country, and the following year reported the success of these. Though the Fund was to have been closed in 1901, the Conference of 1902 was told that promises of £6,000 were still outstanding, and it was not until 1904 that the final figures were announced. The total subscribed was £52,630 3s. 9d. The extra time had raised the costs, and the figures allocated were reduced by 5% below the targets. Part of the allocation to the orphanages duly went towards the cost of establishing a new home for orphans, Craigmore Home near Moira. A century later the equivalent of the amount raised in terms of purchasing power would be in the region of £3,150,000

For many years, in fact since 1826, the Home Mission Fund of the British Conference had been sending money to Ireland in the belief that the Irish Methodists were unable to support themselves. The amount was in the region of £800 per annum. The success of the Twentieth Century Fund suddenly awakened the British to the fact that the Irish were able to maintain themselves, and that the grant should cease. In 1903 they generously offered a single payment of £15,000 in lieu of the annual grant. The Irish Conference happily accepted the offer, and invested the money in the interests of its own Home Mission Fund.

This, however, was not the only subsidy which the Irish church received from London. For many years certain areas where Methodists were very few had been designated 'mission stations', and had been supported by the Wesleyan Missionary Society. At one time there were as many as forty of these, and over a hundred day schools had been established in them. At their peak in 1871 the Missionary Society grant had amounted to £6,664. However, as the number of missions and schools declined this figure dropped to something in the region of £4,000. Irish contributions to the Missionary Society rose to about the same figure, and the payments were therefore effected by book entry. The system came under considerable criticism. In 1905 the Missionary Society proposed to end the grant, and after some negotiation agreed to continue paying £4,200 for ten years only, on the condition that all money raised in Ireland for Foreign Missions would be remitted to the Mission House in London.

The Irish Conference began to look critically at the various missions, assessing their justification, and some were closed and others amalgamated. Much of the continuing grant was capitalised for the Irish Home Mission Fund, and when payments ceased in 1915 the remaining mission stations were merged into the circuits. In the Minutes of the Conference of 1915 they made their final appearance. By 1916 the Irish contributions to Foreign Missions had risen to almost £6,000.

From the earliest days, when a society had acquired a site for a chapel, a school or a minister's residence, it had been customary to establish a trust to hold the property. Such trusts were usually in a prescribed form which ensured that the property was always secured to the Methodist Conference, but the trustees were generally found locally. It was the practice for the first three or four to be the ministers of the circuit and neighbouring circuits, and with them were joined a sufficient number of substantial local members to bring the total to between ten and fifteen. Some property, generally investments rather than buildings, was owned by the Conference to be used for one fund or another, and each holding required its trust. Both Wesleyans and Primitive Wesleyans had such trusts. Their number made legal transactions cumbersome.

During the connexional year 1913/14 legal advice was sought and received to the effect that the easiest solution would be the establishment of a corporate body of Trustees with their own seal, and to do that a private Act of Parliament would be required. The Conference of 1914 approved such a course of action, and in due course the Act was obtained. It was entitled

The Methodist Church in Ireland Act, 1915

5 and 6 George V Cap xlvi

An Act to constitute and incorporate the Trustees of the Methodist Church in Ireland, and to vest in them certain trust properties for the said Church, and to provide for the administration of those properties and for other purposes connected therewith.

The Conference was careful to arrange that the Trustees could hold any Methodist property on behalf of the Conference, or on behalf of any circuit or institution. Through the years many circuits have been encouraged to transfer their property to these Trustees, who have come to be called the Statutory Trustees. In an attempt to ensure that no circuit or institution would put money into property more elaborate than the work required, the Trustees were barred from holding more than thirty acres for any society, more than one hundred for any college or charity, or more than twenty for any hall or offices for the use of the Conference. Nobody ever imagined that less than thirty-five years later the church would open an agricultural college which would require for its work several hundred acres.

The Trustees were to be eighteen ministers and eighteen lay people, and the first appointed by the Act were:

The Revs James M. Alley, Samuel T. Boyd, William R. Budd, Joseph W. R. Campbell, R. Lee Cole, William Corrigan, William Crawford, Henry Evans, Frederick E. Harte, Robert M. Ker, James Kirkwood, William B. Lumley, William J. F. Maguire, J. Oliver Park, James W. Parkhill, John C. Robertson, George W. Thompson, and George R. Wedgwood.

Robert N. Anderson, Richard W. Booth JP, A. Crawford Browne, J. Roberston Coade JP, Alexander M. Fullerton, George H. Fulton, George Hadden JP, William J. Jefferson, David J. Lindsay, Albert V. McCormick JP, Robert B. McMullen, Claude C. Mercier, Samuel T. Mercier JP, Alfred C. Reilly JP, Philip B. Robinson JP, John H. Thompson, Sir William J. Thompson and Sir William Whitla.

If on the one hand the Irish Methodists were feeling self-confident in their church, singing Sankey around the parlour piano, developing social concerns in the cities and raising substantial sums of money for new ventures, on the other they were facing a situation of considerable turmoil. These were the years of the campaign for Home Rule.[12]

We have noted earlier the Methodist record of loyalty to 'King and Country' and the reasons for it. Throughout the nineteenth century that record was maintained, and added to it was traditional Protestant fear of how a Catholic government would treat a Protestant minority. For these reasons they had opposed Catholic emancipation, repeal of the Union and the Maynooth grant. Initially they disliked the national education proposals, but later came to see an advantage in the scheme. The Primitive Wesleyans opposed Disestablishment, but on that issue the Wesleyans were less certain.

The campaign for land reform presented a more difficult question. On the one hand the Methodists were critical of repressive landlords, but on the other they heartily condemned attacks on their persons and property, or on those of their tenants. Some Methodists, however, without condoning the violence of the extreme groups, were happy to support the Land League, and one of these, a man named Stirling gave such valuable service to it that his colleagues raised a monument to his memory in Glasnevin cemetery. Others had to face a more terrible dilemma. If they paid their rent they would be attacked by 'Captain Moonlight' and if they didn't they would be evicted by the landlord. Several resolved the issue by choosing to emigrate.

The plight of the tenants convinced some Methodists that the only solution lay in having an elected government in Ireland, and some moved beyond Home Rule to nationalism. James Sullivan Starkey wrote poetry in Irish using the Irish form of his first name and signing his poems Seamus O'Sullivan. Both of his grandfathers were Methodist ministers. We have noted the name of one of them, William Starkey who died during the Great Famine. The other, James Sullivan was a fluent Irish speaker. J. S. Starkey played a significant role in the Irish Literary Revival.

Alice Milligan, an Omagh Methodist, and educated at Methodist College, was the organising secretary of the centenary celebrations in Ulster of the 1798 Rising. She was a friend of John O'Leary, and an organiser for the Gaelic League. She published a number plays, poetry and other works, and was engaged in journalism. Her sister, Charlotte Milligan Fox, was a noted folk music collector, and Founder of the Irish Folk Song Society.

Frederick J. Allan claimed that it was being asked to participate in a debate in Clonliffe Methodist Church in Dublin that persuaded him to rebel against the Victorian values of his colleagues. He joined the Irish Republican Brotherhood, and rose to a leading position in it, but when Pearse began to lead some of its members towards a policy of violence Allan did not follow him.

Such people were the exception rather than the rule, and a source of embarrassment to most of their fellow Methodists. The *Christian Advocate* made it clear that the official policy of the church was against Home Rule. When in 1886 the newly elected Member of Parliament for West Clare, a Methodist named Jeremiah Jordan, used his maiden speech at Westminster to launch a vigorous attack on landlordism, clericalism, and Orange bigotry, the *Christian Advocate* cast doubts on his right to be called a Methodist. Those Methodists who were supportive of Home Rule without going to the extremes where generally to be found in the rural areas of the south and west, where their livelihood to some extent depended on the goodwill of Catholic neighbours. Where Protestants were sufficiently numerous to be self-sufficient, the Methodists were decidedly opposed to it.

The reasons were less religious than related to Protestant solidarity, and to some extent there was a nervousness as to how Home Rule would affect the missionary work of the church. English Methodists constituted the largest non-conformist denomination in the country, and as such had a major place in the the missionary effort through the British colonies. Irish Methodists did not want to imperil that. However, the attitude of the English Methodists was an embarrassment. They were strongly supportive of Gladstone as a politician, and therefore in favour of Home Rule which he was advocating. The Rev Hugh Price Hughes, in the pages of his *Methodist Times*, was strongly trumpeting its cause. Several Irish ministers made journeys to Britain seeking to persuade their opposite numbers there to change their views.

When the second Home Rule Bill was proposed in 1892 the Revs Dr Oliver McCutcheon and Wesley Guard expressed the official view of the Methodist Church at the Ulster Unionist Convention. The 1893 Bill was seen as worse than that of 1886, threatening to extinguish Protestantism in the south. Methodists organised their own demonstration against the third Home Rule Bill in 1912. Simultaneous meetings were planned in the Ulster Hall and the Exhibition Hall, and special trains were arranged to bring people from all parts of Ulster and elsewhere. So great was the number of those who came that a third venue had to be arranged at the last minute – the People's Hall. Sir William Whitla occupied the chair in the Ulster Hall.

So great was the enthusiasm that those who were in favour of Home Rule were discouraged from saying too much. One of those who had the courage to take a different view was the Rev William Crawford, Liberal and Home Ruler as to his politics, and then stationed in the Kingstown circuit. He said that he had met more intolerance in Ulster than in the rest of Ireland put together, and received a number of abusive letters. The Conference confirmed its opposition when it met in June.

The Ulster Volunteer Force gun running at Larne in the April of 1914 was reported in the *Christian Advocate* without comment.

It would seem, however, to have caused second thoughts in the Conference. It was now very clear that opposition to Home Rule could take a violent form, leading possibly to civil war. When, therefore, a strongly uncompromising resolution was put before the Conference, an amendment was moved expressing the desire for a settlement by consent. It was lost by 143 votes to 110, and the original motion adopted. As violence did erupt in Dublin in 1916, and in many parts of the country in the years immediately after the First World War, the attitude of the church was modified, and in 1920 the *Christian Advocate* was willing to accept the suggestion of partition as a lesser evil than civil strife.

It is significant that both a Methodist in the councils of the Irish Republican Brotherhood, and the majority of the church who had so strongly opposed Home Rule, were at one in the recoil from violence. Not far short of 150 years before, just before the Battle of Lexington in 1775, John Wesley had written to the Methodist preachers in America:

My dear Brethren, You were never in your lives in so critical a situation as you are at this time. It is your part to be peacemakers, to be loving and tender to all, but to addict yourselves to no party. In spite of all solicitations, of rough or smooth words, say not one word against one or the other side … See that you act in full union with each other: this is of the utmost consequence.

In the heightened passions of the thirty five years of the Home Rule agitation, and under the pressure of opinion among neighbours, much of this irenical advice had been forgotten, and Methodists had taken sides, some of them to extremes, but in the last analysis the political extremes were not where the bulk of Methodists were either most happy or most effective. The route they preferred was the route of conference, however difficult, rather than armed conflict. It was not that the church was pacifist. In the face of aggression it was happy to bless those who joined the colours, and place in the churches memorials to those who gave their lives in the war; but for the settlement of internal disputes it was, as it had been in Wesley's time, to the process of law which most of them instinctively turned.

The Home Rule debate was rudely interrupted in 1914, when a maverick student fired the shot which gave some of the European powers the pretext they wanted for war. In Ireland it was the first time since the Napoleonic period when the country was actually threatened with foreign invasion. There had been other wars in which Irishmen had fought, but India, the Crimea, and South Africa were distant, and news travelled slowly. Europe was very close, and the news came more swiftly.

There was an immediate twofold impact on Irish Methodism. The first was in the number of young men who enlisted in the army and in the navy. Their motives were certainly never as straightforward as memory has suggested. Some went from motives of patriotism. As Kitchener's famous recruiting poster said, 'Your Country needs YOU'. For others it was an escape from unemployment, or the dull routine of a boring job, into a life of excitement. For yet others, it was the spirit of the moment in which they had been caught up. Young women enlisted in the nursing services, probably with less diverse motivation. The second was the arrival in Ireland of large numbers of recruits to the army, sent to barracks and camps here for training. Methodist halls anywhere convenient to these training centres were opened to the troops for recreation, and were staffed by volunteers from the membership of the churches. Most of these operated throughout the war.

Cork Harbour and Berehaven further to the west were important naval bases, and here the Methodist Chaplain to the Royal Navy, the Rev Thomas Moran became the first Methodist allowed to conduct a parade service. Twenty-six Irish Methodist ministers volunteered to serve as chaplains to the forces, and served in many fields of action. All of them served in the army, two rising to the rank of Senior Chaplain, and two to Assistant Principal Chaplain. Several were decorated for bravery. For the people of Cork the conflict came very close on 7 May 1915 when the *Lusitania* was torpedoed off the Old Head of Kinsale, and sank with heavy loss of civilian life. Two days later fourteen of the survivors attended the Sunday morning service in the small Methodist church in Queenstown.

Soon Irish Methodist families were among those receiving the news of husbands, sons, fathers, brothers, and others killed in the fighting. It has been estimated that something in the region of eight and a half million people were killed on one side or the other before hostilities ceased in 1918. Nobody has estimated the number of Irish Methodists, but in many churches tablets on the wall record the names of those who died. Probably the longest list is that of the Mountpottinger and Newtownards Road circuit in Belfast with sixty-two names from a membership of 467. One would expect the greatest number to be from Ulster, but the Memorial Porch in Wesley Chapel in Cork recorded twenty-four out of a membership of 450. The little church in Bantry lost only a few, but numbers there were so small that their loss was sufficient to bring about the closure of the church in a generation. Twenty-five of those killed were sons of Irish Methodist ministers.

The Easter Rising in Dublin in 1916 directly involved no Methodists, but had a curious aspect which did. A Methodist family, Fannins of the Centenary church, owned the major firm of medical suppliers in the country, and had the contract for supplying such items to the army. After the suppression of the Rising it became known that one of their employees had for some time been pilfering from the firm, and giving the material to a friend in the IRA. Thus unconsciously Fannins supplied bandages and other medical necessities to both sides in the conflict.[13]

The end of the World War was followed in Ireland by an IRA campaign directed at the establishment of an independent Irish Republic. When this was brought to an end by a treaty which partitioned the country, civil war followed. These years were immensely difficult for the whole population. In large areas of the country law and order broke down, and a guerrilla war was waged. In 1919 a small detachment of the King's Shropshire Light Infantry was billeted in Fermoy. Some of these were ambushed as they marched to the Methodist church in the town on Sunday, one being shot dead and several others injured in front of the building. The minister, the Rev James D. Foster, had been leading a service elsewhere, and did not arrive on the scene until a few minutes later, but his wife rushed from the nearby manse, and had the body of the dead man carried into it. There she also gave first aid to the wounded.

District Inspector Wilson of the Royal Irish Constabulary in Templemore was shot dead on his way to the Post Office. He was a devoted Methodist, and one of the letters he was carrying was addressed to the Secretary of the Methodist Conference. It was afterwards delivered – bearing his bloodstains. Four Methodists were murdered in county Cork, which was the one most deeply involved in the civil war. Thomas Dooly's death in Roscrea was a tragic error. He had been stopped by a sentry as he was returning to the town with his wife in the car. Thinking that he had been given a signal to continue, he drove on, and was fatally shot in the back.

Only one minister suffered serious injury. The Rev Jones Whitla was shot by a sentry as he returned to Enniskillen from a Harvest Festival in Ballinamallard, and had to have his right arm amputated. For a while it was thought that his injury would be fatal, but he fought his way back to a measure of health, and eventually returned to duty. However, two years later he died of the effects of his injury.

The dreadful events of which these were a part came in time to a conclusion, and the forces of law and order again took control. In the Irish Free State, of course, the forces of law and order were now different, and the Irish people settled down to the business of living in two jurisdictions.

CHAPTER 8

Under Two Jurisdictions

It is one of the strange ironies of history that in Northern Ireland the unionists got what they had originally been determined to resist – they got home rule. It was, of course, home rule in a much smaller area, and one in which they could be assured a majority for the foreseeable future, and they set about the business of ensuring that it should be as long a future as possible. The single issue which dominated successive general elections throughout the life of the parliament in Belfast was the constitutional position of Northern Ireland, and the majority of the Northern Irish Methodists wished to remain as part of the United Kingdom. Their voting, therefore, was generally unionist. There were Methodists who thought otherwise, but they were very few.

The Methodist community in Ireland declined in the years from 1925 to 1935, largely due to losses in the Irish Free State which we must consider a little later, but it then resumed its growth to reach a peak in 1955 when there were over 67,000 people recorded in the church's books. The great majority of these – more than 60,000 – were in Northern Ireland, and it was there that the growth had occurred over the twenty years.

Administratively the church had been divided in a number of Districts, of which there were ten in 1920. Fluctuating numbers reduced these to seven at one period, and then increased them again to eight. An examination of their membership statistics reveal both in Northern Ireland and in the Free State a gradual movement into the largest cities – Belfast in Northern Ireland, and Dublin in the free State. In Northern Ireland this continued to the point where, in 1973, the Belfast District was thought to be too large for easy management, and was divided into three. It then became evident that the movement at that time was towards the urban areas south of Belfast Lough and Newtownards. In fact this was probably well established before the division of the District made it evident. The movement to Dublin continued throughout the life of the Free State and Éire and the earlier years of the Irish Republic, but began to change in the 1980s.

One of the Ulster-born evangelists working in Northern Ireland during the 1920s, W. P. Nicholson, was very strongly criticised for his unpolished style. He was capable of making quite candid references to particular people in his audiences if they drew his attention by arriving late, or by odd behaviour. It was probably this candour which attracted large numbers to his meetings. Many were offended by what they saw as rudeness, but many more were impressed by an evangelism that matched the ways in which ordinary working people expressed themselves. They saw Nicholson as a man of the people, forthright, and without any nonsense. His principal influence was on Presbyterian churches. It is impossible to be precise as to the number of people added to the Methodist community, but some of the membership increase was certainly attributable to him.

Tradition has also attributed to him the increase in the numbers of candidates annually received for the ministry during the middle and later years of the decade – eighteen in 1924, thirteen in 1925, fourteen in 1926, eleven in 1927, and twelve in 1928. That is not to say that all of the candidates had been influenced by him, but some certainly were. Such a surge in numbers is always a great encouragement to a church, but it is useful to look at the end of their ministry as well as the beginning. Assuming that a candidate was accepted at an age somewhere in the middle twenties, and retired at about sixty-five, an active ministry of forty years was regarded as the standard. Of the sixty-eight candidates received in these years fifteen either withdrew before ordination, or after ordination transferred to another Methodist church or to another denomination. Nine died in active ministry.

Of the others twenty-five retired during the 1960s and eleven in the single year 1970. Because there was no similar surge in numbers at that time, the number of ministers in active work fell from 168 in 1963 to 147 in 1971. The 1960s were difficult years of circuit realignment, particularly in the Irish Republic, but had it not been for the surge in ministerial recruitment during the 1920s that realignment would have come earlier, though it might have been more gradual, and therefore less painful for the circuits concerned.

The Second World War had a much greater impact on Northern Ireland than had the first. Shortages in supplies of food, fuel and other goods were much greater. It was now the only part of Ireland available to the British and American forces for training, and the presence of troops both for this purpose and for defence met with a similar response from the Methodist circuits as it had done in the First World War. Premises were opened to provide social and recreational facilities for the men – and women. For in the Second World War women were recruited into the auxiliary forces, the ATS, the WRNS, and the WAAF. The greatest impact, however, was in the fact that this war was not confined to the battlefields and trenches. The conflict in the air came home to the population of Northern Ireland, and Belfast sustained a severe, if comparatively brief blitz.

All of these factors affected the lives of the Methodist people as much as any others in the community. Members had enlisted; normal church activities were suspended, except for Sunday worship, to make way for other activities. Sixteen Irish ministers served as chaplains to the forces, one in the Royal Navy, ten in the Army, three in the Royal Air Force, and two, who had gone overseas as missionaries, in forces raised in South Africa and Burma.[1] One achieved the rank of Senior Chaplain. The bombing of Belfast destroyed many homes and businesses, and among the buildings demolished were two Methodist churches. That at Ballymacarrett was rebuilt after the war under the name Newtownards Road, but the church at Duncairn Gardens never was. Its congregation was merged with that of Carlisle Memorial Church on Carlisle Circus.

Wartime travel restrictions affected the church in occasionally quaint ways. If a minister in Northern Ireland was invited to preach at a service in Éire, he was required to submit the full text of his sermon to the censors before he went, just in case something he planned to say would reveal some information about the forces in Northern Ireland. It was necessary for the Conference in 1941, 1942 and 1943 to obtain emergency orders from the governments in Belfast and Dublin to reduce the size of the Conference, which had been fixed by the Methodist Church in Ireland Acts of 1929. It 1941 there were only a hundred and twenty members, and in the other two years only two hundred, instead of the usual three hundred. It was customary for the President of the British Conference to preside over its Irish counterpart, but in 1944 a very tight ban on travel to Ireland prevented the Rev Dr Leslie Church from making the journey to Belfast. The official fear was that a remark about troop movements around England might betray information important to the Normandy landings in the same month. An Irish minister, the Rev George Joynt, presided with grace and good effect.

The War ended in 1945, but it was some years before conditions began to return to normality, and restrictions and rationing ceased. There were then a number of Methodists who began to feel that the government in Belfast suffered from the lack of a 'loyal opposition'. They wanted to move the debate at elections away from the constitutional issue, to issues related to the economic and social needs of the communities, and particularly those concerning the people living in the city centre. Two of them, Vivian Simpson and William R. Boyd, were among the Members of the House of Commons at Stormont elected in the General Election of 1958 representing the Northern Ireland Labour Party. Boyd had contested the Woodvale seat in 1953 and 1955 without success. He was re-elected in 1962, but lost his seat in 1965. He stood for Belfast West in 1973, but again without success. Simpson contested the Larne seat in 1945, and Carrick in 1953 without success in either constituency. In 1958 he was elected for Oldpark, and held the seat for the remaining years of the Northern Irish Parliament. In 1973 he was a candidate for the Northern Ireland Assembly in the Belfast North constituency, but was not elected.

The protests of the Northern Ireland Labour Party that they did not wish to change the relationship between Northern Ireland and Great Britain were ultimately unavailing in face of the conviction that to divide the vote of the unionist interest was to give an opportunity to the nationalist party. His colleagues soon lost their seats, but Vivian Simpson continued to be re-elected for the Oldpark constituency more on account of who he was than of the party he represented. He was a good constituency man. At one stage, when the nationalist members withdrew from Stormont in protest against unionist policies which they could not change, Simpson was the only occupant of the opposition benches. This drew favourable comment from the then Northern Irish Prime Minister, Brian Faulkner, who disagreed with Simpson's politics, but admired his integrity.

Throughout the life of the Stormont parliament, however, most of the Methodists elected to it were unionists. The first of these was Frederick Thompson, who was returned unopposed at Ballynafeigh in 1937. He successfully defended the seat in 1938 and 1945, and retired in 1949. Robert B. Alexander was elected for Belfast Victoria in 1945, and retained the seat in 1949. He did not seek re-election in 1953. A third Methodist was elected in 1945 in the person of Capt R. Austin Ardill, who took the Carrick seat. He did not stand in 1949, but in 1973 returned to Northern Irish government, taking the fourth of eight seats for the Antrim South constituency in the Northern Ireland Assembly. In 1971 he had been elected Chairman of the Ulster Loyalist Association, and 1972 was Deputy Leader of Vanguard, playing an important role in the shifting attitudes of unionism through those years.

W. Basil McIvor, son of a Methodist minister, entered in Commons in 1969 as unionist member for Larkfield. He held the portfolio for Community Relations in 1971 and participated in the negotiations of the Sunningdale Agreement. In 1973 he headed the poll in Belfast South for the short-lived Northern Ireland Assembly, and in 1974 was Minister for Education. He was the first Chairman of Lagan College, the first integrated secondary school in Northern Ireland.

Basil Glass was also the son of a Methodist minister. He was one of the founders of the Alliance Party, and its Deputy Leader. He represented Belfast South in the Northern Irish Assembly, and in the Northern Irish Constitutional Convention, in each case taking the second of six seats. Defeated in 1982, he was Chairman of the party from 1985 to 1987.

These were the Methodists who fulfilled roles in the government of Northern Ireland, either as part of the party in power, or in opposition. Many more were involved in local government, sitting on county and district councils, and city corporations.

In 1968 agitation began in Northern Ireland to demand civil rights for the nationalist minority in the province, a minority which was growing in number. The conflict, which was to cost thousands of lives, leave even more with permanent injuries, and destroy a vast amount of property, has not finally been resolved. It has had a very marked effect on the life of the Methodist Church in Northern Ireland, particularly in Belfast.

There the fear engendered and positive intimidation led to considerable movement of population, and the city divided itself into 'Protestant' and 'Catholic' areas. As a result of this movement seven Methodist churches disappeared. One on the Falls Road was relocated for a time in Upper Falls, but even there failed to survive. The other six were Primitive Street, Carlisle Memorial at Carlisle Circus, Ligoniel, Lynn Memorial on Oldpark Road, Ormeau Road and Crumlin Road. The church at Agnes Street also closed, but this was only partly due to the conflict; it was also affected by the redevelopment of the area by town planners. The Donegall Square church in the centre of the city and that at Osborne Park off the Lisburn Road also closed during these years, but because of congregations dwindling for other demographic reasons.[2]

One of the buildings destroyed by a terrorist bomb in 1971

was the premises of the Irish Methodist Publishing Company in Wellington Street, Belfast. It destroyed the records of the *Irish Christian Advocate*, and made it impossible to continue publication of the weekly paper that had served the Irish Methodists for nearly ninety years. In January 1973, under the auspices of the General Committee of the church a new magazine was launched, appearing monthly instead of weekly. This was called *The Methodist Newsletter*, and was initially edited by the Secretary of the Conference, the Rev Harold Sloan. Within six years two others had followed him, Dr James Smylie and the Rev Ted Lindsay. In 1979 the Rev Dr Eric Gallagher became editor and guided the paper through the next sixteen years. He relinquished office at the end of 1995, since when the paper has been edited by a small team

During this period two Methodists, an Irish minister and an English layman, emerged into prominence. The Rev Dr Eric Gallagher was the superintendent minister of the Belfast Central Mission, and was one of those who took a major role in striving to build understanding between the divided communities. To that end he participated in both church and civil organisations. Dr Stanley Worrall was born in England, and came to Ireland on his appointment as headmaster of Methodist College in Belfast. He gave wholehearted service to the church and the community in Ireland. Gallagher and Worrall were among the small group of churchmen in 1974 who travelled to Feakle in the west of Ireland to meet leaders of the IRA in an effort to persuade them to call a ceasefire and make room for peace. The book which they co-authored, *Christians in Ulster 1968-1980*, is an important record of the role of the churches during those years.

In 1987 an IRA bomb destroyed a building near the War Memorial in Enniskillen, killing eleven people who had gathered for the ceremony of Remembrance on 8 November. One of these was a young nurse named Marie Wilson. Interviewed by the media later in the day, her father Gordon Wilson described holding the hand of his dying daughter as they lay trapped under six feet of rubble. It was a brief, but moving story, which was broadcast by media throughout the world. In the course of it he said, 'I have no ill will. I bear no grudge. Don't ask me for a purpose. I don't have a purpose, and I don't have an answer. But I know that there has to be a plan, and God is good.'

They were the words of a man deeply convinced that vengeance was not the way of a Christian, striving in the midst of deep tragedy to find the way Christ would have him respond. Gordon was the owner of a large drapery and outfitting business in the town, and had played no part in politics, but from this time he devoted himself to the task of making peace. He met with much criticism, and his efforts at times had a certain naïvety, but this was the evidence that he was genuine, and won the admiration of many. He was awarded the World Methodist Peace Prize, was voted Man of the Year in a BBC poll, and was included in Dublin among the list of Irish People of the Year. In 1994 the Taoiseach, Albert Reynolds, appointed him to the Senate in Dublin. He sat as an independant, continuing to speak for peace and reconciliation. In 1994 his only son was killed in a motor accident, and in 1995 Gordon Wilson died suddenly of a heart attack.

We shall come again to the statements of the Methodist Conference concerning the conflict, but for the moment it is important to acknowledge that Methodists were not of one mind. Few were involved in the paramilitary organisations, but opinion varied from the extreme to the liberal. Conference statements, however, represented a conviction rather than a compromise. They were not an attempt to reconcile the possibly conflicting views of different members, but to assert that communities live rather by debate than by confrontation, and that conviction has commanded the support of the great majority of the Methodist people in Northern Ireland and in the Republic.

Between 1916 and 1926 the number of Methodists in the Irish Free State fell from approximately 15,000 to just over 10,000. The underlying cause of this decline was the transfer of government from Westminister to Dublin, but there were several more immediate causes. A number of British people, Methodists among them, had been sent to Ireland to serve in one branch or other of the administration. They were civil servants, coast guards, post office officials, etc. On the withdrawal of the British administration most of these simply went home. Not all did, and the most notable exception was Arthur Dean Codling. Born in Lancashire, he was the son of a Wesleyan minister. In 1900 he was sent to Dublin to work in the Local Government Department where he became an expert in labourers' housing. Given the choice of transfer to London, to Belfast, or to the new Free State government, he chose the last. Neither he nor his wife had any wish to live in London, and as a convinced Gladstonian liberal he was not willing to work with a unionist administration. Transferred from Local Government to Finance, he rose to be Assistant Secretary of the Department, and was regarded as one of the very strong influences on the quality of the civil service in the early years of the Free State.[3]

In 1911 there were 1,021 Methodists domiciled in those counties which were to form the Free State and who were serving in the Army, the Navy or the Police. Soldiers and sailors particularly would have seen it as sensible to transfer their domicile to the United Kingdom, and others would have done so out of a sense of insecurity. Naturally those who were married brought their families with them. Of Methodist families being obliged to leave their homes there are few instances, confined to the areas where the Civil War was most intense. However, such instances did give to others the feeling that they were not wanted under the new regime. That feeling was behind one curious event. The Methodists of Ballineen in Co Cork met to discuss whether or not they should support the new government. It may be asked what alternative they had, but there have been several instances in Irish history of virtually entire church communities emigrating for one reason or another in the eighteenth and nineteenth centuries. Notable were the Presbyterians of Rathmelton, the Methodists of Innishannon, and the Catholics of Killaveney and Annacurra in Co Wicklow. The Methodists of Ballineen took a different decision; they chose to remain and support the new regime.[4]

As we have noted, the membership of the church was reduced by one third in a very few years. In the next thirty-five
years another third went. Behind this slower attrition lay too
main factors. One was the economic situation in the country
which gave rise to general emigration of young people.
Obviously the minority groups were the more seriously affected.
Another was the insistence by the Catholic Church that the
children of Catholics married to Protestants should be reared as
Catholics. This had a double effect. Where Methodists married
Catholics there was, in the early years at least, a strong possibility
that the family would eventually cease to be Methodists. But the
rule persuaded many young Methodists that such a marriage
was impossible, and they either failed to marry or emigrated, in
the latter case the matrimonial factor being added to the economic as motivation. It was in the 1970s that this pattern began to
change. A major shift in the attitude of Roman Catholics following the introduction of the Charismatic Movement into Ireland,
and the relaxation of the marriage regulations brought a change
in the attitude of the Methodists themselves, who became less
defensive and more confident. In some rural areas of the Irish
Republic numbers began to show a slight increase.

In some areas of life, in fact, the confidence returned quite
early. By the late 1920s Methodists were beginning to stand for
election to local councils, and even to Dáil Éireann. The first
Methodist to be elected Cathaoirleach (Chairperson) of a
County Council was Griffith Hinds of Laois in the 1930s. Several
others followed, and Charles Willoughby was Cathaoirleach of
the Dun Laoghaire Borough Council for four terms. The first
Methodist to be elected to Dáil Éireann was Jasper Wolfe in
1927. In fact he was elected in the West Cork constituency three
times between then and 1932. In the 1943 Niall McCormick
stood unsuccessfully for election to the Dáil, and in 1957 Lionel
Booth was successful. Wolfe stood as an independent, and
McCormick for Clann na Talmhan (The Farmers' Party). Booth
was a member of the Fianna Fáil party.

In 1930 Letitia Dunbar-Harrison was chosen by the Local

Appointments Commission for a post as librarian in county
Mayo. She won the position in open competition. However, in
what was to become one of the most celebrated cases of religious
discrimination in the Free State, her appointment was resisted
by the local library committee and the Mayo County Council.
Local Catholic clergy protested that because she was not a
Catholic she would not be capable of deciding which books
were suitable for reading by the young Catholics of Mayo. The
case gave rise to considerable controversy in religious and political circles, and received a great deal of coverage in the news-
papers. The Local Appointments Commission declined to bow
to the protesters, and Miss Dunbar-Harrison remained in post
until 1940, when she was transferred to a post of librarian in the
Defence Forces. She was by then Mrs Crawford having married
a Methodist minister, the Rev R. C. Plaice Crawford.[5]

Castlebar in Co Mayo had been an important centre of
Methodism in the eighteenth century, and the Methodist chapel
on the Green was the only building in Ireland for which John
Wesley laid the Foundation Stone. But Mayo was one of the
counties most seriously affected by the decline in Methodist
numbers during the years from 1935 to 1970. So were neighbouring counties. In 1915 there were eleven Methodist ministers
working in the province of Connacht; in 1995 there were two. In
1915 fourteen ministers lived in the counties of Cavan,
Monaghan and Louth. In 1995 there were none, and the remaining members of the churches there were under the care of ministers living in Tyrone or Longford. Circuits in south Leinster and
Munster, though greatly reduced in membership, have fared
somewhat better, and it is in some of them that the upturn in
numbers has been registered.

The Irish Methodists now lived in two political jurisdictions,
but the church did not alter its administration to accommodate
the new political boundary. Indeed no Irish church did, and in
all denominations dioceses, districts, circuits and congregations
straddled the border. It occasionally caused strains because of
differing perspectives, and in the first fifty years generated a

considerable amount of form filling to enable ministers and others to cross the border in the course of their pastoral duties without infringing customs regulations. These were accepted as irksome, but not seriously troublesome.

Methodists were responsible for one instance of political co-operation involving the two governments. When Wesley died in 1791 he left the control of the Methodist societies and Methodist property to one hundred ministers, who had power to fill vacancies in their number. Ninety of these were British and ten were Irish, and after some years it was agreed that this proportion should be maintained. Both the British and Irish Conferences had considerably more than one hundred members, but the agreement of the hundred was necessary for the acts of each Conference to have legal force. It was quite easy to bring ten Irish ministers to England for the British Conference, but the ninety Englishmen delegated their responsibility to one of their number who came to Ireland to authenticate the Irish Conference decisions.

In the late 1920s three divisions of British Methodism were planning to reunite, and in the course of doing so to abolish the 'Legal Hundred' as it was called. That meant that the Irish Methodist Church was obliged to revise its constitution to remove the role of the Legal Hundred also. When it had wished to create a body of Trustees in 1915, it had been a simple matter for the Conference to obtain a private Act of Parliament at Westminster, but this time it was functioning in the jurisdictions of two governments; two Acts were necessary. The Conference which met at Dublin in 1927 approved the draft of the neccessary Bills, and a few weeks later the British Conference at Bradford gave approval to those provisions which dealt with relations between the two Conferences. In 1928 the Bills were introduced the parliaments in Dublin and Belfast, and passed without difficulty. The Free State Bill was presented in Irish and in English; the Northern Irish Bill in English only. It was the first occasion on which the two parliaments acted identically and simultaneously. It is under the terms of these Acts that the Methodist Church in Ireland continues to be governed.

In the final analysis, however, a church is not a political organisation. Its essential function is to enable people to relate to the things of God. The Methodist societies began as a means by which members might develop their spirituality, and in the twentieth century this remained the primary purpose of the church as a whole. However, the best of all possible systems sooner or later becomes just that – a system and no more. It is possible over the past fifty to note a succession of ways in which Irish Methodists have from time to time sought to renew their spirituality.

The General Mission, originally appointed in 1799, had been designed to draw new members into the Methodist societies, but had also served to stimulate the spiritual commitment of existing members. During the course of the nineteenth century it had developed into a number of 'mission stations', which in 1915 were incorporated into the circuits. Occasional missions in the churches were thereafter left to local arrangement. In 1945 the Conference believed that these needed further stimulus, and appointed a Superintendent of Evangelism, whose task was to encourage circuits in arranging these missions at reasonable intervals, and to conduct them when asked. Each mission might last from a few days to a few weeks, according to local circumstances. Three ministers were successively appointed to the work, James Wisheart (1945-52), Hedley W. Plunkett (1952-55), and W. Sydney Callaghan (1955-62). By then the demand for such missions was beginning to decline, and in 1962 W. J. Wesley Gray was appointed to the work on a part time basis, which he did until 1964 when the appointment was discontinued. It was recognised that changing times needed a different approach.

Another movement, however, had already developed. At the Conference of 1950 in Cork Gerald Armitage of Cloughjordan in Co Tipperary made a plea that the lay men should take a more active and responsible role in the spiritual life of the church. They were more inclined to undertake administrative responsibilities, and women were generally better represented at devotional meetings. Aware that a similar movement had begun in England a few years before, a group of laymen called a conference at Gurteen College near Cloughjordan, and out of this grew what was called The Laymen's Fellowship. At a conference in Greystones in 1958 it adopted the following principles:

The Laymen's Fellowship is within the church, and is *not* a separate organisation.

Every man in the Methodist Church is invited to share in it.

The Fellowship exists for the undernoted purposes:

1. To deepen the spiritual life of the laity in our church.

2. To foster a vital Christian fellowship within the church.

3. To encourage laymen in effective service in the local church.

4. To develop the connexional spirit among laymen.

5. To encourage laymen to take an active interest in the world church.

6. To assist in every way possible the work of our ministers, and to co-operate with them in offering Christ to the people.

7. To strengthen and increase the witness of the laymen of our church in the life of the community.

If the document is a little pretentious, it illustrates the real concerns of many of the most active laymen in the church at the time. It shows the consciousness among the members of certain suspicions which they were anxious to allay, and certainly some ministers saw the Fellowship as implying criticism of their effectiveness. The group did not plan to create an extra organisation in the circuits, and did not propose to become a pressure group in the Conference.

Organisation was minimal. Committees were elected in several Districts, and these organised annual conferences at Bangor in Co Down, at Greystones in Co Wicklow, at Portrush in Co Antrim and at Portadown in Co Armagh. The Fellowship never sought representation in the official structures of the church, though its conferences were reported in the *Irish Christian Advocate*, and won wide approval. It did not arrange regular

group meetings in circuits, but simply provided in its conferences a forum for the exchange of ideas and experiences among
its members. Its ethos was essentially devotional. The driving
force of the group began to wane in the 1960s, and conferences
ceased in the 1970s.

In 1959 the Conference set up a committee to examine the
principles of Christian Stewardship, which had been introduced
into this country from America by a commercial firm, and was
reputed to have revolutionised fund raising in some churches of
other denominations. The committee took two years in the
study, and then recommended that the principles be adopted, at
the same time drawing attention to the fact that it was not merely
a matter of fund raising. It was an opportunity for a church to
consider responsibly all of its resources in terms of time, skills
and financial giving. The British Conference had set up a department with this wide approach, the Methodist Stewardship
Organisation (MSO), and their advice was sought. They suggested that the Irish church should not set up an independent
administration, but should use that already in place in
Manchester. It was agreed that the Irish committee would find a
suitable person, and the MSO would appoint him to their staff.
As Director of Christian Stewardship in the Methodist Church
in Ireland he would be jointly responsible to both the Irish committee and the MSO, he would do all the work in Ireland, and
when not busy there would act as a field director in England.

In 1962 Dudley Levistone Cooney was appointed, with two
main areas of responsibility. One was the advocacy of Christian
Stewardship principles in meetings organised by Districts and
circuits. The other was the introduction of Christian Stewardship programmes in circuits which requested them. Not long
after he began work it became evident that the financial basis of
the appointment had not been fully explored. The funding of the
MSO depended on the conduct by each director of between six
and eight fully directed campaigns each year, and the financial
charges were so structured that fully directed campaigns were
only feasible in circuits with at least two hundred families. The

MSO had assumed that most Irish circuits would be of that size, but in fact very few of them were, and certainly not enough to sustain an Irish director. The Irish committee had assumed that the MSO would fund the director for quite a number of years, but in 1966 it withdrew its funding of the appointment.

The effect of the campaigns during those years was mixed. The organisation insisted that Christian Stewardship was properly concerned to mobilise all resources, but the fact remained that in some places it was seen as a solution to financial problems. Also, there was a strong pietistic strain in the church which disliked the direct confrontation of the individual with requests to be precise about the commitment of money, and to some extent of commitment to particular forms of service. The Irish stewardship committee continued to function until 1971, and where further programmes were to be introduced a member of the MSO staff travelled from England. In 1971 the committee was discharged and its responsibilities taken over by the Home Mission department of the church. By then Mr Cooney had been accepted as a candidate for the ministry, trained and ordained.

It was also from America that the Lay Witness Movement was introduced into Ireland in 1975. It worked on a very simple principle. A group of people from one church or circuit visited another, usually for a weekend of small group meetings and Sunday services, and talked about their experience of Christian faith. They described its effect on their own lives and on the life of their church, thereby encouraging the members of the host church or circuit to do likewise. In the first Lay Witness weekends teams came from America to a number of Irish circuits, and some of the practices derived from American culture caused a measure of adverse comment, but there was no doubt that the basic methods were useful, and effective.

The Lay Witness Movement in Ireland never established a large organisation. Wilson Doran and a small steering group were sufficient to arrange the training of leaders, and the liaison between visiting and visited churches, as well as planning occasional conferences of those involved to exchange ideas and experiences. On that simple basis the work has continued fruitfully for over two decades.[6]

On the negative side, in the 1970s the church saw its second secession, also based in the Fermanagh area, but much smaller than the secession of 1816. During the 1960s a number of people began to express concern about the involvement of the church in the World Council of Churches, particularly after the admission to it of the Eastern Orthodox churches. They opposed what they saw as 'ecumenism, liberalism and modernism' in the church. They formed a group called The Irish Methodist Revival Movement, and published a magazine called *Whither Methodism?* For some time they voiced their concerns through it, and at Conference to which some of them were elected as circuit representatives.

It became evident that they did not command enough support to alter the policy of the church, and in 1970 at a meeting in Fivemiletown they decided to withdraw. They took with them not more than a thousand people, none of them ministers. For a short time they established a link with the Free Methodist Church of North America, which already had a small presence in Northern Ireland. However, within a sort time they learned that the Free Methodist Church was involved in ecumenical relations. Five of the congregations therefore withdrew from it, and formed the Fellowship of Independent Methodist Churches in 1973.

A General Council of ministers and lay representatives meets each month to manage the affairs of the Fellowhip, but each congregation calls its own minister, who has then to be approved and ordained by the General Council. In 1980 Bethel Bible College was established to train ministers. Twenty-five years later the Fellowship had sixteen congregations and two 'outreach appointments', staffed by thirteen ministers and one layman.[7]

During the lifetime of John Wesley a number of women in England began to preach, some of them with Wesley's direct, if cautious, encouragement.[8] Among them were such remarkable women as Sarah Crosby and Mary Bosanquet, the latter subsequently the wife of John Fletcher, the Vicar of Madeley. The practice, given the general contemporary view of the role of women, gave rise to adverse comment, and after Wesley's death the Wesleyan Conference put a stop to it, though women class leaders continued to 'exhort' the women in their own classes. The line between 'exhorting' and 'preaching' was not always clear.

In Ireland the only woman preacher of any note at the time was Alice Cambridge of Bandon in Co Cork. At the age of eighteen she began to attend Methodist meetings, in which she soon developed a very deep commitment and a lively concern that others should share her religious experience. At first she simply invited her friends to accompany her to Methodist gatherings, but then she began to exhort small groups of them, and her success with this led to her being invited to address groups at Kinsale, Youghal, Cappoquin and elsewhere. The inevitable opposition to a woman preacher arose, and she wrote to Wesley for advice. He replied with his usual cautious encouragement.

Thus encouraged, Alice Cambridge continued to preach where opportunity was afforded, and in 1798 addressed a meeting in Charles Fort, Kinsale, which was attended by most of the soldiers billeted there, together with their wives and families. The Irish Methodist Conference was, however, more concerned about appearances than about the success which she achieved, and in 1802 declared it contrary to both scripture and prudence that women should preach in public. Miss Cambridge was excluded from membership.

During the next eleven years she went into business in Dublin and in Cork, but continued to preach. Methodist premises were closed to her, but she found other opportunities. Then in 1813 she gave up her business to devote herself wholly to evangelism. Now Methodist premises were again opened to her, and she was invited to Presbyterian churches, and even to one Church of Ireland parish. After some years during which she preached in all of the Irish provinces, she retired to live in Nenagh, where she died early in 1829.[9]

Anne Lutton had a happier career. She was born at Moira, Co Down in the year 1791, and her childhood home was the venue for the local Methodist meetings. Her preaching began at small meetings for women in Moira, but in later years she travelled to various parts of Ireland and to some parts of England. She avoided opposition largely by confining herself to women's meetings, though some men did attempt to gain admission so that they might hear her. When at one time she visited Tullamore in Co Offaly the local minister was stationed at the door of the chapel to ensure that only women were allowed inside. It was hot and the windows were open, so that a number of men were able to congregate outside and hear her address. She died at Bristol in 1881.[10]

Alice Cambridge and Anne Lutton were outstanding exceptions to the general rule that the role of women in Irish Methodism was generally supportive. Charles Crookshank, in his book *Memorable Women of Irish Methodism,* tells the stories of eighteen women, but only Alice Cambridge was a preacher outside her own immediate society. The others were important in the support they gave to preachers, or in encouraging their husbands to provide accommodation for Methodist preachers and meetings. The nearest any of them got to preaching was in speaking to their class meetings, attended only by a small number of women.

Women, of course, were encouraged to make use of their skills, particularly in needlework, to support certain causes, and by the third quarter of the nineteenth century one of the leading causes was that of foreign missions. This led in 1884 to the formation of the first Irish Ladies' Committee to work for missions. Sewing parties met in various circuits to make clothing for orphan children in India, and this work developed into a wider concern for overseas missions, the groups gathering and disseminating information about missionary work, collecting school books to be sent to the mission field, and praying for missionaries. In 1895 the Conference took note of this development, and added the name of a woman, Mrs J. H. Thompson of Cork, to the Foreign Missionary Committee.

Visits of Mrs Caroline Wiseman to Dublin 1903 and 1905 inspired the next development in this sphere, and Women's Auxiliary was formed to encourage interest in missions, and to raise money and other resources for the mission field. It developed a junior branch called the Girls' League. In 1928 the Women's Auxiliary was reorganised under a new title, becoming the Women's Department of the Irish Auxiliary to the Methodist Missionary Society. Later the words Irish Auxiliary were usually omitted. The Women's Department became one of the strongest organisations in the church, not only fostering missionary interest, but also making a significant contribution to the the life of the circuits at home. There was a further development in 1972 when other women's meetings were drawn together with the Women's Department under the name of the Methodist Women's Association, with a sister organisation for younger women, the Young Women's Association. Both of these have developed quite varied programmes of worship, missionary support, social service and general interest.

It was the Conference of 1910 which approved of the proposal that women should be admitted to its membership, and the first three were elected in 1911. In the manner of the time they were named as Miss P. Holmes of Dublin, Mrs Judge of Londonderry, and Mrs S. T. Mercier of Belfast. The personal names of none of the three were given in the Minutes, and the initials assigned to Mrs Mercier were those of her husband, the well known Samuel T. Mercier.

Because local preachers are appointed by circuits and not by the Conference, it is not easy to trace the growth of the number of women among them, but by the middle of the twentieth century there were several, and the number has steadily increased since. However, no woman was accepted for the ministry until 1976. Resolutions of the Conferences of 1974 and 1975 established the principle than men and women should be admitted to the ministry on terms of equality, and the first candidate was accepted in the following year. She was Ellen Whalley, who went on to establish two other records. In 1980 she was the first

woman to be appointed Superintendent of a circuit, that of
Adare and Ballingrane in Co Limerick, and in 1986 she was the
first to be elected to the Chair of a District, the Midlands &
Southern District.

CHAPTER 9

Structures

In 1744 John Wesley called a conference of the clergy and lay preachers who were then working with him in building up the Methodist societies in England. It was precisely what he called it, a conference. The responsibility for what should happen to his Methodist societies lay with him, and he was enough of an autocrat even at the age of forty-one to wish it so, but he was not so foolish as to think that he could make all the decisions on his own. The others were called to confer with him, and to advise him, and decisions were made by agreement, in which undoubtedly Wesley's opinion carried more weight that that of any of the others, but his mind was not impervious to their influence. It is important, as one considers the structures, to remember that fact, for the governing body of the Methodist Church in Ireland is still a Conference. It is now a Conference with more power, for the Methodist ministers after Wesley's death were shy of accepting another autocrat. The principle of conference runs throughout the structures of Methodism, where no individual has power but many have influence, and decisions are always made in consultation with others.

By 1752 Wesley considered that the work in Ireland was sufficiently strong for the Irish Methodist preachers to meet in Conference in this country. In that year the first Irish Conference met in Limerick on Friday and Saturday, 14 and 15 August. Meeting with Wesley were Samuel Larwood, John Haughton, Joseph Cownley, John Fisher, Thomas Walsh, Jacob Rowell, Thomas Kead, Robert Swindells, and John Whitford. The name of James Morris was added at the end of the Conference, suggesting that he was present on the second day only. He was one of six preachers accepted by the Conference, and would not have been eligible to attend the first day. The other five were John Ellis, James Wild, George Levick, Samuel Hobart and Philip Guier, none of whom were present at any stage. Guier is exceptional in that he was the only preacher among them not to be moved from circuit to circuit. For the rest of his life he ministered to the German community in county Limerick, of which he was one, many of whom had become Methodists.

Of those who sat down with Wesley on that first day, only one was Irish, Thomas Walsh. The others were English preachers whom Wesley had sent to Ireland, and the Irish Conference in its early years was virtually a regional preparatory meeting for the Conference in England. Its decisions could, in theory and very occasionally in practice, be overturned when the English Conference met a few weeks later. Limerick was the venue for two more Conferences, one in 1758 and the other in 1760. Otherwise all the Conferences during Wesley's lifetime were held in Dublin. They, of course, only took place when Wesley himself was in the city, and not always then.

In *A Consecutive History of the Rise, Progress and Present State of Wesleyan Methodism in Ireland,* which was published in 1830, William Smith states that there was a Conference in Ireland in 1782, but no contemporary record of this survives. Wesley was not in Ireland in that year, but Smith tells us that he sent the Rev Dr Thomas Coke to preside in his place. One of Coke's early biographers Samuel Drew confirms the fact. This Conference is interesting for two reasons. Firstly it was the first Irish Conference over which Wesley did not preside in person, and secondly it was the beginning of a series of annual Conferences which has continued unbroken to the present time.

There is also a suggestion that it marked a further development. In the earlier years Wesley had stationed his preachers wherever he believed they would be most effective. In this he paid no regard as to whether they were English or Irish. Several Irishmen gave distinguished service in England, and quite a number of Englishmen served with great effect in this country.

However, as the number of preachers working in Ireland increased, it became too expensive to ship them back and forth across the Irish Sea. Irish preachers, therefore, were left in Ireland, and English preachers in England. At no time was there a formal separation of the two; their independent functioning evolved.

From 1782 to 1790 Wesley and Coke alternated in the Chair of the Irish Conference, Wesley coming personally in the odd years, and sending Coke in the even. Wesley made extensive tours of the country prior to the Conferences. Coke's were rather less extensive. In 1791 Wesley died, and no Irish Conference was held that year. The preachers did meet in Dublin, but their meeting was not official, and no Minutes were published. There was something of a surprise when the British Conference met in Manchester. The obvious choice for President was Coke, who had been Wesley's deputy so often in Ireland, but there was something autocratic about Coke, and the Conference was not prepared to accept the sort of governance from another that they had accepted from their beloved founder. They voted somebody else into Mr Wesley's Chair. That somebody was a gentle preacher with a reputation as a maker of peace, and certainly not self-seeking. He was William Thompson, a native of Cornabrass in county Fermanagh. He fulfilled the expectations of the Conference; he was not worried when they elected somebody else the next year. So by a curious turn of circumstances in the year of Wesley's death an Irishman presided over the British Conference.

Wesley, as we have already noted, had left certain legal rights in Methodism to one hundred ministers. Their names, and their powers were defined in a Deed Poll of 1784. Of the original one hundred eleven were Irish. However, the Legal Hundred, as they were generally called, had the right to appoint new members to any vacancies. Forty formed a quorum. As vacancies arose the initial tendency was to appoint English ministers to fill them, even when the vacancy had been caused by the death of an Irishman, and Irish representation declined. By 1811 it was down to two. The Irish protested at this, and it was agreed that ten of the hundred should be elected by the Irish Conference. This continued until the Methodist Church in Ireland Acts took effect, as we have noted, in 1928.

It was, of course, comparatively easy to bring ten Irish ministers to the British Conference, where they were entitled to sit as members. To bring ninety, or even the thirty necessary for a quorum, from England to Ireland was quite a different matter, but the acts of neither Conference were valid without the agreement of the Legal Hundred. The solution was found by the ninety English members delegating their authority to one of their number, who then travelled to Ireland to give their consent necessary to the Irish acts. It became the custom for 'The Delegate' to preside over the Irish Conference

Coke was the Delegate in 1792, but the British Conference of that year appointed its President, Alexander Mather, to go as Delegate to the Irish Conference of 1793. In the event Mather was unable to travel, and John Crook, who was stationed at Newry was elected the first Irish minister to preside over an Irish Conference. Coke then returned every year from 1794 to 1809. He was not elected President of the British Conference until 1797, but was elected again in 1805. He was appointed Delegate to the Irish Conference of 1810, but declined the office that year, and the Irish elected the Rev Adam Averell as their President. In 1811, 1812 and 1816 the Rev Dr Adam Clarke presided over the Irish Conferences. Himself an Irishman, he had been serving for many years in England. He was also appointed for 1814, but could not travel, and again Averell was elected.

In 1816 the British Conference designated its President, Richard Reece, to attend as Delegate in Ireland the following year, and this became standard practice each year thereafter. Thus in 1816 originates the practice of the President of the British Conference in one year presiding over the Irish Conference in the next. In 1868 he ceased to be the Delegate, for in 1867 the British Conference asked the Irish to elect from among their ten members of the Legal Hundred one whom the British would then appoint as Delegate. The British President continued to come to the Irish Conference and preside, and the duly elected Irishman was termed 'Vice-President of the Conference'. The first to be elected was Henry Price. Initially the President was simply the presiding officer of the Conference with no ceremonial duties at any other time. However, quite quickly the practice began of inviting him to represent the Conference at special events during the year, and this developed into a full programme of Presidential visits. In Ireland the Vice-President began to fill the same office, and in 1921 was given the additional title of President of the Methodist Church in Ireland.

The coming of the British President to Ireland, and his occupying the Chair at the Irish Conference, were matters of courtesy, not of legal requirement. In 1877, when the Conference met in Cork a group of ministers and laymen thought to make this clear, and as proceedings opened, formally proposed that the Rev Alexander McAulay, who was the British President, should be invited to take the chair and preside over the Conference. McAulay had had some warning of their intention, and refused to put the motion. Further, he went on to say that if it were pressed, he would go back to England immediately. The matter was dropped, most people believing that his presence was necessary to validate the acts of the Conference, though in fact since 1868 that had not been the case.

By the late 1920s attitudes had somewhat changed, and when the Methodist Church in Ireland Acts of 1928 were drafted a clause was included giving the British President the right to preside over the Irish Conference. This was seen as preserving the link with Wesley, and so continues. It gives rise to some confusion among the uninitiated, as the Irish Methodist Church is quite independent of its British sister.

Apart from the three early Conferences in Limerick, every Conference met in Dublin until 1824. It was then thought that it should meet in more than one venue, as its British counterpart had been doing for many years. The Conference of 1825 therefore met in Cork, and that of 1827 in Belfast, thus establishing a rota. Meetings were in Dublin in even years, and alternated between Cork and Belfast in odd. This four year cycle continued until 1881. Belfast had by then became a more important Methodist centre, and wished to welcome the Conference more often. An eight-year cycle was then introduced in which Cork took the meetings every fourth year, and Dublin and Belfast alternated in the other six.

This rota was broken in 1921, when the Conference should have gone to Cork, but the south west of Ireland was then in the grip of the Civil War and so the meetings were transferred to Belfast. To meet changing circumstances in the three venues, another rota was agreed by which Dublin and Belfast alternated for four years and Cork hosted the Conference in the fifth. The years of the Second World War again changed the rota and after that Portadown Methodists wished to be included. The Conference first met there in 1947. The next change came in 1980, when it went to Bangor in Co Down. Enniskillen welcomed it for the first time in 1983, and Londonderry in 1989.

The Irish Wesleyan Conference maintained the tradition of having only ministers present until negotiations for reunion in the 1870s put pressure on it for the admission of the laity. The Primitive Wesleyans had always had lay members. The Constitution of the Methodist Church in Ireland requires an equal number of each in the Representative Session. However, the admission, training, discipline and exclusion if necessary of ministers are debated in a Ministerial Session which takes final decisions on all such matters except one. The vote which admits ministers and authorises their ordination is taken by the Representative Session on the recommendation of the Ministerial. Lay people sit on the Board of Examiners which recommends to the Ministerial Session who should be received as candidates, monitors their training, and recommends their acceptance and ordination.

Wesley referred to his societies as being 'in connexion' with him, and as a form of verbal shorthand Methodists refer to 'the

Connexion' and to the boards, councils and committees through which the Conference manages its various activities as 'connexional', using the eighteenth century spelling. Those parts of the World Methodist Church under the jurisdiction of other Conferences would be described as 'the appropriate Connexion'. Over the years the number of Irish connexional boards and committees has increased, in spite of periodic efforts at reduction. However, the tradition of 'conference' continues to influence the way in which business is done, whether in the Conference sessions or in smaller groups. This means that procedure is comparatively simple, 'set speeches' apart from those introducing business are rare, and there is a real engagement of minds.

The first Conference, meeting in Limerick in 1752, divided the Irish societies into six rounds, or circuits – Dublin, Wexford, Cork, Limerick, Athlone and the North. The word 'round' was soon dropped in favour of 'circuit'. The name of the circuit was that of the city or town where the preachers were based, and the fact that the sixth was simply 'The North' indicates that development there was still at a very early stage. To each of these circuits one or more preachers was appointed, whose business was to travel around all the societies in turn, and when he had completed the circuit, to repeat the process. The term circuit therefore clearly indicated the way in which the work was organised. As the numbers of societies and preachers increased it was possible to divide the circuits so that each preacher had a smaller area to cover. It is now possible for any minister to visit all of the societies under his or her care in one day, but the name circuit continues in use for traditional reasons.

The governing body of a circuit is called, from the frequency of its meeting, the Quarterly Meeting. It comprises all the ministers appointed to the circuit, and the lay officials of each of the societies belonging to it. There may be only one minister in a small circuit, or as many five in a large one. The number of lay members is very much greater, depending on the number of societies. The circuit is the basic local unit of the church, and is the one which is represented at·Conference, and does business with the Conference or its boards.

In the early years a Quarterly Meeting was a much larger affair than it is now. It generally lasted for a full day, and was attended by as many members of the circuit as could get to it. Intended as a source of inspiration, it was addressed by one or two preachers, possibly invited from neighbouring circuits, and was probably the only time in the quarter when most members saw each other. It afforded an opportunity for the stewards responsible for the circuit finances to settle accounts. In the course of time the business grew, and other means arose in smaller circuits to gather the members together, so that the meeting became the administrative gathering that it now is.

Quarterly Meetings regularly deal with membership statistics, matters of circuit finance, and arrangements for circuit meetings and mission. They take an overview of the property. As occasion arises they appoint local preachers, recommend members needing assistance from certain Methodist funds, recommend candidates for the ministry, and consult with the appropriate authorities about the appointment of ministers to the circuit. All dealings with the Conference on behalf of the circuit are managed by the Circuit Stewards (senior lay officers) on the instructions of the Quarterly Meeting.

Each congregation in the circuit is still, by tradition, called a society, and is governed by a Leaders' Meeting. This comprises the minister responsible for the society, and the various lay officials responsible for pastoral care, property, finance, etc. It can meet with greater or lesser frequency as circumstances demand. Leaders' Meetings deal with pastoral oversight of members, arrangements for Sunday services, society finance, and the appointment of local lay officials.

In 1791 the British Conference grouped all of the circuits in Britain and Ireland into Districts, and the six Irish Districts were Dublin, Cork, Athlone, Clones, Londonderry and Charlemont. For some unknown reason the Irish Conference did not introduce the division into the list of preachers' stations until 1798, when there were eight districts. In that year they were not named, and in the following year they were numbered and named: Dublin, Cork, Athlone, Clones, Londonderry, Belfast and Newry. As the numbers of Irish Methodists have fluctuated Districts have been realigned, increased in number and amalgamated. In 2000 there were eight again: Dublin, Midlands and Southern, Enniskillen and Sligo, North West, North East, Belfast, Down, and Portadown.

District meetings were held to exchange news and ideas, and one of the ministers was appointed to preside over these meetings. He came to called the Chairman of the District. As is the case with such meetings, the District Meeting developed as a means of organising inter-circuit activities, and processing business in preparation for the Conference. In or about 1905, by general usage rather than by legislation, the name of the District Meeting was changed to District Synod, as more truly representing its function. In the 1990s the agenda of the Autumn Synod was modified to allow fuller discussion of important issues related to mission, discipline and social responsibility, though the Spring Synod remained largely administrative.

Increasingly in the twentieth century the Chairman became a representative of the church on civic occasions in the District, and a pastor to the other ministers. In 2000 the title was changed to District Superintendent, an American term which was seen as less sexist.

CHAPTER 10

Smaller Connexions

It is not often remembered that a very real rivalry existed in the third quarter of the eighteenth century as to who should control the Methodist revival in England. Since the term is now applied only to the church which derives from Wesley's work, it is often thought that he was the unchallenged leader, but it was not so. We have seen how he was influenced by George Whitefield at Bristol to begin field preaching, but Wesley was not persuaded of Whitefield's theology, which was strongly Calvinistic. Whitefield also exerted a strong influence on Selina, Countess of Huntingdon, widow of the 9th Earl, who became an ardent Calvinist. As Wesley set about the conversion of the working classes, Lady Huntingdon gave her attention to the nobility. As a peeress she claimed the right to have a private chapel in her residences, a right she stretched beyond the limits when the chapel she built at Spa Fields was larger than the residence. Her religious reputation prompted Horace Walpole to dub her 'The Queen of the Methodists'.[1]

In 1768, with the assistance of Howell Harris, she opened a college at Trevecca in Wales to educate preachers who would disseminate Calvinistic theology through the Church of England. Two years later the uneasy relationship between the Countess and Wesley came to a head. In 1770 Wesley published the Minutes of Conference which made clear his rejection of Calvinism, and Lady Huntingdon and her friends were out-raged. Her cousin, the Rev and Hon Walter Shirley, who was rector of Loughrea in Co Galway, was her most active agent in the protest, and called upon all her supporters to gather in Bristol in the following year, and oblige the Wesleyan Conference to retract these Minutes. In the event the Calvinist forces failed to muster, and only a small group met Wesley. The emendations which Wesley was prepared to make did not satisfy the Huntingdon party, and the uneasy friends became rivals.

The Countess and her Calvinistic friends were endeavouring to defend the sovereignty of God, and therefore argued that a person's salvation depended on God's election alone. Nothing that the person could do would be able to alter that. Wesley agreed that a person could not earn salvation by doing good, they had to depend on God's grace, but he went on to say that how one behaved was nonetheless important. The principal defence of his position was made in the five pamphlets published in the immediate aftermath of the dispute by John Fletcher, the Vicar of Madeley. These were entitled *Checks to Antinomianism,* and made clear that what Wesley was contesting was the belief that if actions did not matter, then people were free to commit any immorality without prejudice to their eternal bliss. There is a sense in which each side was attacking the extreme of the other side, while not wishing to defend the extreme of their own, but that is the nature of controversy.

One of the effects of the controversy in so far as it affected Ireland was that Lady Huntingdon sent some of her preachers to Dublin, where they began to hold meetings in the Merchant Tailors' Hall in Back Lane. In 1773 they acquired the use of a former Presbyterian Meetinghouse in Plunkett Street, where on occasion the preacher was Walter Shirley. In 1774 they extended work to Limerick, Cork, Waterford and Sligo. In Sligo they succeeded in getting possession of the Methodist chapel, and the Methodists who remained loyal to Wesley were obliged to build another in the following year. This, however, was the farthest extent of their work.

In 1782 the Countess seceded from the Church of England, and the Countess of Huntingdon's Connexion became an independent denomination. At this point her cousin Walter Shirley parted company with her, and returned to his parish in Loughrea. Galway was preferable to dissent. Lady Huntingdon's

Connexion was never strong, and most of its congregations, including that in Sligo, joined the Congregational Church. A few congregations of the Countess of Huntingdon's Connexion still remain in England.

It was, as we have observed, the negotiations for the reunion with the Primitive Wesleyan Methodists in the 1870s that persuaded the Irish Wesleyans to admit lay members to their Conference, but that was not the first time the question had arisen. Years before the Primitive Wesleyans had come into existence the question had been raised in Lisburn. In 1795 the Lisburn circuit petitioned the Conference to permit the administration of the sacraments by the preachers. This was refused. However in the following year the preacher at Lisburn, David Gordon, bowed to the demands of the circuit and administered the Holy Communion. For this he was reprimanded by the Conference in 1796, a reprimand which annoyed the leaders of the circuit. In an attempt to put a stop to the agitation, thirty-two of them were expelled. In 1798, these appealed to Conference for reinstatement, and petitioned for lay representation at District Meetings and at Conference. Again the petition was refused, but in the political climate then prevailing the petitioners were accused of 'Jacobinism' and their expulsion confirmed.[2] Two hundred members of the circuit withdrew in support of them.

In 1796 Alexander Kilham was expelled by the British Wesleyans after he had published a succession of pamphlets criticising the establishment, and advocating reforms including the admission of lay representatives to the Conference. He and a number of others came together in the following year to form the Methodist New Connexion (MNC). The Lisburn Methodists who had been excluded or had withdrawn made an approach to the MNC, which responded positively. Work was commenced in the Lisburn area. In 1800 John McClure extended their work to Dublin, forming a society in the Weavers' Hall. In 1815 this moved to the Merchant Tailors' hall, becoming the second Methodist body to make use of that premises. Meanwhile chapels had been opened in Belfast and Newtownards, and sometime later another commenced in Bangor.

In 1821 Matthew Lanktree of the Irish Wesleyans made an attempt to heal the breach and bring the MNC back into their fold, but the attempt was unsuccessful. In 1824 the MNC Conference in Britain designated Ireland as a mission field, but nothing much seems to have happened at that time. Six years later, however, there were six chapels in Belfast in addition to those in the vicinity of Lisburn, in Newtownards and in Bangor, with their own Irish Conference.

Between 1836 and 1841 William Cooke took charge of the Irish MNC Mission. He was their greatest theologian, one of his students being William Booth, who later founded the Salvation Army. Cooke sent missionaries to Cork, Limerick, Waterford, the Aran Islands, Dromore, Galway, Ballyclare and Lurgan. William McClure was sent to Dublin, and established a congregation in Aungier Street. Success in most of these areas was small, and the premises at Queen Street in Lurgan were sold to the Primitive Wesleyans in 1856. A year later the MNC work in Ireland was reduced to the status of a District of their British Conference.

Through the next fifty years numbers declined, and some of the smaller societies ceased. In 1905 the last nine were transferred to the Methodist Church in Ireland, which purchased the buildings from the British MNC for £4,000. In 1907 the Methodist New Connexion in Britain united with the Bible Christians and the United Methodist Free Churches to form the United Methodist Church, which in turn united with the Wesleyan Methodists and the Primitive Methodists in 1932 to form the Methodist Church. Thus most of the Methodists in Britain came once more under the one Conference.

In the early years of the nineteenth century American evangelists introduced the 'camp meeting' to Britain. A camp meeting was an evangelistic campaign conducted in a large tent, with auxiliary meetings in a number of smaller tents. It was not the fact that the meetings were held in tents which worried the Wesleyan Conference, but the strong emotion which the meetings engendered. Wesleyan Methodism was becoming respectable,

and did not wish to return to the sort of emotion that was observed in some of the Methodist meetings of fifty years before.
Hugh Bourne and William Clowes, on the other hand, were inspired by the new revivalism and their advocacy of it led to their
expulsion by the Wesleyans. In 1811 they founded the Primitive
Methodist Society, adopting the name in token of their belief
that they were returning to the early Methodist experience. In
that year their first chapel was built at Tunstall. The Primitive
Methodists grew quite rapidly, and while their greatest strength
always remained in Yorkshire and Durham, they had a good
measure of success among the agricultural communities of East
Anglia and the South. Though both the Wesleyans and the
Primitives were involved in the foundation of the early trade
unions in Britain, the Primitive contribution to these was the
greater, because more of their membership was then found
among the working classes.

The spread of Primitive Methodism was due to the initiatives
of their circuits in developing offshoots rather than to any extension policy on the part of their Conference. Their coming to
Ireland was no different. In 1832 two of their circuits quite inde-
pendently sent missionaries to this country. The Shrewsbury circuit sent William Haslam to Belfast in April, and the Preston
Brooks circuit sent Francis N. Jersey to Dublin in May. On arrival Jersey was immediately discouraged from work in Dublin,
and moved to Newry, where the work he began later extended
to Banbridge, Loughbrickland and Dromore. Sometime later a
third missionary went to Lisburn. Haslam had a dispute with
the Primitive authorities in England, and resigned from their
ministry. He joined the Methodist New Connexion. Jersey later
became a Baptist and moved to America. By 1838 the Primitive
Methodists were also working in Carrickfergus.

Numbers in Primitive Methodist circuits in Ireland were
never large, and in the late years of the nineteenth century began
to decline. In 1910 their remaining congregations were transferred to the care of the Methodist Church in Ireland. The fact
that between 1832 and 1878 there were three separate Methodist

Churches working in Ireland bearing the very similar names of Wesleyan Methodist, Primitive Wesleyan Methodist, and Primitive Methodist has caused a great deal of confusion, which even historians have not escaped.

Samuel Hay of Carrickfergus was the youngest child of a couple who had entertained John Wesley and the early Methodist preachers when they had visited that town. The boy did not inherit their religious zeal, and had a chequered career in Ireland, England and America, failing in business more than once. He eventually returned to Carrickfergus, bringing with him his wife and family. A visit from one of the Methodist leaders led to a change in his life, and he became as devout as his parents had been, but not so unquestioning. There was in Methodism in the 1830s a widespread questioning of the way in which Wesleyan Methodism was governed in Britain, and something of this spirit crossed the Irish Sea.

In 1832 Abraham Mason, a wealthy ironmonger, and a member of the Methodist society in Dublin, died leaving a legacy of £1,000 to assist in the foundation of a Theological Institution for the training of young preachers. The Irish delegates to the British Wesleyan Conference of the following year spoke of this, and it may have been the fact that money had been given for the purpose which persuaded them to form a committee to examine the possibilities. The committee in 1834 recommended that the Institution be established, but went beyond its brief in suggesting that Dr Jabez Bunting should be appointed its head. One of the committee, Dr Samuel Warren, strongly objected to this latter proposal. In all fairness to him he was probably worried about putting more power into the hands of Bunting, who had already been Secretary of the Wesleyan Conference and twice its President, and was still the most powerful minister in the connexion.[3]

Warren was forceful in his criticism, both during the Conference and afterwards, and was suspended from his office as superintendent of his circuit. By the end of the year, 1834, he had withdrawn and formed what came to be called the

Wesleyan Methodist Association (WMA). He did not remain very long at its head. Failing to get what he wanted in its constitution, he resigned, and was ordained for a parish in the Church of England. Meanwhile one of those who was present at the first Assembly of the WMA was Samuel Hay of Carrickfergus, who may have met Warren while visiting Manchester on business. Through this contact a small WMA congregation was established in Carrickfergus.

Joseph Thompson was sent from England as minister of this group, with the intention of extending the work, but progress was slow. Hay died in 1842, and therefore did not see its extension into a number of areas around Carrickfergus. It was in the time of a later minister, Mark Bradney, that a handsome little chapel was built by the WMA in the town. In 1857 the WMA formed a union with some Wesleyan Reform societies, and the united body adopted the name United Methodist Free Churches (UMF). In 1868 they acquired an opening in Belfast, when an existing congregation at Ligoniel joined them. Numbers, however, declined and an approach from the Irish Wesleyans in 1872 afforded them the opportunity of transferring their work to it.

We have mentioned Howell Harris as assisting Selina, Countess of Huntingdon in the establishment of her college at Trevecca in Wales. Harris was in fact a native of Trevecca. Influenced by George Whitefield, he began a preaching ministry in Wales out of which grew the Welsh Calvinistic Methodist Church. In the 1960s this adopted the name Presbyterian Church in Wales.

By the end of the first quarter of the nineteenth century there was a significant Welsh presence in Dublin, largely composed of sailors working between Dublin and the Welsh ports. In 1831 the Welsh Calvinistic Methodists leased a disused Lutheran chapel in Poolbeg Street, and began to send a minister from Wales each week to conduct services for the Welsh in the city. On occasion a minister stayed for two Sundays. This arrangement proved to be unsatisfactory in more than one respect, and in 1832 a minister, Robert Williams, was sent to Dublin on a permanent basis. He renegotiated the lease of the Poolbeg Street chapel for some years, but in 1838 obtained a better site in Talbot Street. There, using money largely raised in Wales, the Welsh Calvinistic Methodists built a chapel of their own. In Welsh tradition they called this 'Bethel', but to the population of Dublin it was usually simply 'The Welsh Chapel'. For some years there was a smaller chapel in Kingstown (Dun Laoghaire), which was known as 'Bethel Bach'.[4]

Williams left Dublin in 1841, and the practice was resumed of sending preachers from Wales for one or two Sundays at a time. In 1862 a gallery was built at the back of the Welsh Chapel to accommodate the sailors, who were now a minority of the congregation. The gallery pews were fitted with spittoons, as it was believed that the sailors would be more likely to come to church if they were allowed to smoke during the services. The chapel preserved the original Methodist tradition of men sitting on one side of the building, and women on the other.

A minister was again appointed to reside in Dublin in 1865. This was Edward Jones. He reported that there were then fourteen Welsh families in the city. Several of the wealthier families in the city employed Welsh menservants, and quite a number of Welsh girls were in domestic service there. These made up the greater part of the congregation. In addition Welsh students found it easier to cross the sea to Trinity College, Dublin rather than to take the long overland route to the English universities. These too worshipped in Bethel. In fact not all of these were Welsh Calvinistic Methodists. Nationality seemed to be more powerful than denominationality, and there was a tendency for all of the Welsh in Dublin, regardless of denomination, to resort to the chapel in Talbot Street on Sundays.

A succession of ministers followed Edward Jones, but the last of these returned to Wales in 1934. The church, in fact, found it cheaper to send a different minister from Wales each Sunday than to carry the cost of keeping one in residence. The Second World War sounded the death knell of Bethel in Dublin, and the building was closed in 1939, and sold. It still stands, much defaced.

PART III

Preachers and People

CHAPTER 11

The Life of the Preachers

In the early years of Methodism in England John Wesley was supported by a small number of Church of England clergy who were sympathetic, but were not able to give all of their time to the Methodist movement as Wesley did. The expansion of Methodist work throughout the country only became possible when Wesley was convinced of the value and validity of laymen sharing in the preaching work. Anxious on the one hand not to be thought a rival to the Established Church, or on the other hand to be associated with dissent, Wesley called them 'preachers', which was what they primarily were.

At one time there were three classes of Methodist preacher. There were the itinerant preachers. These were men of particular ability whom Wesley called from other work to move to a different circuit each year. They were fulltime Methodist preachers, and were paid a living allowance by the Methodist societies. In the nineteenth century they came to be called 'ministers'. In the second class there were half itinerant preachers. These were men who conducted businesses of their own, but travelled about preaching as Wesley directed them. This class of preacher was always small, soon fell into disuse, and was never introduced into Ireland, though the appearance of Philip Guier's name in the Minutes of the first Irish Conference (1752) may indicate that Wesley had some idea of using him in this way. Finally there were local preachers, who had businesses or professions of their own which provided their livelihood, and who preached in the limited area which they could reach from home. They were unpaid. Local Preachers are still appointed, and still exercise a ministry in many Irish circuits.

The Local Preacher was generally somebody with a rather better education than the other members of the societies to whom he preached. Often the master of an elementary school in the circuit would add this work to his responsibilities. Others might be successful shopkeepers, or artisans. Some, like Christopher Tidd of Cloughjordan, were minor landowners and magistrates. Only three tests were generally applied in the early years – do they have a call to this work? do they have the gifts for it? are they effective? Their appointment and use was a matter for the local circuit, though the Conference did establish criteria for both. It was only in 1902 that the Conference established a committee to oversee the local preachers throughout the country, and to raise their standards. The first thing it did was to produce a reading list for the guidance of local preachers. Later it introduced an examination in scripture, theology, and homiletics, but preparation for this was generally a matter between the prospective preacher and the superintendent minister of the circuit.

It was when Wesley learned of local preachers who were particularly gifted that he 'called them into the itinerancy', and they became itinerant preachers. In these cases also Wesley considered the questions of call, ability and effect. The church still requires that a man or woman shall be a local preacher before he or she can be considered as a candidate for the ministry. This is one of the ways in which ability and effect are recognised.

After Wesley's death it fell to the Conference to devise a way in which new itinerant preachers should be admitted. Wesley's principles continued to apply, but now the candidates were brought before the Conference, questioned as to their Christian experience, call and doctrine, and if satisfactory were placed 'on trial' for a period of years, generally four. During these they worked on circuit in association with an experienced preacher. If after a further examination they were then found to be fully satisfactory, they were 'received into full Connexion', that is to say, into the company of preachers in the Connexion established by Mr Wesley.

In time it became necessary to establish a committee to make preliminary examination of the candidates, and the advice of local Methodists who knew the candidate was also sought. Thus there grew up the present system by which the candidate is first examined by the quarterly meeting of his or her own circuit, then by the ministers of the District, and finally by the Board of Examiners. Medical and aptitude tests are taken into account, and on the basis of all of these the candidate, if all is satisfactory, is accepted for years of training and 'probation', the latter being the modern term for working in circuit on trial.

Augustus Montague Toplady, the Calvinist pamphleteer and hymn writer, who was vicar of Broadhembury in Devon, owed his religious to a Methodist preacher in Co Wexford, James Morris. He wrote:

> Strange that I, who had so long sat under the means of grace in England, should be brought nigh to God in an obscure part of Ireland, amidst a handful of God's people met together in a barn, and under the ministry of one who could hardly spell his name.[1]

Comments such as that have given rise to the suggestion that the early Methodist preachers were ignorant men. It must, however, be remembered that Toplady was writing in the year in which he adopted Calvinistic opinions, and he was therefore at pains to belittle those who did not share his convictions. Indeed there is a trace of snobbery about Toplady's tone; a graduate of Trinity College Dublin, he was emphasising by exaggeration the fact that Morris had had no university education at all, but Morris was by no means illiterate.

The need for preachers to develop the work certainly led Wesley to call men who in later years would have been allowed time to get more experience, but Wesley did not tolerate ignorance. The Large Minutes, first published in 1744, and periodically revised up to 1789, form the definitive document of Methodist discipline. It includes the following:

Q. 29 What general method of employing our time would you advise us to?

A. We advise you 1st: As often as possible to rise at four. 2. from four to five in the morning, and from five to six in the evening, to meditate, pray and read; partly the Scriptures with the Notes; partly the closely practical parts of what we have published. 3. from six in the morning until twelve (allowing an hour for breakfast) to read in order, with much prayer; first the Christian Library, and the other books which we have published in prose and verse, and then those which we have recommended in our Rules of Kingswood School.

Q. 32 But why are we not more knowing?

A. 1. Read the most useful books, and that regularly and constantly. Steadily spend all the morning in this employ, or at least five hours in four and twenty.

The Notes on the Scriptures were contained in two works, *Notes on the Old Testament* and *Notes on the New Testament*, which Wesley had compiled and published in 1765 and 1755 respectively. Wesley twice revised the latter, and it remains one of the foundation documents of Methodist doctrine. The *Christian Library* was a collection of fifty volumes which Wesley published between 1749 and 1755. It contains potted biographies and excerpts from the writings of the Apostolic Fathers, the Puritan divines, high churchmen such as George Herbert and Jeremy Taylor, the Cambridge Platonists, latitudinarian and dissenting theologians, and mystics. The 'other books which we have published' would include Wesley's collected sermons, his various collections of hymns (mostly written by his brother Charles), and pamphlets on a variety of doctrinal and ethical issues.

That is not the sort of diet that one recommends to semi-literate men. Gordon Rupp is quite correct in drawing attention to the facts that the *Christian Library* was the one publishing enterprise on which Wesley lost money, and that this, added to the frequency with which he urges people to read it, suggests that it was not as much used as he would wish, but that is not to say that his preachers would not have understood it. If they failed to fulfil Wesley's demands as to their reading it was more probably because they were differently constituted from Wesley, who failed to appreciate that not many people could function efficiently on as little sleep as he himself apparently could.

Some of his preachers were noted scholars. Thomas Walsh, born near Limerick, was described by Wesley as one of the finest biblical scholars he had ever met. Walsh destroyed his health by his strenuous work and died before he was twenty-nine. Adam Clarke, whose birthplace was near Portrush, became one of the most noted polymaths of the eighteenth and early nineteenth centuries. He published a notable commentary on the Bible, and a Bibliographical Dictionary in eight volumes. It was he who began the cataloguing of the State Papers from the Norman Conquest to the reign of George II in Windsor Castle.

To suggest that the early preachers were ignorant men is certainly a libel, but it would be equally false to suggest that the situation was so good that it could not be improved. From as early as 1744 the British Conference was asking, 'Can we have a Seminary for labourers?' and the fact that it had not proved to be possible may have been one of the considerations which prompted Wesley's demands that the preachers spend so much time in educational reading.

Abraham Mason was a well-to-do ironmonger in Dublin. He died in 1832, and bequeathed a sum of £1,000 towards founding a 'Theological Institution' for the training of young preachers. When the Irish delegates reported this fact to the British Conference of 1833, the latter established a committee to examine the prospects, and we have already observed how their suggestion that Jabez Bunting should be its first head resulted in the secession of the Wesleyan Methodist Association. The disruption delayed any action towards the establishment of the institution.

In 1838 the British Conference raised a Centenary Fund to celebrate the centenary of Methodism, and in the distribution of this, the first consideration was the training of preachers. £72,000 was set apart for the purpose. To this sum the Irish Conference added the Mason bequest, and in the event two institutions were established. One, near London, developed into Richmond College, and the other, at Manchester, was named for the district in which it was located, Didsbury. In acknowledgement of the Irish contribution four places were reserved annually at one or other of these colleges for Irish preachers. This provision, of course, was for Irish Wesleyans.

The Primitive Wesleyans never had a college for their preachers, but in 1841 they introduced a syllabus of preliminary reading for their candidates, and began requiring them to sit a written examination in English literature, history, geography, the scriptures, ecclesiastical history and Methodism, as well as an oral examination in piety, talent, knowledge, zeal and usefulness as before. In 1869 they introduced a reading list for those seeking admission to their 'ministry', this word having by then superceded 'preachers' in general usage.

Nineteenth century Methodism was very good at finding pretexts for the raising of special funds, and in 1863 it was the Jubilee of the Wesleyan Missionary Society which provided another pretext. The Irish Wesleyans raised almost £10,000. At that time the English Wesleyans saw Ireland as still a mission field, and they returned the Irish contribution to the Irish Conference. This formed the nucleus of the fund needed to establish a college in Belfast, called Methodist College. This was opened in 1868, and was constituted for two main functions – the education of boys, and the training of Wesleyan ministers.

The Theological Hall occupied one wing of the building, and the Principal of the College was the Theological Tutor. The first occupant of this post was the Rev William Arthur. Curiously, the first theological student was not sent to the college until 1870, when William Smiley became the sole ministerial candidate in residence. Nine more joined him in 1871. The dual arrangement continued for fifty years through the reigns of four more principals.

By then the secondary education department of the college was expanding, and the Theological Hall was feeling the need for more space, but the two demands could not be met in the

same building. Sir William Whitla, a prominant Belfast
Methodist, was then a member of the college's Board of
Governors, and was living in a house at the end of Lennoxvale,
off the Malone Road. He suggested that a house beside his
would make a suitable location for the Theological Hall, and
happened then to be on the market. In the April 1918 this house,
which happened to be called 'Edgehill', was purchased, and the
tutor and twelve ministerial students moved in. The principal
who oversaw the transition was the Rev Joseph W. R. Campbell.
However, he got into poor health and asked to be relieved of his
post.

In 1920 the Rev John C. Robertson was appointed principal,
with the Rev Alexander McCrea as tutor. The Rev William L.
Northridge was appointed to the Belfast Central Mission with
the proviso that he also act part time as an additional tutor. In
1926 the building was extended by the addition of a lecture hall.
Two years later the Conference separated the Theological Hall
from Methodist College, and constituted it a separate body with
the name Edgehill Theological College. In 1933 a house was
built adjoining the college, and this housed the principal and his
family, whose former flat then became available for additional
student accommodation. The generous gift of Dr Hugh Turtle in
1937 enabled a small chapel to be built.

The next major step in the life of the College came in 1951
when it became a recognised college of the Queen's University,
Belfast. This in turn facilitated a growing co-operation with the
Presbyterian Assembly's College, so that the resources of a larger
faculty benefited the students considerably. Students preparing
for the Irish Methodist ministry now regularly undertake degree
or diploma courses.[2]

Wesley maintained a tight discipline over his preachers, and
the rules which they were asked to observe were at times pedan-
tic. Wesley's intention was to preserve their health and their
effectiveness. How closely all of the rules were observed it is not
possible to determine, but that preachers made a serious attempt
to observe them cannot be doubted. The Large Minutes speak of

the chief preacher on any circuit as the Assistant; after Wesley's death this title was changed to Superintendent. The other preachers on the circuit are termed Helpers. Under Question 26 they set forth the Rules of a Helper:

1. Be diligent. Never be unemployed for a moment. Never be triflingly employed. Never while away time; neither spend any more time at any place than is strictly necessary.

2. Be serious. Let your motto be 'Holiness to the Lord'. Avoid all lightness, jesting and foolish-talking.

3. Converse sparing and cautiously with women, particularly with young women.

4. Take no step toward marriage without first consulting your brethren.

5. Believe evil of no one; unless you see it done, take heed how you credit it. Put the best construction on every thing. You know the judge is always supposed to be on the prisoner's side.

6. Speak evil of no one; else *your* word especially would eat as doth a canker; keep your thoughts within your own breast, till you come to the person concerned.

7. Tell every one what you think wrong in him, and that plainly as soon as may be, else it will fester in your heart. Make all haste to cast the fire out of your bosom.

8. Do not affect the gentleman. You have no more to do with this character than with that of a dancing-master. A Preacher of the Gospel is the servant of all.

9. Be ashamed of nothing but sin; not of fetching wood (if time permit) or drawing water, not of cleaning your own shoes, or your neighbour's.

10. Be punctual. Do everything exactly at the time. And in general do not mend our rules, but keep them, not for wrath, but for conscience sake.

11. You have nothing to do but to save souls. Therefore spend and be spent in this work. And go always, not only to those that want you, but to those that want you most.

It should be noted that in the last rule Wesley is using the word 'want' in the sense of need, not merely of wish. Later in the Minutes the duties of an Assistant are listed. These are mainly administrative, and were, of course, in addition to his observance of the Rules of a Helper. His primary duty was to see that the other preachers in the circuit behaved well, and lacked nothing. It is at point 6 that Wesley lists three books which he believes ought to be used in every Methodist household: *Kempis, Instructions for Children,* and *Primitive Physic.* The Kempis book was, of course, *The Imitation of Christ. Instructions for Children* was Wesley's condensation of works by Abbé Fleury and M. Poiret, translated into English. Wesley first compiled and published *Primitive Physic* in 1747, and it went through twenty-three editions in his lifetime. In an age when professional medical help was expensive and rudimentary, it was ahead of its time in the advocacy of hygiene, and a healthy regimen of exercise and diet. The remedies are mainly folk and herbal cures, though Wesley hails electricity as a great new panacea.

The concern for health inspired much of his more personal advice to the preachers. In 1763 he was urging them to eat only three meals a day, and no flesh suppers. In 1769, writing to Richard Steel, who was then in Armagh, he advised that supper should be confined to a little milk or water gruel. Thinking more generally he gives Steel a long list of advice for preachers, which includes the following:

2. Be steadily serious. There is no country upon earth where this is more necessary than Ireland; as you are generally encompassed with those who with a little encouragement would laugh or trifle from morning to night.

4. ... on this and every other occasion avoid all familiarity with women ... You cannot be too wary in this respect ...

5 (1) Be active, be diligent ... (2) Be cleanly ... Do not stink above ground ... (3) Whatever clothes you have, let them be whole ... (6) Use no tobacco unless prescribed by a physician. It is an uncleanly and unwholesome self-indulgence ... (7) Use no snuff unless prescribed by a physician ... (8) Touch no dram. It is liquid fire. It is a sure though slow poison ...[3]

The curious advice 'Do not stink above ground' may allude to the fact that in the eighteenth century city streets were so befouled that it was impossible not to have malodorous shoes. A note of wry humour enters the advice which Wesley gives at the British Conference at Leeds in 1778:

1. Touch no dram, tea, tobacco or snuff.
2. Eat very light, if any, supper.
3. Breakfast on nettle or orange-peel tea.
4. Lie down before ten, rise before six.
5. Every day use as much exercise as you can bear: – Or
6. Murder yourself by inches

His concern for the well being of the preachers extended to their horses:

Be merciful to your beast. Not only ride moderately, but see with your own eyes that your horse be rubbed, fed and bedded.[4]

If Wesley had no illusions about the failings of his preachers, when commendation was due he did not stint it. In 1767 he wrote from Sligo to Mrs Crosby:

There is an amazing increase in the work of God within these few months in the North of Ireland. And no wonder; for the five preachers who have laboured there are all men devoted to God, men of a single eye, whose whole heart is in this work, and who 'Constantly trample on pleasure and pain'.

The five preachers were James Dempster, John Johnson, James Morgan, James Rea and Robert Williams.

Wesley could also be very compassionate. In 1780, when Samuel Bradburn was appointed to Keighley having worked for some time in Dublin, Wesley wrote to him from Bristol advising him to delay his sea crossing until his children were a little stronger, and to spend the intervening time at Athlone. In 1781 or 1782 (the letter is undated and entered under both years in the standard edition) he directed Hugh Moore to exchange with the Lisburn preacher, Thomas Rutherford, for a period of six or eight weeks. Rutherford's wife, a native of Coleraine where

Moore was stationed, was expecting a baby, and Wesley thought it would help her to be near her family at the time of her confinement.

Much of his advice on the practical business of preaching is as relevant today as when it was written:

1. Be sure never to disappoint a congregation, unless in case of life or death.

2. Begin and end precisely at the time appointed.

4. Always suit your subjects to your audience.

5. Choose the plainest texts you can.

6. Take care not to ramble …

8. Take care of anything awkward or affected, either in your gesture, phrase, or pronunciation.[5]

During Wesley's lifetime it was he who administered discipline. The recurrence of his complaints about preachers who were lazy, or too fond of drams, tobacco or snuff suggests that the ideal was greater than the achievement. Individual enquiry into the efficiency of each minister remains a part of Methodist discipline in Ireland, though now administered through the District Synods.

At the spring meeting of the Synod each year the roll of ministers is called, each standing in turn. Some other minister says 'No objection!' This is in answer to an unasked question 'Is there any objection to this minister on the grounds of health or character?', and if there is any such objection, it ought to be raised at this moment. In that case an enquiry has to be made into the nature of the objection. If there is no objection the minister makes three affirmations: 'I believe and preach our doctrines. I accept and administer our discipline. I am not in debt.' If any minister cannot make any one of those affirmations, again there must be an enquiry. At the ministerial session of the Conference, the District reports on any misdemeanour and the Conference takes any action necessary to deal with the matter.

At the end of the eighteenth century they were Methodist preachers; at the end of the nineteenth they were Methodist ministers. The change of title represented a change of function.

For our understanding of the role of the preachers at the beginning we turn again to the Large Minutes:

Q. 25. What is the office of an Helper?

A. In the absence of a Minister, to feed and guide the flock: in particular

> 1. To preach morning and evening. (But he is never to begin later in the evening than seven o'clock, unless in particular cases.)
>
> 2. To meet the Society, and the Bands weekly.
>
> 3. To meet the Leaders weekly.

Let every preacher be particularly exact in this, and in the morning-preaching. If he has twenty hearers, let him preach. If not, let him sing and pray.

The conditional reference to the minister is an expression of Wesley's wish that his preachers should not usurp the role of the clergy. He uses the term to describe the minister of the Established Church, be he rector, vicar or curate. He then goes on to be particular as to how the flock is to be fed and guided, and first names preaching in the morning and in the evening. Anyone who was not capable of preaching twice in the one day remained a local preacher. The weekly meetings with society bands and leaders was again the statement of an ideal, and in the early years in Ireland was certainly impossible of achievement in many places.

In 1767, for instance, the Castlebar circuit included the counties of Mayo, Sligo, Leitrim and Roscommon. It took the preachers six weeks to go the round of the societies and preaching appointments. They were at home in Castlebar for only three days in the six weeks and otherwise did not sleep in the same bed for any two successive nights. At one stage of the round two successive appointments were so far apart that it took two days to ride from one to the other. It was sheer physical impossibility for the preacher to meet any one society more than once in the six weeks. Such was the severity of the toil, and the exposure to all sorts of weather, that William Pennington, who was appointed to Castlebar in the August of that year, was dead by Christmas.

It was the size of the circuits that imposed the strain, and that had been the case for twenty years. In 1755 Thomas Walsh had written to Wesley saying, 'I am quite weak and spent, although I endeavour to preach once a day, sometimes twice.' He went on to report that James Oddie was ill of a fever in Dublin, James Morgan was running away from the work from a consciousness of his own inability, and John Fisher had left Athlone to go to Dublin, apparently also ill. Morgan was only nineteen at the time. The wonder is not that so many preachers stayed the pace, but that they sustained a great enthusiasm for the work.

As time passed two things relieved the pressure to some degree. Increasing numbers of preachers made it possible to appoint two or three to each circuit, when it became the practice for each in turn to remain in the circuit town while the other(s) went around the outlying places. The weeks in the town were by no means idle with the society there to be tended, but they did afford some opportunity for the preacher to read, study, and prepare for his next round. The increase in the number of members led to the division of circuits so that rounds became shorter. Two consequences flowed from this.

In the earlier years preachers were moved to a different circuit every year. As Wesley wrote to Mrs Elizabeth Bennis in July 1770, '... it would never do to let one man sit down for six months with a small society; he would soon preach himself and them as lifeless as stones.' The simple fact was that the amount of travelling left the men insufficient time for reading and the gathering of fresh material; if they moved to a new circuit each year they could use the same material again. Increasing opportunity for study enabled the time spent in one circuit to be extended to two, and then to three years. The maximum time that any minister was permitted to stay in one circuit remained at thee years until after the First World War, when it was extended to five, and in 1967 it was further extended to eight. Certain specified appointments were excepted from this rule.

The second consequence was the development of a pastoral role for the preacher. He was able to meet the members of the circuit more frequently, and gradually the pastoral function originally exercised by the class leader was transferred to him. This was certainly encouraged by the reintroduction into Methodism in 1836 of ordination by the laying-on of hands. Between 1784 and his death in 1791 Wesley had ordained twenty-seven of his preachers in this way, but the Conference did not immediately follow his example. As early as 1818 some had been ordained on the foreign mission field, but the practice only became general in England and Ireland in 1836. The term preacher over the next twenty or thirty years was superseded by that of minister. With this came the adoption of the courtesy title 'Reverend', and the wearing of the clerical collar.

After the '59 revival the pattern of the minister's week changed. In a city circuit he would have a morning and an evening service, possibly in the same church, each Sunday and a regular mid-week service, often called a 'Prayer Meeting'. Otherwise he would be expected to support other church meetings, though not necessarily to lead them, and to undertake pastoral visitation of the members and others associated with the circuit. In country circuits the minister might be responsible for two or three services on Sunday, and each would probably be in a different church. Certain weeknights would be taken up with cottage meetings.

Cottage meetings were so called whatever the status of the building in which they took place, and they were more likely to be in reasonably substantial farm houses. Each house would have a cottage meeting on a certain day each month, such as the third Wednesday or the second Thursday. A common pattern of this event began with the arrival of the minister to have lunch with the family in the house. He would then spend the afternoon visiting houses in the locality reminding people that this was the evening of the meeting, and inviting them to be present. Invitations would already have been issued by the family, so that in the evening probably two rooms would be filled with people, and the company might even overflow some of the way up the stairs.

The form of worship would be similar to that of the Sunday service, but conducted much less formally. The minister would station himself wherever he could best be heard by all of the company. Hymns would be sung to whatever accompaniment was available, prayers would be said, and a short passage would be read from the Bible. On this the minister would base his address. It was not uncommon for the minister to interpolate individual questions into the address. On referring to the saving grace of Christ, he might ask of one or another, 'Have you put your trust in Jesus, Michael? Have you, Annie?' The answer might be no more than a nod, a smile, or a somewhat uncomfortable shift in position, and the preacher would continue. This sort of approach was quite acceptable in the manners of the time.[6]

When the meeting was over, if the house was at some distance from the minister's own residence, he might stay overnight, talk to the children before breakfast in the morning, and leave after the meal to return home. The advent of the motor meant that even the furthest journey in the circuit could be done in a very short time, and there was never thereafter any need for the minister to stay overnight. The cottage meeting survived until the Second World War, but as the members of the circuits acquired cars, they gradually ceased.

The development of psychology and psychiatry were taken up in the middle years of the twentieth century by two ministers, Dr William L. Northridge and Thomas M. McCracken. His initials led to the latter being affectionately known to his colleagues as 'Tim' instead of Tom.

William Northridge was born at Ballineen in Co Cork, and after some years in business he entered the ministry in 1910. He became Principal of Edgehill College in 1943. His particular interest was the relationship between psychology and the pastoral ministry of the church, and his writings in this field won him wide recognition. He introduced the subject to the curriculum of the college, and applied it to the college management. This was seen as a renewal in contemporary terms of Wesley's approach to the 'whole person' rather than a concern limited to the state of the soul. It was he who initiated the closer co-operation with the Presbyterian Assembly's College. He died in 1966.

Thomas McCracken was a native of Belfast, and entered the ministry in 1924. He was given permission to withdraw from pastoral work for some years in order to qualify in medicine. He returned to circuit work for some years, but his psychiatric expertise led a number of Dublin business men to fund the establishment of the Kylemore Clinic, and there worked for the rest of his life in a healing ministry. For many years he conducted the psychological assessment of candidates for the ministry, and he also lectured in the Church of Ireland Theological College and in Dublin University Medical School. He died in 1994.

The next important change in the role of the minister came in last quarter of the twentieth century. Through the middle of the century better relations had been developing between the several denominations, and the Second Vatican Council gave an added impetus to this. Local authorities became aware of the development. Where it had been customary to invite the Catholic parish priest or the Church of Ireland rector to a civic function, or possibly even both, it was now seen to be important to have each of the religious communities represented. Increasingly, therefore, ministers have found themselves filling a representative role at functions that are not in any way religious.

For many years in the nineteenth and twentieth centuries a distinction was made between ministers and junior ministers. The latter were those who had not yet completed ten years of service in the ministry. They were not entitled to a manse supplied by the church, and therefore found lodgings wherever they could. In practice successive junior ministers in the same circuit generally stayed in the same house. Junior ministers could not marry without the prior permission of the Conference, which was rarely sought as the junior minister's stipend was not adequate for the support of a wife. Junior ministers were never elected to the Conference. All of this bred a certain degree of frustration among them, and in 1888 the Rev John Hickey Moran took the initiative in inviting a number of others to meet him in Pettigo, where he was stationed.

Twelve accepted the invitation: James M. Alley, John Chambers, W. Loftus Coade, P. Ernest Donovan, Nathaniel R. Haskins, John W. Johnston, William E. Maguire, Francis Moran, William J. Russell, James Stewart, George L. Webster and James White. They formed the Junior Ministers Convention. This became an annual event, and has met every year since with the exception of a few years during the First World War. It continued to meet throughout the Second in spite of wartime restrictions on food and travel.

The tradition was to gather on a Monday evening early in November, and to disperse on the following Thursday. Members addressed private sessions on topics of current interest, and public meetings were held each evening. Occasionally a speaker from outside the membership would invited to speak on a subject in which he or she had particular expertise. After the partition of the country an effort was made the arrange that the Convention would meet alternately in each jurisdiction.

The distinction between minister and junior minister was abolished in the 1970s, but the Convention was seen to be too valuable to stop, and it continues to provide a forum for those within the first ten years of ministry.

The work of the early preachers was particularly strenuous and stressful, and they did it purely out of a conviction that it needed to be done, and was valuable to God and to people at large. They certainly did not do it for the pay. Indeed it was true then, and is true now, that if ministers were paid what they earned, no church could afford one. That is not peculiar to Methodists; it is a fact of church life.

The first Irish Conference, meeting at Limerick in 1752 directed that preachers were to be allowed £8 a year, and if possible (!) £10 for clothing. It was expected that living quarters should be provided, though this was not always done. If the preacher was married, he was to be allowed £10 for his wife, and something additional for any children. If these figures seem dreadfully small, they amounted, in fact, to about twice the average wage of a labourer. In 1785 the allowance to the minister was in-

John Wesley
at the age of sixty-two.
Portrait painted by
Nathaniel Hone the Elder
in 1765, the only portrait
of Wesley by an Irish
artist.

Charles Wesley

Thomas Walsh

Henry Moore

William Thompson

Dr Adam Clarke

Early Irish Preachers

Adam Averell   Thomas Coke

Gideon Ouseley

William Lunell's house,
15 Francis Street,
Dublin, at which Wesley
stayed in 1747.
[Sketch by S. J. Hurd]

The exterior of Whitefriar Street Chapel in Dublin, the first Methodist
building in Ireland. *[Sketch by S. J. Hurd]*

Ballingrane Methodist Church, built on ground which had belonged to Barbara Heck's husband, Paul, in 1766, and renovated in 1885. [*Sketch by Peter Murray*]

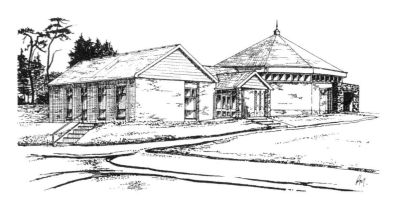

Cullybackey Methodist Church, built in 1969.
[*Sketch by Peter Murray*]

Brookeborough Methodist Church

Donegall Square Methodist Church, Belfast

Rathgar Methodist Church, Dublin, built in 1874, extended to the rear in 1924.

Rev Ellen Whalley

Dr Eric Gallagher

Dr Stanley Worrall

Gordon Wilson [*Photo courtesy RTÉ Stills Library*]

Ernest Walton

Dr Edith Loane

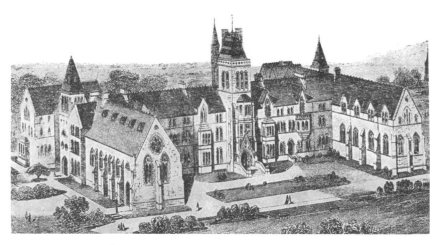

Methodist College, Belfast in 1868, from an etching
(Marcus Ward)

In the library at Methodist College, Belfast

Wesley College on St Stephen's Green, Dublin, built in 1879.

Wesley College at Ballinteer, Dublin. A game of hockey in 1999.

The main entrance of Gurteen Agricultural College

Fund raising at Gurteen Agricultural College

Barbara Heck
[Portrait painted by Joseph Barnes 1773, now at St John's Church, New York]

Philip Embury
[Portrait painted by Joseph Barnes 1773, now at St John's Church, New York]

creased to £12, and the allowance for each child was specified at eighteen pence. The stipulation that the allowances be paid in English money, meant that if the preacher was paid in Irish he received an extra £1. 15s. 9d. for himself and his wife. The circuits were required to defray the expenses of their own preachers travelling to and from the annual Conference.

To make rules is one thing; to enforce them another. In 1767 it was recorded that the stipends of the preachers in the North-East amounted in the first quarter of the year to £9. There were four of them! At the March meeting of that circuit it was agreed that each member of the societies in it should subscribe one penny per quarter towards the extraordinary expenses of the circuit. In 1771 the wife of Jonathan Hern, then the preacher in Limerick, refused to take her allowance as the circuit was so poor. She worked to keep herself and her children in spite of the fact that the youngest was only an infant.

The English Conference of 1753 had set up an Annuitant Fund to provide for 'old and worn-out' preachers. The description might have seemed rather offensive, but a consideration of the sort of work they did, the conditions under which they did it, and the scant remuneration they received for it, suggests that the terms were at least apt.

Throughout the nineteenth century and after it the Irish Conference seems to have taken very little interest in what ministers were paid, leaving it to be settled between individual ministers and their circuits. Alexander Fullerton, who entered the ministry in 1860 and died in 1922, makes reference in his memoirs to several occasions on which the circuit in which he was serving found itself short of funds, and he was not paid his full allowance. It was only after the First World War that the Conference took up the matter seriously, and having noted with pleasure the efforts of some circuits to bring the figures up to date, decided to set standards. In 1920 it determined that the minimum stipend of all ministers on dependent circuits should be £200. Dependent circuits were those which required assistance from the Home Mission and Contingent Fund to meet their yearly costs. They went on to say that every minister should be paid at least twice the pre-war stipend, that no married minister should receive less than £250, and that the minimum payment to an unmarried minister should be £150. They did not attempt to put a ceiling on the amount paid if the circuit could afford more, but in practice few did.

In 1948 the minimum stipend for a married minister in Northern Ireland was £310, and in the Irish Republic £320, due to a higher cost of living. The rate of post-war inflation was greater this time, and a minimum of £400 was fixed in 1951, and £530 in 1959. The minimum passed £1,000 in 1971 and £10,000 in 1995. The difference in amounts paid to married and unmarried ministers was abolished in 1977.

CHAPTER 12

Circuit Life

In the early years the members of any given Methodist society in rural Ireland may have seen the circuit preacher as seldom as once in six weeks, depending upon the size of the circuit and the number of appointments involved in it. His visit would have involved a meeting at which he would have preached, and to which anyone in the community would have been welcome, a field meeting at a different hour, and a private meeting of the members at which an enquiry would have been made into the fitness of each, whether present or not. For this reason the regular meetings for worship and discipline would have been conducted by Local Preachers and Class Leaders, who were lay members of the society and circuit.

Each society was divided into classes and bands. Classes were small groups of members, divided according to sex and age, each with its appointed leader. The ideal was a different leader for each class, but this was not always possible, and there are cases where one leader took responsibility for two classes which met separately. There are instances of classes meeting immediately after the Sunday service, but the great majority of them met on a convenient weeknight, either in the preaching house premises or in the home of the leader. Each meeting would have included the singing of hymns, an 'exhortation' by the leader (which was virtually a sermon), an opportunity for members to speak of particular religious experiences during the preceding week, and the collection of moneys. The leader was regarded as a lay pastor of the members of his or her class, and was required to take an interest in and assist the development of their religious experience.

Bands were smaller, and were seldom larger than six or seven persons. Again, they were divided according to sex and age. The purpose of these was mutual examination and encouragement of holy living. After an opening hymn and prayer each member in turn was required to speak of 'the true state' of his or her soul, confessing faults and temptations. The former was purely for their own correction; in the latter there would also have been the consideration that one member's tale of temptation resisted would encourage another on a similar occasion. In the rules which he drew up in 1738 Wesley proposed eleven questions which would guide the band meeting:

1. Have you the forgiveness of your sins?

2. Have you peace with God through our Lord Jesus Christ?

3. Have you the witness of God's Spirit with your spirit, that you are a child of God?

4. Is the love of God shed abroad in your heart?

5. Has no sin, inward or outward, dominion over you?

6. Do you desire to be told of your faults?

7. Do you desire to be told of all your faults, and that plain and home?

8. Do you desire that every one of us should tell you, from time to time, whatsoever is in his heart concerning you?

9. Consider! Do you desire we should tell you whatever we think, whatsoever we fear, whatsoever we hear, concerning you?

10. Do you desire that, in doing this, we should come as close as possible, that we should cut to the quick, and search your heart to the bottom?

11. Is it your desire and design to be on this, and all other occasions, entirely open, so as to speak everything that is in your heart without exception, without disguise, and without reserve?

This was a very strict discipline indeed, and membership of the Methodist society depended upon it. Only those who met in band were regarded as members, others being welcomed as 'hearers' to the services. It is not surprising that not everyone was willing to accept the discipline and there were generally more hearers than members. What is surprising is the number of people who did accept it: by 1789 there were over 14,000 people in membership in Ireland. It must, of course, be remembered that Methodism was not then a church, but a society within the Church of Ireland, and its appeal was to those who wished to take their religion very seriously.

If the thought of telling even so select and trusted a group as seven people the faults you have committed in the past week sounds daunting, it must not be forgotten that the discipline had a preventive effect as well. The knowledge that you would have tell this group on Thursday the temptation to which you yielded on the previous Saturday was a powerful aid to your resistance on the Saturday.

In the event it is very difficult to determine when the bands ceased to meet. Such records were not kept, and we have to rely on chance references in correspondence or other sources. The probability is that they had ceased by the end of the eighteenth century. Membership then began to depend on the class ticket – a small ticket bearing a text chosen by the Preisdent of the Conference, which was distributed quarterly to each member. Class meetings became less frequent during the nineteenth century, and survived into the twentieth, but generally ceased as other religious meetings crowded the weekly programme. Where class leaders have continued to be appointed, their function has been visitation, and possibly alerting the minister to pastoral needs.

The early pattern of life for the members of society revolved largely around Sunday and the weekly class and band meetings. Sunday was expected to begin with a meeting for worship at five o'clock, which would not have seemed so extraordinarily early to an eighteenth-century group of people as it does to their twenty-first-century successors. In the days when light was provided in most houses by rushlights or tallow candles, people made the maximum use of daylight, and rose and retired earlier than is now general. They were then expected to attend Morning and Evening Prayer in the Church of Ireland, the latter then usually at mid-afternoon. There was another Methodist service in the evening which Wesley directed should never start later than seven o'clock.

If this sounds a very intense programme for one day, it did hold a balance between the direct evangelical appeal of the Methodist services and the liturgical depth of the Church of Ireland Prayer Book. However, there is good reason to question how often it was observed. Wesley's complaint about fervour flagging because the five o'clock service had been neglected does tend to suggest that it was the occasional ideal rather than the usual practice. Again, in the rural areas it was not always possible to find a parish with two services on Sunday. In urban areas where the four services were available, it is reasonable to believe that most Methodists made a selection.

It is often forgotten that the Methodist revival was not only evangelical – it was also sacramental. When Wesley celebrated Holy Communion for the local Methodists there are records of hundreds, and on occasion more than a thousand, attending. In the long time which it took for all of these to receive the bread and wine it would have been every easy for the atmosphere of worship to be lost. To remedy this hymns were sung as the people moved to the communion rail and back again. This is one of the reasons for the great length of some of Charles Wesley's communion hymns.

John Wesley himself was a frequent communicant – in general weekly – and he urged his people to follow his example. That was not always easy to do. Holy Communion in many parish churches was infrequent. The eight o'clock celebration every Sunday only came into use after the influence of Newman and the Tractarians reached this country in the second half of the nineteenth century, and then not in more rural areas. Generally on the Sundays when it was observed it replaced Morning Prayer. This may be one of the reasons for the fact that after Wesley's death Methodists in both Britain and Ireland received the sacrament less frequently. Rattenbury argues that the decline in frequency in England arose from two causes. The first was the tendency of new groups to emphasise the points on which they differ from the group they have left rather than the points which they retain, so that class meetings, love feasts and the like were stressed in preference to the sacrament. The second was a reaction against the Tractarian Movement, which was seen to stress the ceremonial of the sacrament, at the expense of the central truth.[1] The first of these would certainly have applied to the Irish Methodists; it is doubtful if the latter did to any significant extent.

When, in 1816, the Conference gave permission for the celebration of the sacraments by the preachers no frequency was specified, and certainly varied from place to place. In the twentieth century it generally settled into the pattern of Holy Communion on the first Sunday of each month. It has also been traditional in many circuits for Holy Communion to be celebrated on Easter Sunday, but not usually on Christmas Day. Baptisms were administered to infants as occasion arose, though there are records of the simultaneous baptism of several children in the one family which suggests that the members were not always as careful on this point as might have been wished.

A distinctive feature of Methodist worship was the 'Service for the Renewal of the Covenant with God'. Based on the biblical understanding that God had given great blessings to us, and therefore should receive the commitment of our lives, this was first introduced by Wesley at Spitalfields in London in 1755. In modern practice it is observed at the beginning of a new year, always in association with the sacrament. It has passed through several revisions, though the main form and substance of it remain. It includes acts of adoration and confession, the proclamation of the word, and the covenant itself reaching its solemn climax in the words:

> I am no longer my own but yours. Put me to what you will, rank me with whom you will; put me to doing, put me to suffering; Let me be employed for you or laid aside for you, exalted for you or brought low for you; let me be full, let me be

empty; let me have all things, let me have nothing; I freely and wholeheartedly yield all things to your pleasure and disposal. And now, glorious and blessed God, Father, Son, and Holy Spirit, you are mine and I am yours. So be it. And the covenant now made on earth, let it be ratified in heaven. Amen

The pattern of Sunday services, band and class, with their calls to Christian commitment and their rigorous discipline were, of course, designed to encourage and assist the members in holy living. Did they succeed? There is enough independent evidence to suggest that in many cases they did. However, the comment of the late Dr Donald English is probably most accurate. The real achievement of the early Methodists was not that they were holy, but that they took the effort seriously.

Because prayer books were not used it is not easy to discover the form of early Methodist worship. Some of those who underwent deep spiritual experiences at one or other of them have left accounts which can be quite detailed up to the point when they became deeply moved – generally during the sermon. Thereafter they are so generally absorbed with their own sense of guilt, forgiveness or joy that they are unaware of what completed the service. We can say with some certainty that services began with the singing of a hymn, after which a extempore prayer was offered. A very short passage from the Bible was then read, after which the sermon based on the reading was given. Probably this was followed by another prayer, and a second hymn would conclude the worship.

Wesley advised his preachers never to pray for more than eight minutes without intermission, and the second prayer was probably shorter than the first. The singing of two hymns would not take more than another eight minutes, and as the reading was very short, the total time taken in singing, praying and reading would be little more than twenty minutes. The fact that he advised preachers not to protract the service beyond an hour suggests that they had a tendency to do so. The sermon, therefore, could have lasted for anything between thirty-five and forty minutes, or even longer on occasion. In the eighteenth century audiences would have had little difficulty in maintaining attention for that length.

Towards the end of Wesley's lifetime there was growing pressure in some places in England, and in Dublin, for the Methodist services to be held at the same time as Morning Prayer in the parish churches, to which fewer and fewer Methodists were going. Indeed there was a major argument over the matter in Dublin in 1788, which cost Wesley the friendship of one of his dearest friends in the city, Arthur Keene. Where there was a strong argument in favour of the change Wesley allowed it, but on the condition that Morning Prayer was read at the Methodist service. For this purpose he produced a somewhat modified version of it. The Abbey Street society was the first to avail of this, but afterwards Whitefriar Street took it up, and their successors, the Centenary society, continue the practice. A second condition was that the society had no meeting of their own once a month, and went to the parish church for the sacrament. Pursuant to that, the Whitefriar Street Methodists went to St Patrick's Cathedral until the Conference permitted the administration of the sacrament in their own premises.

The separation of Irish Methodists from the Church of Ireland is dated from 1816, when the celebration of the sacraments in the Methodist chapels began, but for some time before that an increasing number of them were not going to the parish churches. In most cases it was not that they stopped doing so; it was more the case that they saw no reason to start, having never done so before becoming Methodists. Thus the number of those experiencing the richness of the Prayer Book was declining. It was almost certainly in an effort to balance this loss, though the matter was never officially debated, that the form of Methodist service began to be enlarged and developed. The readings from the Bible were generally lengthened, and the custom began of reading two of them, one from the Old and the other from the New Testament. The number of hymns increased to four or five. The first prayer, generally of adoration and confession, was shortened, and the second, of intercession for a variety of people in need, was extended. Later still it became the custom to introduce a short talk or story designed to give the children a place in the worship. Sermons were shortened, but the service lengthened to last for fifteen or twenty minutes beyond the hour.

A regular, though less frequent feature of early Methodist devotion was the love feast. The feasting element in this ceremony did not lie in the amount of food consumed, which was usually no more than a biscuit. The feast was a spiritual one. A loving cup of water was passed from person to person, and as it came to each they had an opportunity of telling the assembly of some religious experience that had received since the last occasion. The intention was that other people might be encouraged and inspired by hearing how people like themselves had felt the blessing of God. Love feasts in the eighteenth century are noted as the final event of a quarterly meeting of the local Methodist societies, but they were sometimes arranged at other times, to mark a special date or a visit from a special preacher.

One of the significant features throughout the years was, and is, the singing of hymns. Initially these were 'lined out'. The preacher read two lines of the hymn, which the people then sang, and he read two more, and so continued until the whole had been sung. As literacy improved in the societies, and hymn books became available, the lining out was happily abandoned. John Wesley's younger brother Charles was a prolific hymn writer, his output having been variously estimated at between six and seven thousand. Inevitably many of these were of poor quality and were never published in his lifetime, but some were among the finest hymns which have been written. They included 'Jesus, Lover of my soul', 'O for a thousand tongues to sing my great Redeemer's praise', 'Hark! The herald angels sing',[2] 'And can it be that I should gain an interest in the Saviour's blood?', 'Love divine, all loves excelling' and 'Christ, whose glory fills the skies'.

It was mostly hymns written by John and Charles Wesley that the Methodists sang. Saturated in biblical language and imagery, they were an extraordinarily effective means of teaching people doctrine. One remembers far more of what one sings than one does of what one reads or hears. The power of music is well known, though curiously John Wesley appears to have had no appreciation of music for its own sake. He valued it as a vehicle for the words and was anxious that the music should not obscure the sense. His disliked repetition of parts of lines, and was annoyed if different singers were required to sing different words at the same time.

Wesley's advice on the matter to congregations is characteristic:

1. Sing *all*. See that you join with the congregation as frequently as you can ...

2. Sing *lustily*, and with a good courage ...

3. Sing *modestly*. Do not bawl ...

4. Sing *in time*.

5. Above all, sing *spiritually*. Have an eye to God in every word you sing.

At first congregations sang hymns to whatever tune they knew which would fit the measure of the verses. The same hymn could be sung to a dozen different tunes in as many different circuits. When in 1780 Wesley published his definitive collection of hymns a particular tune was recommended for each hymn, most of the tunes being recommended more than once, and these were not published in the same volume. The idea of printing a tune with each hymn did not arise until the latter half of the nineteenth century. The first Methodist hymn book to do so was the edition of 1877.

The proportion of Wesley hymns in successive Methodist hymn collections has reduced, as the riches of other writers has been recognised, but they still constitute the core of doctrinal hymns in the most recent, *Hymns & Psalms*. This book, published in 1983, includes a good representation of the very fine hymn writers working in the second half of the twentieth century, a fair proportion of them Methodist.

The early singing was certainly unaccompanied unless there

chanced to be somebody present who could play some sort of instrument. In time it became general for any members of the society who could play suitable instruments to be formed into a small band. In city churches, where congregations were larger, it was possible to gather what amounted to a chamber orchestra to accompany the hymns. At the end of the 1860s fashion moved away from the band, and those congregations which could afford it began to acquire pipe organs, sometimes of very high quality. The first such was installed in the Methodist Centenary church on St Stephen's Green in Dublin inn 1869. It was a two manual and pedal instrument which cost £450. The choirmaster, Richard W. Booth, who raised the money for it, was criticised for extravagance and novelty. When the Carlisle Memorial church was built in 1876 a very fine organ was installed right from the beginning. Before long organs were installed in every church that could afford one, including those in the larger provincial towns.

Those smaller churches in the cities, and rural churches who could not afford the expense, acquired harmoniums. By the end of the nineteenth century it was virtually unthinkable that hymns should be accompanied by any other sort of instrument. The disadvantage of the harmonium, not considered at the time, was that the player had to pump into it with foot bellows throughout the whole time he or she was playing. Improved technology after the Second World War saw the introduction of the electronic organ, which had the double advantage of not requiring to be pumped, and being capable of a variety of tones.

History has a curious habit of moving in circles. By the 1980s fewer people were learning to play the organ, and a new style of singing was being introduced into the churches by young people. This was accompanied by groups – the church orchestra by another name, and with different instruments.

So long as the Methodist societies regarded themselves as part of the Church of Ireland the so-called occasional services presented no difficulty. When Methodists wished to marry they did so in the Church of Ireland, and when they died it was natural for them to be buried by the parish rector or curate. When they separated from the church, the difficulties began. The civil law did not recognise Methodist marriages, were such to have taken place, and so although they did not now worship in the Church of Ireland, the Wesleyans were obliged to return to the church if they wanted their marriages to be legal. It was not a satisfactory arrangement.

In 1845 there was a measure of relief. Under the terms of an act passed in that year it became possible for Methodists to marry in their own chapels, but only in the presence of the civil registrar for the district; and it was the civil registrar who held the registration of the marriage in question. It was not until 1863 that it became possible to register Methodist chapels for marriages. Most were immediately registered. Weddings could thereafter be conducted in the chapels by the ministers, who were effectively registrars for the purpose. They were required to maintain registers of marriages, sending copies to the district registrar and the Registrar General. Where the requirements regarding residence before the event were not possible, special licences could be issued by the Secretary of the Conference.

If the difficulties with marriages arose from a discriminatory legislation, the difficulties with burials were social. Most Methodists wished to be buried in the Church of Ireland graveyards where their deceased relations lay. Many rectors raised no objection to this, but there were others who prohibited Methodist ministers from performing burial ceremonies in these graveyards. Numbers did not often justify the Methodists opening graveyards of their own, and some quite unseemly disputes arose. In 1865, for instance, the Rev Edward Best of Armagh was curtly refused permission to bury one of his people in the graveyard at Richhill. He had to perform the ceremony in the public road outside the graveyard, after which the coffin was buried without graveside ceremony.

Mr Best's complaint to the Lord Lieutenant was one of very many, which eventually led to the passage of an act in 1868 which permitted those who had burial rights in a Church of

Ireland graveyard, but who were not members of that church, to bury their deceased without hindrance, provided due notice was given to the rector. A question submitted to the Solicitor General in 1878 elicited two legal opinions, that the right of burial belonged to every resident in the parish, and that the disestablishment of the church in 1871 had not in any way diminished the rights given under the 1868 Act. The presence of three extensive Methodist graveyards in Co Fermanagh, at Sydaire near Ballinamallard, at Maguiresbridge, and at Tierwinney near Irvinestown, are reminders of these disputes. The last occasion on which the Act had to be invoked was in 1989, when the Rev Dudley Levistone Cooney had recourse to it in order to bury a Methodist lady in the grave of her Church of Ireland husband.

While Methodist worship was generally conducted without a prayer book, forms of service had to be used for weddings, and ministers generally drew on such for sacraments and other special occasions. In 1932 three Methodist bodies reunited in England, and shortly afterwards published a *Book of Offices* which provided revised forms of service for these special occasions, some of them based on services in the Church of England *Book of Common Prayer*. Copies of individual services were made available, and were quite quickly adopted in Irish circuits. They served the Methodist people for forty years.

In the third quarter of the century liturgical reform was developing in all churches, and there was a considerable exchange of views on the matter. The result was the remodelling of many services on the basis of what were believed to be the forms used in the early Christian centuries. Accordingly the language used in churches of different denominations began to be quite similar. In 1975 the British Methodist Church published *The Methodist Service Book*, of which individual services had been used experimentally for some time. This volume in a few years replaced the *Book of Offices* in general use in Ireland. The traditional extempore form of service, however, remained the staple in all circuits.

The late years of the nineteenth and earlier years of the twentieth century saw the steady decline of field preaching, largely for reasons related to the political situation in those years. Some ministers still conducted meetings at fairs, but interest in these was declining. There were, however, those who were determined that the tradition should not completely disappear. Wesley had preached on more than one occasion at a field in Sydaire, the property of the Armstrong family in Co Fermanagh, and an annual service at that place was believed to have been held in unbroken succession since then.

The place where he had preached on the Dunraven estate at Adare in Co Limerick was also known, and early in the nineteenth century a Field Meeting was started on the site. When Lord Dunraven developed a golf club in the estate the Wesley site was in the middle of it, but the tradition of the Methodist meeting on the first Tuesday of every June is maintained, and the Adare Manor Golf Club is proud of its record as the only golf club in the world which closes play to facilitate Christian worship.

Other field meetings are of more recent origin, but all now combine two features, the preservation of a unique preaching tradition, and the annual reunion of friends and former members of the circuits in which they are located.

For most of the nineteenth century the life of an Irish Methodist followed a pattern of Sunday services and class meetings, with the addition in the country of the cottage meeting. That pattern began to change towards the end of the century. The cottage meeting lasted somewhat longer, eventually disappearing as people began to be more mobile and to find other ways of spending evenings. It has been suggested that the class meeting died of tedium because the members had too little fresh to say. But there was another factor at work. The number of activities for particular groups within the circuits was increasing.

We have already noted the development of the Women's Department. Though primarily designed to increase and channel support for overseas missions in general and the work of women missionaries in particular, it met a wider need. Meetings not only provided missionary interest, and planned missionary support, but were conducted in a devotional atmosphere, with prayer for the work on the mission field. It was, in short, less introverted than the class meeting.

The greatest proliferation of organisations, however, was in the work with young people. One of the first of these was Christian Endeavour. The first Young People's Society of Christian Endeavour was formed by the Rev Francis E. Clark, the young minister of Williston Congregational Church at Portland in Maine in 1882. Designed to channel into Christian service the enthusiasm and energy of a number of young people who had made responses at a recent mission in the congregation, Clark did not expect it to go beyond his own congregation, but with remarkable speed it was taken up in other congregations and other denominations, and crossed the Atlantic. The first society in Ireland was formed at Agnes Street Presbyterian Church in 1889. A young man named Newman Hall heard of it while visiting friends in Canada, and on his return home persuaded the Rev James D. Lamont, minister of Knock Methodist Church in Belfast, to allow him to form a society there. This was the first Methodist CE society in Ireland.

Within a very short period the character of the organisation commended it to the Conference, and in 1895 it became the official youth movement of Irish Methodism. This position it held officially until the late 1960s, when the Methodist Youth Department proposed that the Conference should not accord that status to any particular organisation. There were a number of features which appealed to the Conference in 1895. One was the devotional nature of the meetings, and the fact that the society centred its work on Christian commitment and witness. Another was the fact that the members were encouraged and trained to conduct their own meetings, gaining experience in public speaking, public prayer and organisation. A third was the balance of the programme between worship and study, missionary interest, social responsibility, and recreation.

The societies were associated with others through local,

national and international unions, each of which organised gatherings with greater or lesser frequency. Thus members found opportunity of meeting young people from other churches. In Ireland societies were affiliated to Church of Ireland, Presbyterian, Baptist, Congregational and Quaker congregations as well as Methodist. There were those who thought that the church's youth work should be more specifically Methodist, and in Britain a Wesley Guild was formed, with a similar programme of worship, missionary support, social responsibility and recreation. A few Irish ministers formed branches of the Guild in this country, but they tended to be short lived. That sort of activity was well provided by CE. (In general conversation the initials virtually became the name, being one of the early examples of this in the life of the church.)

The next organisation for young people to be introduced into Irish Methodism was the Boys' Brigade. The first Irish company had been established in Belfast in 1888, but the first Methodist company did not commence activity until 1899. The Girls' Brigade was founded in Dublin in 1893 in connection with Sandymount Presbyterian Church. It too was taken up by the Irish Methodists before many years had passed. The uniforms, for all their simplicity in the early days, appealed to boys and girls, and the programme of drill was beneficial for their health and deportment. However, one of the features which appealed to the Conference was the fact that each company was obliged by the constitutions of the Brigades to conduct a Bible class as part of its programme.

Scouting and Guiding, with their stress on healthy outdoor activities, discipline and consideration for others, while opening their meetings with prayers, did not have quite the same religious aspect as the Brigades, and fewer Methodist circuits formed packs of either. There were, however, many who found the Scout and Guide programmes preferable, and reckoned that the religious development of the children was adequately served. Between Christian Endeavour and one or other of the uniformed organisations most Methodist children did, in fact, have a varied and valuable programme.

The Gold Triangle was a different sort of organisation in that it did not require its members to attend meetings. Introduced in 1943, it was officially the Association of Christian Citizenship and Total Abstinence, but to members and others alike, it was simply 'The Gold Triangle'. Members undertook to abstain from alcoholic drink and from gambling, and to maintain sexual morality. In witness to this they wore a small badge comprising a gold triangle containing a blue cross on a white field.

The 1970s were years when young people began to move away from the structured organisations. They disliked much of the planning, and felt restricted by the traditional youth activities. The new development of that decade was the Youth Club, to which they were welcomed, and where activity was much more casual. Music and sports began to play a large part in what was happening, and opportunities for discussion of topics of current concern were less formal. In time the annual gathering of the Irish Methodist Association of Youth Clubs became a major event extending over a weekend of sporting activities and worship events.

PART IV

Social Concerns

CHAPTER 13

Education

We have already noted Wesley's concern about the education of his preachers, and his encouragement of them in reading habits. This concern extended to all the members of the Methodist societies, and from very early in the work he encouraged his preachers to carry Methodist publications in their saddlebags, and sell them to the people. It was to encourage the members in reading that Wesley published his *Christian Library* of fifty volumes, containing extracts and abridgements of pious works from a wide variety of writers, ancient and recent. Produced and sold in such numbers, it was possible for the prices to be kept within the reach of almost all of the members. It is seldom recognised that Wesley was the pioneer of the 'condensed book' and the cheap edition.

What the people read in those days was generally pious literature. The theological works in the *Christian Library* were read by only a small number of the better educated; the majority would have read magazines and leaflets exhorting them to ethical living, including Wesley's *Words*. These included *A Word to a Freeholder*, about responsible voting; *A Word to a Sabbath-Breaker*, about Sundays, *A Word to a Smuggler*, which would discouraged the use of smuggled goods as well as the actual smuggling of them; and *A Word to a Swearer*. The magazines would have been those which Wesley published. There was an Irish edition of the *Methodist Magazine* which reproduced the content of the London edition of two months previously and added items of Irish interest. The magazine appeared every month, and contained news of Methodist successes, brief biographies of distinguished Christians, episodes from church history, accounts of evangelical conversions, sermonettes, and other minor pious writings. The only illustration in each was a steel engraving of a portrait of one or other of the preachers, and these were only included in the issues between 1806 and 1822. The last Dublin edition was issued in 1822, after which the English edition circulated.

Wesley established his Irish headquarters at Whitefriar Street, Dublin in 1752, and the site was gradually extended by further leases to include several buildings. In one of these, 13 Whitefriar Street, in 1802 the Conference established a Bookroom. The 'Book Steward', one of the preachers, was responsible for this, his task including the sale and distribution of literature, and the printing and circulation of the Irish edition of the magazine. The first Book Steward was Matthias Joyce, who had served an apprenticeship as a publisher and bookseller before becoming a preacher. His successors were John Kerr and Thomas Wade Doolittle.[1] This Bookroom operated until 1830, when it became a distribution centre for the Bookroom in London. For some years the Special Evangelistic Agency operated a Bookroom in the Abbey Street Church, and then in a small room in O'Connell Street, but the number of other Christian bookshops in the city made its continuation unnecessary. It closed in 1968. The Primitive Wesleyans throughout their existence operated a Bookroom in South Great George's Street, and published their own *Primitive Wesleyan Methodist Magazine*, the content of which was generally similar to that of the Wesleyan publication.

As Belfast developed bookrooms were opened there at May Street, and at Arthur Street. When the Irish Methodist Publishing Company was formed for the publication of the *Irish Christian Advocate*, it took over the business of the bookroom, and developed Epworth House in Wellington Street into one of the leading bookshops in the city. This flourished until 1971, when the building was destroyed by a bomb. A Bookroom operated in Aldersgate House on University Road for several years, but it was closed in 1999, and a Resource Centre in the same building now acts purely as a distribution centre for Methodist publications.

The chapel in Whitefriar Street had over it a large apartment with the same floor area. The pillars which supported the gallery in the chapel were carried up through the ceiling into this apartment, and so to the roof. Partitions between these pillars and the walls divided the sides of this upper floor into small rooms, leaving in the centre a large apartment which was called 'The Lobby'. The partitions could be opened to bring the rooms into use with the lobby if necessary. It was here that the first Methodist school in Ireland, the Free School for Boys, was opened early in 1784 with Richard Condy as its first teacher. He had been a preacher for some years, but ill health forced his retirement from circuit. He taught for less than a year, when his continued ill health necessitated his withdrawal from this too. However, the complete rest of several months seems to have restored his energy, and he returned to circuit in 1785.

His successor appears to have been unsuitable, for in the February of 1785 Wesley was writing to Arthur Keene, the principal lay steward in Whitefriar Street, urging the appointment of one Patrick Fox. He wrote:

> If you are wise secure Mr Fox at any price. That man is sterling gold. But you will have no blessing from God and no praise from wise men if you take that vile sordid measure (especially at this time!) of so reducing the salary. You must give £40 a year at least ... I abhor the thought of our master's keeping an evening school. It would swallow up the time he ought to have for his own improvement. Give him enough to live comfortably upon without this drudgery.

Fox was appointed, and ran the school successfully for eight years. It was during his time in office that it was moved from the lobby over the chapel to a building erected for the purpose behind one of the preachers' residences. He retired or resigned in 1793.

His successor as schoolmaster was an exceedingly colourful character by the name of Roger Lamb, who received a salary of £60 a year. Lamb had been born in Dublin in 1756, and walks along the quays with his father gave him the urge for foreign travel. At the age of sixteen he joined the army, and because of his education, which was better than average among soldiers, was soon promoted to corporal. In 1776 he was sent to America under the command of General Burgoyne, and after the surrender at Saratoga in the following year was made a prisoner of war. Twelve months later he escaped, and was posted to a regiment under the command of Lord Cornwallis. In the course of one battle Lamb saved Cornwalllis from being captured by the Americans. However Lamb himself was again captured, and put into Philadelphia Gaol. From this he escaped with four others by digging a tunnel under the wall. At the end of the war he returned to England with his regiment and was discharged at Winchester.

Refused a pension on the grounds that he had been less than twenty years in the army, he decided to return to Dublin. There he heard John Wesley preach, and himself became a Methodist. He married a widow with several children and decided to take up school teaching. In Whitefriar Street he enjoyed very considerable success and the numbers of boys rose until the school premises were crowded. Indeed, he had some quite unruly lads to tame, some of them from criminal backgrounds, but his romantic military background was an asset, and he was popular with his pupils as well as with the members of the Whitefriar Street society, in which he played a very active part.

Later masters were less notable. The school was eventually terminated by the expiry of the lease which scattered the various institutions from Whitefriar Street to other locations.

The Free School catered only for boys. Nothing was done for the education of girls there during Wesley's lifetime, and for some years afterwards. However, there was one person who was concerned about them. This was Solomon Walker, a silk manufacturer of Bridge Street, and one of the wealthiest members of the Whitefriar Street society. He was not able during his lifetime to do anything practical about his concern, largely because of a storm which he created in 1777. In that year he accused Samuel Bradburn, then the second preacher in the city, of false doctrine. Bradburn was vindicated by his senior colleague, John Hampson, and by Wesley, but shortly afterwards when Hampson called a meeting to appoint a new trustee for the Widows' Almshouse a charge of peculation was laid against the treasurer, James Martin. This too proved to be false, but the ill feeling caused by the two accusations led to the resignation from the society of thirty-four members. In the October Wesley hurried to Dublin for a brief visit to make peace, but did not quite succeed. The thirty-four refused to return to membership, and preferred to meet as a separate class. However, they continued to worship with the Whitefriar Street society on Sundays. One of them was Solomon Walker.

In 1804 Walker met an untimely death when he was thrown from his horse. In his will he left £2,150 'to furnish and provide a room with proper beds and furniture for a Female Charity School, in or near the Preaching-house, Whitefriar Street, and to be called *The Methodist Female Orphan School* and to consist of ten female children'. In 1806 this school came into being with its own house on the corner of Whitefriar Street and Whitefriar Lane. It opened with five girls, who had to be between the ages of seven and fourteen, and who qualified for admission if either of their parents was dead. It was not until 1812 that the number of girls was increased, not to the stipulated ten of Mr Walker's intention, but to twelve. Through the years the number fluctuated, but the average was ten.

One of the benefactors of this institution was John Barret, Professor of Oriental Languages and Vice-Provost of Trinity College, Dublin. Known as 'Jacky' Barret, he was one of the city's most noted eccentrics, whose monumental parsimony accumulated a sum of £80,000 which, at his death in 1821, he bequeathed entirely to charity. The Methodist Female Orphan School received £500 of this.

When it became necessary to move from Whitefriar Street temporary accommodation was found at No 47 Charlemont Street, the house next door to that which had been the residence of Arthur Keene with whom Wesley had stayed on occasion.

Here the school remained for five years. In 1852 a site was acquired in Harrington Street, and a building erected to provide a permanent home for it. The Booth family of the Centenary church built a residence next door, and in 1899 presented this to school to enable it to admit a greater number of girls. The Booths also bought a house at Skerries, which they gave to the school to be used as a summer holiday home for the girls.

In the 1930s the State began to make allowances to widows and orphans, and the demands on the school declined. The premises in Harrington Street became too large for the number of girls. The buildings were sold in 1938, and the school moved to Northbrook Road where there was accommodation for ten girls. However, it stayed here for only five years. In 1943 it seemed more economical to avail of the boarding facilities in Wesley College. So in their turn the Northbrook Road premises were sold, and the money used to endow the Methodist Female Orphan School Trust which paid for the education and maintenance at Wesley College of girls who would otherwise have qualified for the school.

This arrangement continued until 1976 when the Trustees found themselves with a steadily increasing endowment because there were too few girls eligible to benefit from it. Application was made to the High Court to vary the terms of the Trust, and it became available to boys as well as girls. It was given a new name: The Methodist Orphan Education Fund. The fund is administered by the Methodist Orphan Society.

These two schools marked the entry of Irish Methodists into the field of elementary education, but their involvement was not limited to the two. Wherever a suitable teacher could be found, and money to support him, circuits opened schools, most of which were patronised by many more than Methodist children. In some cases a school was built beside or near to a chapel, the same building serving as school during the day and meeting hall in the evening. In a few rural areas, where it was not practicable to build a chapel, the local people built a school, which was used for worship on Sundays. The exact number of these schools may never be known as some were never reported to the central authorities and in other cases records have been lost.

In 1831 the Board of National Education in Ireland was formed to administer primary education throughout the country, but the Wesleyan Conference, in common with the authorities of other churches, was reluctant to lose its schools. It feared that the policy of nondenominational religious education in the 'National Schools' would lack 'a sound scriptural' basis. At the time quite a number of schools in mission areas were supported by the British Wesleyans. In 1841 the Conference established a Wesleyan Methodist School Society to encourage the opening of more schools, but progress was hampered by the lack of funds.

It was this that eventually convinced the Conference that the advantages of transfer to the National Board would outweigh the disadvantages, and by 1865 sixty-five schools had been transferred. A further 48 schools were maintained as before on the mission stations. In 1871, however, an arrangement was made by which this funding was reduced to extinction by 1915. In many places the remuneration of the teachers was extremely small, whether the schools had been transferred or not. Of necessity many teachers had other sources of income, including farming. The standard of education given, however, would seem to have been very satisfactory. The census of 1861 reveals that only 9% of Methodists were unable to read or write, a figure well below the national average.

In Northern Ireland the transferred schools were intended to serve the whole community, but the Roman Catholic Church preferred not to transfer its schools, which it used for the religious formation of its children, and the transferred schools became 'Protestant' by default. Methodists participate in the management of many of the transferred schools, but there are no Methodist primary schools as such there. In the Republic the government adopted a policy of supporting denominational management of schools, and there were some under Methodist management in many parts of the country. Economic factors, both in terms of finance and in terms of efficient teaching, led to the closure of most of these, pupils being transferred to those managed by another Protestant denomination. The only surviving Methodist primary school in the country is, therefore, Rathgar National School in Dublin. It is funded by the State, but managed by a committee over which the circuit superintendent minister presides. Methodists are officially represented on the boards of some others. In both jurisdictions ministers have *entrée* into schools for religious education classes or assemblies.

For some years the Irish Wesleyans had their own teacher training institution. The address was 38½ Hardwicke Street, and the site had a curious history. It had at different times been a private residence, a convent of Poor Clare nuns, and a Jesuit chapel and school. When they took it over in 1816 the Jesuits remodelled the chapel to include apartments for resident priests in the upper storey. In a very short time it proved to be too small for their work, and by 1825 they were seeking an alternative. They were given a site by the Irish Sisters of Charity in Upper Gardiner Street, and there they built their present church. In 1840 the school moved to nearby Belvedere House, and adopted the name of its new home. Thus provided, the Jesuits had no further use for the building in Hardwicke Street, and in 1841 the Wesleyans bought it and adapted it for their own purposes. It was opened for Wesleyan worship on 18 June 1843, when the preacher was the Rev Thomas Waugh, then superintendent minister of the Dublin circuit.

A primary school was opened in connection with this chapel in 1845.[2] Ten years later the Wesleyan Conference met in Belfast and inaugurated a Fund for the Increase of the Wesleyan Agency in Ireland. Its objectives were threefold: the development of education, the increase of the number of ministers, and the improvement of ministers' residences. In 1858 a sum of £3,000 was allocated to the first of these. The bulk of this sum was used for the establishment of a training college for teachers based on the Hardwicke Street school.

Unfortunately the records of this college have been lost, so that it is impossible to say how many teachers were trained there, or who the instructors were. It survived for only fourteen years, during the latter part of which its principal was Samuel Hollingsworth. He was later accepted for the ministry, and in 1891 became principal of Wesley College in Dublin. He has the distinction of being the only Methbodist minister to have received a DD from Trinity College, Dublin by examination. The training college was closed in 1872 and an arrangement made with the Model School in Marlborough Street that Methodist teachers should be trained there.

The school in Hardwicke Street had, at the time when the college closed, just 28 pupils. However it survived into the early years of the present century, closing its doors in 1910. It was then sold at auction, subject to a head rent of £30 a year for the unexpired period of the lease of 69 years. The purchaser was Countess Plunkett, who was interested in the Irish drama movement. She let the chapel part of the building to a group led by her son Joseph Mary Plunkett, Thomas MacDonagh and Edward Martyn, who had withdrawn their support from the Abbey Theatre because they believed that its policy was too restrictive. The hall at the back was let to the Dun Emer Guild for arts and crafts. The building was demolished in the 1950s to make way for a Corporation housing scheme.

It is an interesting indication of the seriousness with which the Methodists took education that at one time there were forty Wesleyan teachers in training, a far greater number than the proportion of Methodists in the country would have suggested. In recent years Methodist teachers for Northern Ireland have been trained at Stranmillis College in Belfast, and those for the Republic in the Church of Ireland College of Education.

When Robert Raikes started a Sunday School in Gloucester in 1780 his primary intention was to give some basic education to children whose parents could not afford to pay for schooling. The children were taught to read, to write, and to do simple arithmetic. The basic reading book was the Bible, so that a measure of religious teaching was included with the business of learning to read. In the course of time the basic education element of the programme was left to the day schools as these came to be funded by the State, and the Sunday School became purely a vehicle for teaching faith to the children.

Irish Methodists very quickly recognised the value of the Sunday school movement, and have continued to operate such in every place were there are children to be taught. In 1809 Thomas Parnell,[3] superintendent of the Sunday School at Maryborough (now Portlaoise) Methodist chapel, raised with the Rev Adam Averell the suggestion that a Sunday School Society should be established in Ireland, similar to that in England, to assist in funding the smaller schools. This led to a meeting in Dublin in the November of the same year at which the Hibernian Sunday School Society was founded. Alexander Boyle of Kirlish Lodge was in the chair, and among the other Methodists elected to the committee were Mr Parnell, Martin Keene and Dr Isaac D'Olier. Under the name Sunday School Society for Ireland this body still continues its work, though now largely confined to Church of Ireland Sunday Schools.

By the late 1830s Wesleyan parents were beginning to ask why their church did not cater for the education of their children beyond the primary stage. The first attempt to do anything about this was made in 1839 by four ministers, the Revs James B. Gillman, William Ferguson, William Stewart and Thomas Waugh. They did not succeed in establishing a college, but they encouraged the idea, and in the following year the Conference gave some consideration to the establishment of a grammar school. Nothing happened beyond the discussion. In 1843 a Wesleyan minister from Belfast, the Rev John Kerr Johnston, was teaching in one of the English Wesleyan schools, and he wrote to Thomas Averell Shillington, a prominent member of the Portadown circuit, suggesting that such a school would be practical in Ireland. Shillington read the letter at a breakfast meeting in Portadown, and it inspired on of the company present, the Rev Robert G. Cather to take up the project.

Through his initiative in 1844 a provisional committee was formed, which proposed the establishment of a boarding and day school for boys in Belfast. The location was soon changed to Dublin for two reasons: there were more than twice as many Methodists in Dublin as there were in Belfast; and Dublin, as the capital city, was the hub of the country's transport system. The committee's plans were laid before the Wesleyan Conference which met in Cork in 1845. The Conference approved, and set up a committee to give effect to these.[4]

A somewhat delapidated building at No 79 St Stephen's Green was leased, and made ready to receive the Wesleyan Connexional School, as the new institution was called. It opened its doors on 1 October 1845 with three boarders and nine day pupils. For reasons related to the transport of boarders from and to their homes, the school originally operated on a year of two terms, separated by a four week holiday at Christmas. The first Governor and Chaplain of the school was the Rev Dr Robinson Scott. In 1851 the adjoining house, No 78, was leased to relieve the congestion as the number of pupils rose.

Of the pupils who were educated in the Wesleyan Connexional School, two are outstanding. Sir Robert Hart was there from 1848 to 1852. He achieved fame, and his knighthood, through his service in China, where he was Inspector General of Customs, and founder of the postal and lighthouse services. Of his time in the school his biographer, Stanley F. Wright, records:

> The curriculum then was on the old-time classical model, and Hart came in for the usual drilling in Latin and Greek, as well as for a thorough grounding in English subjects, French and mathematics. Organised school sports did not exist, and competitive athletic contests with other schools were un-heard of.

The other pupil, George Bernard Shaw, was both better known, and much less complementary. In 1928 he wrote:

> I have not a good word to say for it. It could not even teach Latin, and it never seriously tried to teach anything else. A more futile boy prison could not be imagined. I was a day-boy: what a boarder's life was like I shudder to conjecture.

At the School between 1865 and 1868, Shaw was a shy and lonely boy, which coloured his view of the place.

The leases of the two houses on St Stephen's Green, which adjoined the Guinness residence on the side nearer to Earlsfort Terrace, were due to expire in 1877, and it was by no means certain that the landlords, the trustees of the King's Hospital, would be willing to renew. For one thing the Guinnesses were anxious to purchase both and extend their house. The Board of the School began to think of alternative plans. In 1872 they bought a piece of land a little distance along the Green, partly behind the Methodist Centenary church, and partly behind adjoining houses. Here they spent £20,000 in building a new school. It was in Gothic style, and was designed by Alfred Gresham Jones.

The leases of 78 and 79 were extended for three years, because the new premises were not ready in 1877, but in 1879 the transfer took place. In fact it was virtually a re-foundation, as the name was changed to Wesley College. The Wesleyan and Primitive Wesleyan Connexions had reunited in the previous year and to retain the original name would have been discourteous to the former Primitive Wesleyans. The first Governor of Wesley College was the Rev Dr Thomas A. McKee, and the first Headmaster was Dr Maxwell McIntosh. Twelve years later, in 1891, to offices of Governor and Headmaster were merged in that of Principal, the first Principal being the Rev Dr Samuel Hollingsworth.

In was not until 1911 that Wesley College admitted its first girls, quite some years after its younger sister Methodist College, Belfast. They could not live in the same building as the boys, and so the former Epworth Club, at No 110 St Stephen's Green was purchased to serve as a girls' hostel. The house next door at No 111 was bought later to double the accommodation. At various dates between 1918 and 1948 premises were acquired in Leeson Street, Burlington Road and Winton Road to serve as residences for pupils. In 1927 a handsome War Memorial Chapel was built to a design by George F. Beckett.

For many years most of the children of rural Methodists in the south of Ireland attended Wesley College. At the beginning and end of each term a whole carriage was reserved on the Cork train to bring pupils from that county to and from school.

In 1947 the Rev Gerald G. Myles was appointed Principal, and immediately initiated a programme of development to enable the college to meet the challenges of educational development in the years after the Second World War. In 1956 a campaign was launched to raise £100,000 to provide new classrooms and laboratories, the latter to cater for the demands of science teaching. These were opened by Professor Ernest T. S. Walton, the Nobel physics laureate, who was a member of the College Board.

The scattered accommodation remained a problem until 1964 when Mr Myles seized upon a change in government capital funding policy. Ludford Park, a house on fifty acres of ground at Ballinteer, was purchased, and all the other premises sold. On the new site a college was built to a design by Robin Walker of Michael Scott and Partners. It was opened in 1969. Since then a number of other buildings have been added to enhance the teaching programme, sports facilities, and student welfare.

The establishment of the Connexional School in Dublin did not satisfy some of the Wesleyans in Portadown and Belfast, who thought that their numbers, which were growing, justified a similar foundation in the north of the country. Discussion on the point developed in the 1850s with some disagreement as to whether it should be at Belfast or at Portadown. Nothing was actually done until 1864 when James Carlisle bought the fourteen-acre Vermont Estate just outside Belfast to the south of the city, and offered all or part of it to the committee which was considering the project. A native of Castledawson, Carlisle had come to Belfast as a journeyman carpenter and had developed a business as builder and contractor which earned him a considerable reputation. After his death two of his leading employees continued the business under their joint names, McLaughlin & Harvey.

The Committee, with unusual foresight, opted to take the whole fourteen acres, an action for which their successors have constantly blessed their memory, for it made possible a great deal of expansion in later decades. The principal member of this committee was William McArthur, son of a Wesleyan minister, who had been born in Donegal. He began a woollen business in Londonderry which he later transferred to London and extended to Australia. Knighted, he became Lord Mayor of London in 1880. He continued to take an active role in the affairs of the college throughout his life. His father-in-law, Archibald Mc Elwaine, had many years previously offered £1,000 towards the building of a grammar school in Belfast, and this was the first subscription to the new project.[5]

The architect, William Fogarty of Dublin, designed a building in the fashionable gothic style, with a central block and two wings. The foundation stone was laid in 1865, and the institution was intended to provide an education for boys, and theological training for Wesleyan ministers, the latter carried on in the East Wing. The Principal was to have overall charge of the college, with the Theological Tutor responsible for the theological department, and the Headmaster responsible for the school. This division of purpose and responsibility was a source of tension for the next fifty years. A strip of land at the northern side of the site was sold for the building of houses, the street being called College Gardens. The houses were to be of uniform height, and solely residential. The ground rents provided some income for the college.

The year 1868 saw the opening of the Wesleyan Methodist Collegiate Institution, with the Rev William Arthur as Principal, the Rev Dr Robinson Scott as Theological Tutor, and Dr Robert Crook as Headmaster. Arthur, an Irishman, had spent some years as a missionary in India, and later at the headquarters of the Wesleyan Missionary Society in London. He was a prolific writer. Scott and Crook had both been associated with the Connexial School in Dublin. Crook's successors as Headmasters were all laymen. In 1885 the name of the college was simplified to Methodist College, Belfast, but it has been generally known with affectionate respect as 'Methody'.

One of Crook's first actions in the new institution was to form a kindergarten department. Only three months after the opening he made his most significant innovation, he persuaded the committee to admit 'young ladies'. The college was to be co-educational almost from the start. There were other differences with Wesley College. Recreation was being given a fuller role in education, and the fact that there were several unused acres in the college site enabled a rugby pitch to be laid out, surrounded by a running track. Initially boarders were all required to attend the Methodist Church at University Road, which had been opened in 1865, but this requirement was later altered to allow them to attend a church of the denomination to which they belonged.

In 1886 Sir William McArthur proposed to give the college a residence for girls. He died very suddenly in the following year, but the money for the project had already been set aside, and the McArthur Hall, as it was named, was opened in 1891 near to the Lisburn Road end of the site. In 1917 James W. Henderson became Headmaster, and began a programme of development. In 1919, as we have already noted, the theological department was moved to a new location, a house called 'Edgehill' in Lennoxvale. The eventual separation of Edgehill College from Methody put an end to the tensions between the two aspects of the original foundation. In 1932 a piece of ground containing forty acres was purchased from Harland & Wolff, then suffering a period of recession, and to this, named Pirrie Park, the sports pitches were transferred. Building of a preparatory school immediately began on a part of this ground, and Downey House School was opened the following year. It was named for John Downey of Cavan, whose bequest had made the building possible.

The removal of the sports pitches made possible a series of developments which soon covered a large proportion of the original site. The first building was a new assembly hall, called the Whitla Hall after Sir William Whitla, who had been a member of the college Board, and whose generous bequest funded the project. In 1960 Dr Stanley Worrall was appointed Principal, and growth continued through his term of office. A convinced pacifist, he threw himself wholeheartedly in his off duty hours into efforts to establish peace in Northern Ireland, and was one of the prominent churchmen who travelled to Feakle in an effort to persuade the leaders of the IRA to call off their campaign in 1974. The college celebrated its centenary in 1968, and part of the celebration, owing much of its inspiration to Worrall, was the building of a new chapel, designed by a former pupil, Gordon McKnight. This small, but very fine building was called the Chapel of Unity, and has been used for multi-denominational worship.

Two generous benefactors of Methodist College were Sir William McArthur and Sir William Whitla. Methody was not the only object of their generosity. Willliam McArthur was a Donegal man, born at Malin, the eldest son of a Methodist minister. He opened a business in Enniskillen, and later moved it to Londonderry. In Enniskillen he financed the building of the McArthur Halls adjoining the Methodist Church in Darling Street. In Londonderry he was instrumental in the development of the city quays. He superintended the Sunday School in the Methodist church there and promoted the building of a Methodist church on the East Wall. In 1857 he moved the centre of his business to London and was soon involved in civic affairs there, becoming Sheriff in 1867, Member of Parliament for Lambeth in 1868 and Lord Mayor of London in 1880. He was knighted in 1883. He was one of the founders of the London Chamber of Commerce. He was a man of strong personal faith. He died in 1887.

William Whitla was born at Monaghan in 1851. He won the highest honours as a student of medicine at Queen's College in Belfast, and later bacame Professor of Materia Medica and Therapeutics in the Queen's University, and then Pro-Chancellor of the University, where he is commemorated in the Whitla Hall. A noted physician of great skill and understanding, he was President of the Irish Medical Association and of the British Medical Association. He was knighted in 1902 and died in 1933. His Christian commitment was expressed not only through the Methodist Church, but also through the YMCA, of which he was President, and his generous support of the work of the Salvation Army.

The most recent enterprise of Irish Methodists in field of education has been the establishment of Gurteen Agricultural College in North Tipperary. Given the fact that many people thought of Methodists in terms of trade and industry it is probably their least expected venture. In 1940 the Conference appointed a new council, the Council on Social Welfare, which was asked to consider and report of matters of social and ethical concern. One of the first things it did was to convene a small conference on rural youth, and it was suggested that if Protestant young people were to remain in rural Ireland they would need training in the best agricultural methods. To achieve this the other Protestant churches were approached, as the foundation of an agricultural college was thought to be beyond the resources of the Methodist Church on its own. The reaction of the other churches was negative, and the matter was shelved on the outbreak of the Second World War.

In 1945 the Rev Dr William L. Northridge was elected President of the Methodist Church in Ireland, and his observation of the rural communities during his countrywide presidential tours moved him in the May of 1946 to revive the question of agricultural training. Reckoning that the only possibility for the Methodist Church to manage on its own was a model farm, the Council on Social Welfare set about seeking one. The day after their meeting with some rural representatives one of the latter, Ted Armitage of Cloughjordan, observed an advertisement in the paper for a farm of some 300 acres in the townland of Gurteen to be sold at auction in August. The Council was successful in buying the land.

Meanwhile the Department of Agriculture had been advised of what was being planned, and discouraged the notion of a model farm. It offered financial support with lecturers' salaries if the Methodist Church would open an agricultural college instead. Over the next few months stables were transformed into lecture and dining rooms, and the lofts into dormitories. A flat was created for the principal and his family on the upper floor of the farm house. And so Gurteen Agricultural College was brought into being. It was opened on 11 October 1947 with forty-one students, and the Rev J. Wesley McKinney as Principal. The Taoiseach, Éamon De Valera, took a great interest in the project, but was unable to attend the ceremony, and the college was opened by Patrick Smith TD, the Minister for Agriculture.

The farm had been neglected for several years, the land was in poor condition and the hedges and fences in poor repair. It was said, only half in jest, that the main thing the students learned at Gurteen was the rehabilitation of land. From the beginning it was co-educational. In the early years the girls did a rural economy course, including poultry management and such skills as butter making. As demand for these declined the girls began to follow the same general course as the fellows, which included animal husbandry, grassland management, arable crops and maintenance of farm machinery and buildings.

Methodist students always formed a small minority of the students at the college, the largest number being members of the Church of Ireland. In 1970 the Governors changed the college policy, and admitted students without religious distinction, thus coming to serve the whole community.

For the first forty years of its life the college struggled constantly with debt, largely arising from the need to develop its buildings. The farmyard was renewed and enlarged, and other facilities were added. A new college building was erected in 1969, and then extended in 1983. Éamon DeValera, then President of Ireland, attended the opening of the new building, but the ceremony was actually performed by the Minister for Agriculture, then Neil Blaney TD. Residences built for the principal and farm manager relieved the pressure on the buildings in which they had been living. In 1980 the generosity of Patrick and Julia Trench of Sopwell Hall provided the college with a second farm of nearly 300 acres five miles away from the Gurteen farm.

Then in 1988 a substantial benefaction freed the college from its then burden of debt, and enabled it to use the profits of several years of profitable farming to embark on a programme of renovation of older buildings, and construction of new. In the following year a new equine course was introduced. The second half of the 1990s saw a sharp decline in farm incomes, and a resultant decline in the number of students applying for places in agricultural courses. True to its original purpose of assisting the young people of rural areas to earn their living there, Gurteen College had embarked on a programme of further diversification of its courses.

Many Methodist have been involved in the work of the Irish universities, but possibly the most distinguished has been Ernest T. S. Walton, the only Irish Methodist to be awarded a Nobel Prize. The son of a Methodist minister, he was born at Dungarvan in Co Waterford. Educated at Methodist College and at Trinity College, Dublin, he went on a travelling scholarship to the Cavendish Laboratory in Cambridge. There in 1932 he and John Cockroft achieved the transmutation of atomic nuclei – in popular parlance, 'they split the atom', a phrase which Walton disliked as it was not an accurate description of the process. He returned to Trinity as a Fellow, and in 1946 was appointed professor of natural and experimental philosophy. He and Cockroft were awarded the Nobel Prize for Physics in 1951.

A man of great personal charm and humility, he was happy not to be involved in the exploitation of nuclear power for warfare, always hoping that if a love of peace could not restrain the use of nuclear weapons, fear would. He was a warm advocate of the potential of nuclear power for good, in that it provided a source of renewable energy. A man of deep Christian faith, he died in 1995 at the age of 92.

At all three levels of education, primary, secondary and third level, in one way or another the church continues to offer service to the younger members of the community.

One of the important elements of education is the study of history. We are shaped by the events that have gone before. The most important contribution to Irish Methodist history was made in 1926 when a small group of men founded the Irish Branch of the Wesley Historical Society. Its purpose was to conserve and study the history of the church, and to encourage others in the learning of it. A small committee of thirteen ministers and laymen was formed, with Robert Morgan as Secretary and Treasurer. He was the only officer of the Society for ten years, his successor in 1936 being a minister. The offices of secretary and treasurer have been separated at times, but have more often been held by the same person. A President was not appointed until 1942, when the first holder of the office was Francis J. Cole. In 1967 the Society appointed and Honorary Archivist. In the fashion of the time she was announced as Mrs Victor Kelly. It was not until 1987 that her own name appeared in official lists, as Mrs Marion Kelly. She managed the Society's collection of memorabilia, and added to it faithfully until ill health obliged her to retire in 1995.

The foundation of the Society's collection was that of David B. Bradshaw, a Dublin banker who had accumulated a large number of very important documents and artifacts. Through other generous gifts, both large and small, the Society as acquired an unrivalled archive of Irish Methodism. The Conference in 1926 noted that this was housed in Wesley College, Dublin, and thereafter seems to have been happy that it was safe-keeping wherever it was housed. The Minutes make no further mention of the location. When Aldersgate House on University Road was opened in 1960 to provide accommodation for youth work in connection with Queen's University, part of the building was to house some church offices. On the ground floor space was provided behind secure doors to house the Wesley Historical Society's collection.

The Society publishes a *Bulletin* of papers and queries on

Methodist history, arranges visits to places of historic interest, and organises occasional lectures.

CHAPTER 14

Poverty and Suffering

Right from the time of the Holy Club at Oxford John Wesley had a concern for the poor and the suffering. He discovered during those years that he could live on £28 a year, and this he continued to do, whatever his income may have been. Anything that he earned or received by way of gift above that figure he gave away, either to the work of the Methodist societies, or to the poor. What he did himself he encouraged the Methodist people to do. His sermon on the use of money was preached under three headings: Gain all you can (provided you do it honestly), Save all you can, and Give all you can. In the twentieth century people concerned about worldwide starvation coined the slogan 'Live simply that others may simply live'. It was another way of saying what Wesley had said two and a half centuries earlier.

The first Methodist preachers to visit Cork arrived in that city at the beginning of June in 1748. Two months later a young Quaker in the city, Susanna Pim, wrote to her aunt, Deborah Fuller at Timolin. The letter has survived in the Quaker archives at Donnybrook in Dublin. Among other things Susanna Pim wrote:

The Methodists are here these some weeks. There is a great reformation wrought amongst the people. They preach twice a day, at five in the morning and seven in the evening. It is thought there was ten thousand yesterday. They go every day to the jails to preach to the prisoners. They are now gathering money to release the poor debtors. Yesterday, after they had done preaching, they desired that the people might contribute to it, and lest it should be imagined that it was for themselves, they appointed men to stand one on each side of the [Hammond's] Marsh where they preached to collect the money. They collected yesterday evening upwards of twenty pounds, which was the first time of gathering.

At that time people could be imprisoned for quite small debts, and remained incarcerated until such time as the debt was paid. To raise funds which would clear these debts restored the poor debtors to their families, and enabled them to resume normal life. It was an act of charity with very important ramifications.

The eighteenth and nineteenth centuries, of course, different-iated between what were called 'the deserving poor' and the others. The deserving poor were those who gave some sign of being industrious, and could demonstrate that their poverty was due to circumstances beyond their control. The others were deemed to be poor as a consequence of their own idleness, or waste, and had the sympathy of nobody. To help the deserving poor to remain free of debt or indeed so to improve their lot that they could help to relieve others, Wesley established what he called a lending-stock in London. From this fund small sums could be lent to needy people to be repaid over a period of three months. From an amount of only £50 some 250 people were as-sisted in the first year. There is no record of a similar fund hav-ing been established in Dublin, but we shall observe that Dublin had a fund which went somewhat further in its charity.

One of the constant causes of poverty was sickness, which prevented people from earning a living; but even without that consequence sickness was a problem in itself. Medical knowl-edge was rudimentary, and most doctors knew little if anything more than the average educated gentleman about the cause and cure of disease. Their efforts quite often were inspired by guess-work, and their remedies as dangerous as the maladies they were supposed to cure. Possibly the most celebrated instance of this is the death of Princess Charlotte, daughter of the Prince of Wales (later George IV) from the mismanagement by her doc-tors of her difficult childbirth. For these hazardous treatments doctors charged substantial fees. The poor, therefore, went to the clergy for advice about their illnesses, or to 'wise women' who knew something about herbal medicines.

It is therefore not surprising to find Wesley venturing into the field of medicine. In 1747 he first published *Primitive Physic or an Easy and Natural Method of Curing most Diseases*, a volume which went through twenty-three editions in his lifetime, and in the end offered more than 800 remedies for nearly 300 ailments. In various places in England he established centres from which simple medicines were distributed to the poor. There is no evidence of his doing so in Ireland, but there is no doubt that *Primitive Physic* circulated widely here.

Wits have loved to fasten on the sometimes quaint, and occasionally dangerous remedies which he recommends. For instance he suggests that baldness may be cured by rubbing the place with a raw onion. To cure the ague, he recommends pills made from cobwebs. For the iliac passion (a kind of colic) he quotes Dr Tissot's remedy, 'take ounce by ounce a pound or a pound and a half of quicksilver', but cautiously adds his own comment, 'This is a very dangerous medicine.' Indeed! It would be guaranteed to kill rather than cure.

The eighteenth century saw the development of experimentation with electricity, and Wesley was quite enthusiastic about its possibilities. He is careful to stipulate that it should be applied 'in a proper manner', but goes on to list fifty complaints it could cure or alleviate, including certain types of blindness, deafness, gout, headache, weakness of the legs, menstrual obstructions, sciatica, stiff joints and toothache.

But these quaintnesses are the exception rather than the rule. He was aware that much disease arose from dirt, and careless eating. It is interesting how often the simple process of washing enters into his cures. Sometimes it is in the form of a bath, at other times simple washing of the affected part. Occasionally he recommends some herbal or medicinal element be added to the water, but mostly he recommends simply cold water. In fact he lists no fewer than sixty-six ailments which he believed would be relieved or prevented by the habit of taking cold baths. For drinking he recommends rain water, which would have been a wise precaution in eighteenth century towns. His concern about

diet is largely for the avoidance of over-indulgence. He is not a
vegetarian, but does advocate the avoidance of meat in late
meals. There is a certain amount of common sense in his advice
on what would today be called preventive medicine. For instance, to avoid infection by flat worms, he counsels, 'Avoid
drinking stagnated water.'

Generally speaking Wesley and the early Methodists were
less concerned with the causes of poverty and disease in the
community at large than with the alleviation of individual cases.
Much of this was done by individual members, or by circuits,
but a number of charitable institutions were also created. We
have already considered the story of the Methodist Female
Orphan School, which combined the dual purposes of housing
the girls and educating them.

The first purely charitable institution which the Irish
Methodists founded was an almshouse for elderly women in
Dublin. The idea was originally suggested in 1764, but it took
two years to raise the necessary funds. In 1766 a plot of ground
adjoining the Whitefriar Street chapel was leased, and seven
trustees were appointed to supervise the building, and the management of the institution. Two houses were built, each of two
stories over the ground floor, and each floor was divided into
two rooms. The almshouse was to cater for 'twenty reduced
widows'. Each widow was provided with her own bed, but two
occupied each room. This was the usual pattern at the time,
though in some widows' almshouses in the city the residents
lived four to a room. Presumably the other two rooms were to
accommodate the warden, but no warden was appointed, and
the number of residents was soon increased to twenty-four. One
servant, presumably coming into the house daily, was employed to look after all of the residents. Coal and candles were
supplied for the heating and lighting of all of the rooms, but here
was no communal sitting room, and no meals were supplied.
Each lady was given two shillings and sixpence a week for sustenance, an amount which did not allow anything for luxuries.
The first widows went into residence in 1767.[1]

When Warburton, Whitelaw and Walsh wrote their history of Dublin in 1818 they listed twenty-three almshouses in the city, but gave most space and the greatest praise to the Methodist institution. They said:

> We have frequently visited its truly venerable inhabitants, and though not exempt from the usual maladies of infirm old age, we never heard one murmur of discontent. They appeared to live in the most perfect harmony and seemed anxious by every little emotion of tender sympathy to soothe each other's sufferings.

Things had not always been as idyllic. In 1777, when the trustees met to elect a successor to William Gaskell, who had died, Patrick Geoghegan and William Hall laid a charge of peculation against the treasurer James Martin. Three prominent members of the Whitefriar Street society were asked to investigate the matter. They made two discoveries. The one was that far from taking money from the almshouse, Martin had used his own money to make up the deficit between the expenses of the house and its income. Without his generosity the place would have been heavily in debt. The second was that certain false entries had been inserted into the books in an attempt to justify the charges. These disclosures led to recriminations as a result of which, as we have already seen, thirty-four members were lost to the membership of the society.

In 1773, visiting Enniscorthy, Wesley had preached from the doorway of Hugh McLoughlin's house in the town. In the 1798 Rising McLoughlin's widow only narrowly escaped with her life from the consequences of the fighting there. The Rev Adam Averell heard of her plight, and sought her admission to the widows' home in Whitefriar Street. The trustees refused to admit her because she was not resident in Dublin. Averell had subscribed generously to the institution, and was annoyed when the refusal was repeated several times. He rashly commented that God would find some way of showing his displeasure at the trustees' hardness of heart. When, shortly afterwards, two more of the resident widows died, alarm spread among the survivors, and a delegation of them called on the leading trustee, Arthur Keene, to beg that 'Mr Averell's widow' be admitted before they were all dead. Faced with this situation, the trustees relented, and Mrs McLoughlin was duly welcomed to Whitefriar Street.

After the secession of the Primitive Wesleyans the almshouse remained in Wesleyan control. The next upheaval came in 1857. The Whitefriar Street lease was coming near to expiry. The trustees did not wait for this to happen, but acquired a site in Grantham Street, where they erected a new building for the widows. They still provided one room for each two women, but now they appointed a warden, who had accommodation in the house.

Perhaps the most surprising aspect of the Widows' Home was the fact that for over a century and a half it was managed by a self perpetuating Trust, all the members of which were Methodists, but over which the Conference had no control. This anomaly was rectified in 1926 when, at the request of the trustees, the Conference took over the home, and appointed a committee to manage it. It is under the constitution of 1926 that the home is still managed.

Shortly after this another change followed. Standards had been rising in the care of the elderly, and it was no longer acceptable that two women should share the one room. In 1934 a large house called 'Eastwell' on the corner of Palmerston Park and Palmerston Road, was purchased, and to this the residents moved. Each woman now had her own room, and single ladies were admitted as well as widows. A communal sitting room was provided, as well as a dining room in which lunch was served to all the residents each day. They were responsible for their own morning and evening meals. A generous bequest from Dr Eustace Fannin in 1985 enabled the committee to considerably improve the accommodation.

At the annual breakfast meeting of the Dublin circuit on New Year's Day of 1808 John Dedrich Ayckbowm, a prominent member of the society, suggested that some provision should be made for old men, similar to that provided for women in the Widows' Home. One of those present was the Rev Joseph Stopford, FTCD, who very warmly supported the idea. This time the Methodists did not act alone. Support was forthcoming from other Protestant churches, and as a result the Old Men's Asylum in the city had its beginning. Located for most of its life on Northbrook Road in the Leeson Park area of the city, it provided for elderly men for the greater part of two centuries.[2]

The care of the elderly became a major feature of late twentieth century Methodist work in Ireland. The North Belfast Mission, which later became the Newtownabbey Mission, and the Belfast Central Mission both provided sheltered housing for men and women within a few miles of the city. The Dublin Central Mission provided two sheltered housing developments and a nursing home with facilities for Alzheimers patients and day care. The Cork circuit, when it moved its city chapel from Patrick Street to the Douglas Road, allowed space in its plans for sheltered housing, which was built a few years later. In Limerick a project was developed at Adare. In all of these projects residence is no longer confined to Methodists.

In 1783 the Peace of Versailles ended the American War of Independence, and at the same time peace was concluded with France and Spain. Regiments returned to England and were disbanded. The country was flooded with ex-soldiers, able-bodied and disabled, for whom there was little livelihood. It was a Methodist ex-soldier, somewhat more fortunate, John Gardner of London who thought of an idea to relieve the want of at least some of these. He and five others committed themselves to give one penny a week to a fund out of which some assistance might be given to the poor in their neighbourhood. Gardner wrote to Wesley about it, and Wesley replied offering a gift of one guinea, and a subscription of threepence a week. With this encouragement Gardner developed what he called the Strangers' Friend Society. He himself had had a good education, and this enabled him to become a doctor. He died in 1807, and his grave in the churchyard of St Leonard's, Shoreditch bears the curious inscription:

Dr John Gardner
Last and Best Bedroom
1807

In 1786, probably through the initiative of the Rev Dr Adam
Clarke, a similar society was established in Bristol, and it was
Clarke who encouraged the formation of a third in Dublin in
1790.[3]

For quite different reasons poverty in Dublin was even more
clamant than that in London, in spite of the lively charity of the
Dublin people, and there was more than enough scope for the
activity of another charitable society. The Strangers' Friend
Society in Dublin was formed with an initial membership of
more than thirty men, who undertook a double commitment.
On the one hand, they were to visit the hospitals, gaols, convict
ships, schools and villages in and about the city, preaching, exhorting and praying wherever opportunity afforded. On the
other, they pledged themselves to the raising and distribution of
a fund for the relief of the poor. The members met in the
Whitefriar Street lobby each Friday to report on what they had
done, and to plan their activity for the following week. The
Society maintained a strict discipline, and a meeting every quarter enquired into the efficiency and devotion of each member.

From the beginning the Society established two basic principles for its charity. Though the membership was confined to
Methodists, it determined that aid should be given without any
religious distinction, the only qualification being need. The second was that grants should be made in cases where an immediate crisis could be relieved and the beneficiary enabled to gain a
livelihood, and that nobody should be allowed to become dependent on the charity. The early records give some indication
of the sort of crisis that prompted the society's actions.

A grant was given to one woman, near her lying-in, to buy
flannelette. Another was assisted because the son on whom she
depended had been killed at Vinegar Hill. A grant to one man
secured his release from the Marshalsea debtors' prison. Small
grants enabled people to buy thread, tape, baskets and eggs,

oranges, lemons, or fish, and so set up as peddlers. There was a grant to an emigrant priest. A woman had her clothes redeemed from pawn. References to buying a loom, or a wheel, suggest that a craftsman or woman had, probably through illness, been obliged to sell the loom or spinning wheel on which their occupation depended, and the Society gave them a replacement. 'Fainted in street for want' tells us nothing of the particular circumstances, but a great deal about the depth of poverty in the city.

In the aftermath of the Great Famine the Society gradually surrendered its preaching and exhorting activities to others, and concentrated on the relief of the poor. The amount of work needed and carried out necessitated the lease of an office in 1876, and the employment of a paid secretary to staff it. Seven years later, in 1883, the first ladies were admitted to the Society, under exactly the same conditions as the men. In funding its work the Society in Dublin had from the beginning raised funds from outside its membership. There were many generous people in the city who gladly contributed. In the Methodist churches collections were made annually, and a variety of fund raising activities helped.

By the end of the nineteenth century a routine of work had been established, which continued to the end. An applicant went to the office with a recommendation from his or her minister, priest or clergyman, and these applications were briefly considered at the next weekly meeting. They were distributed among the members, who during the following week called at the homes of the applicants, or at the hospital if they were in one, to discuss the situation. At the next weekly meeting they reported on what they had seen and heard, and recommended action. Through the years the sort of people who did this work were Bennett Dugdale, the largest bookseller in Dublin at the time, Patrick Fox, whom Wesley so highly valued as a schoolmaster, Martin Keene, son of Arthur and son-in-law of Bennett Dugdale, Isaac D'Olier, John Ouseley Bonsall, nephew of Gideon Ouseley the evangelist, Arthur Dean Codling, Assistant

Secretary in the Department of Finance, and members of the Booth, Fannin, Crawford, and White families, who ran substantial businesses in the city.

In 1923 the Society formalised its constitution, which was registered in the High Court. For more than 130 years it had worked informally, but changing laws on liability necessitated the registration. The work continued for another fifty years, but it was then becoming more difficult to recruit visitors, and in 1977 the Society merged its work in that of the Dublin Central Mission. Possibly nobody at the time recognised the significance of this, but it was the end of a long and important tradition. It was at Oxford in the Holy Club that Wesley and his friends began to relieve the poor, visiting them where they lived. To the poor the gift brought may have been the most important, but to the Methodists the visit was even more so. It gave them some insight into the nature of poverty which taught them a greater sympathy that the writing of a cheque can do, and that sympathy developed in them a humilty. With the growth of State assistance, and the number of charities working among the destitute in the city, the poor may not have lost much by the closure of the Society; the Methodists did.

At the same time as the Strangers' Friend Society was being formed in Dublin the Waterford Methodists were establishing a charitable society of their own. This was the Association of Friends of the Sick Poor whose foundation date was also 1790. The original suggestion was made at an evening social gathering, and one of the local leaders, Robert Mackee, drew up a plan of management. The city was divided into districts, to each of which a visitor was appointed. Each visitor was required to investigate any cases in the district where help was sought, and relief was given without religious distinction. Funds for the Association were subscribed by individuals of all denominations in the city. Later it undertook the task of raising funds for the establishment of a fever hospital. This is believed to have been the first such hospital in Ireland to be founded by voluntary subscription.[4]

It was the Waterford District Meeting, forerunner of the Waterford District Synod, which first suggested to the Conference the creation of a Methodist Orphan Society. The Conference adopted the suggestion, and in 1870 the Society was duly organised. The Methodist circuits were to supply the fund from which grants would be paid to Methodist Orphans. In this way the Society worked for almost a century, but the pattern of life began to change, and the death of one or both parents was no longer the only reason why children were in need. There were children who, with one of their parents, had been deserted by the other. There were children of single parents. Believing that the need of the child was of paramount importance, the Society first altered its criteria, and then its name, to meet the new situation. In 1985 it became the Methodist Child Care Society. It never established an orphanage; that happened another way.

In 1902 T. Foulkes Shillington, one of the lay officials of the Belfast Central Mission, presented to the Conference the Shillington family home, Craigmore at Aghalee in Co Antrim. With the house went a farm of about 140 acres. He had talked to the Superintendent minister of the Mission, the Rev Dr Crawford Johnston, about the possibility of a boy's home similar to the Methodist Orphan School for Girls in Dublin, and it was with this in mind that the gift was given. It was not strictly speaking to be a part of the Mission, but several of those whom the Conference appointed to the Board of the new home were also members of the Board of the Mission, and the Mission office in Belfast did the office work of the home.[5]

Necessary alterations were carried out, and early in 1903 Craigmore Home admitted its first two boys. It had been designed to accommodate twenty, but demand soon exceeded this, and by 1905 it had been adapted to house thirty-four. Each boy was to be given a basic education, and training in some craft, such as carpentry. It was intended that the farm would supply food to the house, and would also afford a measure of agricultural education. The Methodist National school at Aghalee was moved to Craigmore and continued to take children from the neighbourhood, as well as the boys in the home.

The gift had been a generous one, and the vision admirable; the problem was funding for maintenance. The home was always in a state of financial stringency, and this was only temporarily relieved by the sale of one hundred acres in 1919, and the remainder of the farm in 1932.

Meanwhile in 1915 the civil authorities had approached the Belfast Central Mission with the request that it undertake residential work with children of soldiers and sailors. It had two houses at Whitehead which had been used as holiday homes for young women from the city, and decided to use these for the new purpose. In 1916 there were sixty children in residence there. The demand, however, was enormous, and of necessity there was a great deal of overcrowding. To judge from the numbers who were admitted, even allowing for the overcrowding, the stay of each child seems to have been quite short

In 1928 the difficulties at Whitehead were solved by the generosity of Mr & Mrs Hugh Turtle, generous benefactors of various Methodist causes. They gave the Mission Templepatrick House at Millisle in Co Down. This stood in spacious grounds, and was soon adapted to provide for the children who were moved from Whitehead. Renamed Childhaven Children's Home, it was officially opened in June 1930. Six years later the financial problems of Craigmore brought about its closure, and the boys there were transferred to Millisle. Again there was a change of name in order to perpetuate the memory of the 1902 gift. The place was now called Childhaven & Craigmore Home. It continues to carry on work, now in co-operation with the State welfare authorities.

During the nineteenth century in England the Methodist concern for social holiness began to find a new expression in the development of trade unions. In 1833 George Loveless formed a lodge of the Friendly Society of Agricultural Labourers in the village of Tolpuddle in Dorset. In the March of 1834 he, his brother James, Thomas Stanfield and his son John, James Hammett and James Brine were charged with administering an unlawful oath. Found guilty by a hostile judge and jury they were sentenced to be transported for seven years to Van Diemen's Land. They became known as the Tolpuddle Martyrs, and a public outcry eventually led to their receiving a full pardon (in effect an admission of their innocence) and return to England. Of the six five were Wesleyan Methodists, and three of these, including George Loveless, were local preachers.

In his Wesley Historical Lecture, *Methodism and the Trade Unions,* published in 1959 Robert F. Wearmouth refers to a recent survey of eighty fulltime Trade Union leaders whose involvement in Trade Unionism arose out of their Christian convictions. Of these seventy were Methodists, fifty-five of them local preachers. Of the seventy, nearly two thirds were Primitive Methodists, though the Primitives constituted only one third of the Methodist population in England. No fewer than twenty-nine of them had started work, generally in the mines, by the time they were twelve, and owed the completion of their education to the Methodist societies which gave them encouragement and opportunity.

This was facilitated by the simplicity of the agenda which Wesley devised for all meetings. For the list of subjects which constituted a traditional agenda, Wesley substituted a series of questions. In some cases the answer may have been a single statement, as for instance in the Leaders' Meeting, 'Does any class require the appointment of a leader?' In others the answer might emerge from a period of discussion, as for instance, 'What is the amount of the Poor's Fund, and how shall it be allocated?' This is the easiest form of agenda to follow even if one has no previous experience of participating in meetings. It is also the chief factor which preserved for all Methodist business meetings the nature of a conversation. That is not to say that there was never any element of confrontation in meetings. Where opinions are strongly held confrontation is always possible, but the agenda sought to promote the exchange of opinions rather than formal proposal and opposition.

That so many Methodists took leading roles in the formation of the unions is not surprising when one remembers the sort of training they received in public speaking as local preachers, and in the conduct of business in quarterly and leaders' meetings. No other denomination had made as much use of the working class laity in the management of church affairs. In fact the Methodists brought their structures into the unions, and some at least of their language. When one trade unionist calls another 'Brother' he is talking like a Methodist. The combination of a zeal for justice, a concern for the well being of workers and their families, and skills in persuasive oratory and administration was an asset that their fellow workers quickly appreciated.

A story is told concerning one of them, Tommy Hepburn. He formed a union of miners in the north of England in 1831, and in the following year organised a strike for shorter hours. Negotiations in the course of this necessitated his going to Newcastle to meet Lord Londonderry, the proprietor. At the outset of the meeting Hepburn informed the noble gentleman that he never entered upon matters of that kind without first asking for divine guidance. He asked his Lordship to kneel down while he prayed. Lord Londonderry knelt. The outcome of the negotiation was the reduction of the working hours to twelve in the day!

That the Irish Methodists were not involved in that sort of campaign for social justice was, of course, due to the fact that the situation in Ireland was so very different. In the first place the industrial revolution which had taken place in England in the eighteenth century was not paralleled here. The political campaigns of the nineteenth century in Ireland were related to Catholic emancipation, repeal of the Union, land reform, and home rule. We have noted already the Methodist involvement in these. There was also the fact, often remarked, that while England divided along class lines, Ireland divided along religious. The working class Irish Protestant, at least until the latter half of the twentieth century, tended to feel a greater affinity with his Protestant landlord or employer than with his Catholic fellow tenant or employee.

In the twentieth century Irish Methodists have tended to

organise no agencies for social reform, but to throw their energy into nondenominational societies. Towards the end of the century the Conference directed that 1% be added to the budget for the maintenance of the church's administration, and that this sum be devoted to world poverty and development work. It urged all members of the church to give 1% of their income to the same purpose. That target has not yet been realised, but the ideal is still annually promoted.

CHAPTER 14

Manners and Morals

Among the key points in Wesley's ethic were industry, integrity and thrift. They were a recipe for commercial success, though such was not Wesley's intention, and he was fully alive to the danger of affluence, which was apt to breed self-satisfaction, self-indulgence and arrogance. In his advice to the Methodist people, therefore, there is a constant balance between commendation of productive industry, and warning against wealth.

Extravagance was discouraged because it diverted into trivialities that which could have been used to relieve the needs of the poor. Early Methodists did not develop a particular style of dress, as did the Quakers, but they dressed as simply and their lifestyle was equally simple, and continued to be so even after they began to be prosperous. It was a lifestyle which revolved around religious observance, work and domestic pleasure.

However, it must be said that few if any of them adopted Wesley's ideal. His first host and hostess in Ireland were William and Anne Lunell. Anne Lunnell's niece was the wife of Arthur Guinness, the founder of the brewery. In her account of the Guinness family, Michelle Guinness comments on the fact that Arthur regularly went to hear Wesley when he preached in Dublin, and records two family traditions. One was that in brewing an ale with a low alcohol content which provided the Dublin workman with an alternative to whiskey they were following Methodist principles. That is a view which Wesley would have endorsed.

The other tradition is that the family followed Wesley's advice to gain all you can, and save all you can – a certain recipe for wealth. What the Guiness family forgot was that to these two Wesley had added a third – give all you can. This was Wesley's

concern for the poor, and it would have kept his people from becoming wealthy, but it was the point which most of his people
either forgot, or reasoned away on grounds of prudent provision for an uncertain future. Methodists who became wealthy
were generous; of that there is no question. Their gifts to education, to charitable organisations within their own denomination
and outside it, and their known responses to need are evidences
of that. But they did not embrace the frugality which Wesley
practised and advocated in order to give away even more.

In the course of this history we have noted the names of some
individuals whose benefactions did much for a number of
Methodist institutions. They are representative of a great many
others whose generosity was more localised, possibly for no
other reason than that of circumstances at the time. However,
one benefactor does deserve to be mentioned, who was not Irish,
but whose generosity has done a great deal for Irish Methodists.
This was Joseph Rank

Rank was the proprietor of a large English flour milling concern with branches in Ireland. Wartime restrictions between
1940 and 1950 gave him a virtual monopoly of the flour milling
business in England, and he could not but make millions out of
it. Much of this money he then used to set up a number of charitable trusts. On of these was dedicated to Methodist work. For
half a century the Rank Trust has given valuable aid to
Methodist churches and institutions throughout Britain and
Ireland. Some of the projects have been very large and others
quite small, but always the gift was linked to some particular
service to the community. New churches and halls have been
grant aided, and some small churches have been helped with
renovation programmes where the contribution of the congregation to the local community was seen to be important. Workers
have been funded for the development of imaginative youth
work, or pastoral programmes. Aware of the dangers of encouraging dependence on outside sources of money, the Rank Trust
has often coupled the amount of its grant to what could be locally
raised by other means.

Incidentally to this, it is not insignificant how many Methodist businesses in Dublin and Belfast became household names, and how often in the provincial towns one of the largest businesses is Methodist owned. The variety of business is wide – grocery, outfitting, drapery, hardware, timber, linen and poplin weaving, bakery, car sales and repairs, medical supplies, and building and contracting. They have not engaged in the wine trade, brewing, or distilling. Though pawnbrokers were as welcome as any to attend Methodist meetings, a rule debarred them from holding any office in the church, on the ground that they profited from the misfortune of the poor. In all fairness it has to be admitted that a different view has been expressed in recent books about life in the Dublin slums in the early years of the twentieth century, when the pawnbroker was seen as a valued friend of the poor.

It was this same ethic of industry, integrity and thrift which lay behind the exclusion of gambling. To gamble was to seek money without earning it. That undermined the conviction that people should earn and contribute to the community where possible. There was the further problem that people were tempted to squander what little they had on the slight chance of becoming rich. Still today not even the mildest forms of gambling are authorised in Methodist premises.

The ethical stance for which Methodism is probably most widely noted is that of total abstinence, and it is a source of surprise to many Methodists as well as to others that it was not always so.[1] Wesley himself was not a total abstainer. He deplored drunkenness which ruined the health and happiness of so many people. The celebrated notice alleged to have been displayed in some eighteenth-century inns, 'Drunk for a penny; dead drunk for tuppence; and clean straw to lie on for nothing' gave expression to one of the less pleasant realities of life. But it was on gin or whiskey that people got into that state. Wesley himself favoured sweet ale. During his lifetime it was becoming common for hops to be added in the brewing of ale to give it a bitter taste, and Wesley disliked it. When somebody advanced the argument that hops were a preservative, Wesley went to the bother of keeping two barrels of ale in London, one with hops and the other without. He proved that they kept equally well. The fact was that the real reason for their addition was a matter of taste. Fashion was moving to a bitter ale, and Wesley could not put back the clock.

He abstained from wine for two periods of about two years each, from 1735 to 1737 and from about 1747 to 1749. In 1771 he described wine as 'one of the noblest cordials in nature'. His concerns about it were related to health, and it was when he thought that his health would benefit that he abstained from it. When convinced otherwise he resumed his use of it. It is interesting to compare this with his comments on tea drinking, from which he abstained, also on health grounds, for a longer period. While at Oxford he developed a tremor in his hand, which disappeared when he reduced the quantity and strength of tea he was taking. In 1746 he expressed regret at the time and money spent by the poorer Methodists on tea. Tea prices fluctuated, but towards the end of his life it was selling at between eleven and twenty shillings a pound. In the values of 2000, that would be something between £29 and £55 for a pound of tea. It is small wonder that he was concerned about the expense to the poorer members. Ale was a great deal cheaper.

In his directions to the bands in 1744 Wesley says, '… taste no spiritous liquor, no dram of any kind, unless prescribed by a physician.' In 1769 and 1784 he was affirming the same, 'Touch no dram. It is liquid fire. It is a sure though slow poison.' He was, of course referring to spirits. That was an ideal to which most of the Methodists did adhere, though not all of them. Several letters in the 1770s give voice to Wesley's concern about William Brammah, one of his English preachers, who suffered from dropsy. Wesley deplores his refusal to be advised on the subject of spirits, which he continued to drink in spite of Wesley's exhortations. But the bibulous Brammah remained a preacher to his death in 1780. It would seem that Wesley was more tolerant in practice than tradition or the tone of the Large Minutes would have us believe.

Wesley's attitude to alcohol was compounded of several social factors. One of these was health. He gave up the drinking of wine on two occasions, one at least for reasons of health, as we have seen. But he abstained from tea on the same argument for much longer, and when convinced that he was mistaken, resumed the drinking of both. Another was economics. He lived frugally, and urged his people to do the same. Ale had been the staple drink of the English peasant for generations; Wesley saw no excuse to question it. Tea was an import, and expensive; he thought that money could be put to better use, though his diaries suggest that he was not as successful in following his own precept here. A third factor was class.

There was certainly excessive consumption of wine among the nobility and gentry, but Wesley was not greatly concerned about them. He very early recognised that if they came to hear him, it was from mere curiosity, which was quite soon satisfied. It was all that he was likely to arouse in them, and he soon turned from them to more responsive sections of the community. A few of the nobility and gentry did became Methodists, and he probably regarded them as something in the nature of a bonus, unexpected, but none the less welcome, and valuable for the educated leadership and financial strength they could bring to the societies. His real work lay among the working classes, who rarely if ever tasted wine. It was spirituous liquors which took a working man's money and made him poor; took his reliability and made him unemployable; took his health and made him wretched; and brought misery to his wife and children. It was spirituous liquors which were, therefore, anathema to Wesley.

For quite some time after Wesley's death the Irish Methodists followed Wesley's principle, and until nearly the end of the nineteenth century it was the custom to broach a keg of ale for the refreshment of the members after a quarterly meeting. The first sign of change came in 1829, when a Belfast Presbyterian minister, the Rev John Edgar, who had observed temperance work in America, organised a meeting at Donegall Square Methodist Church, made available to him by the minister, the

Rev Matthew Tobias. At this the people who crowded the building were invited to sign a pledge against drinking spirits.
Though the issue was still temperance, and not total abstinence,
the fact that a pledge was signed indicated a tightening of the
discipline. Previously it had been a matter of general exhortation. In 1830 the Conference endorsed the new development.

As it continued, the movement against alcohol moved from
temperance – the moderate consumption of beer or wine – to
total abstinence, until it reached the point where the distinction
was lost, and many people now use the word 'temperance' to
mean total abstinence from alcoholic drinks of any kind. It was
developing rapidly outside Methodist circles as well as within,
and in Strabane in 1834 the first Irish total abstinence society was
formed. Four years later Father Theobald Mathew, a Capuchin
priest, began his total abstinence crusade which exerted a powerful influence on people of all denominations in the south and
west of the country. At about the same time total abstinence was
introduced into England by American evangelists, two of
whom, Charles Caughey and Phoebe Palmer, were Methodists.
It is significant that both of these were barred from using
Wesleyan premises in England. Total abstinence had not yet become, as it soon was, virtually synonymous with evangelical
Christianity.

Dr Kent had drawn attention to the not entirely altruistic factors in this growth. He says:

> To become a teetotaller showed that one had sacrificed for
> one's religious beliefs and also enabled one to distinguish, with
> overtones of superiority, one's own social group from others.[2]

That was true of the English middle classes, and to some extent
true of the Irish. That it was less true here was probably due to
Father Mathew's ability to penetrate lower in the social scale.

By the 1870s total abstinence had gained sufficient strength
in Methodist societies for members to be concerned as to
whether they were breaking their pledge each time they went to
Holy Communion. The debate was at times heated and occasionally verged on the ridiculous. In Conference of 1875, the historian
Charles H. Crookshank ventured the observation:

He hoped he was not heterodox but he thought a Greenlander would be observing the ordinance if he used fish and oil, or a Hindu if he used rice and milk.

The Conference was not legislating for Greenlanders or Hindus but for Irish Methodists. It gave more weight to the plea of the Rev Dr Joseph McKay that to allow a non-alcoholic beverage to be used would be to hand over to the weaker brethren the exclusive right to govern the church. By 85 votes to 11 it refused to make any change. In fairness to Crookshank, whose choice of language was unfortunate, he was raising the serious principle as to which was more important, the fact that Christ used bread and wine at the Last Supper, or the fact that he used the customary food and drink of the local peasant.

This refusal by the Conference proved to be a temporary check, and by the end of the nineteenth century total abstinence had won the day. The rule remains that the consumption of alcohol is not permitted in Methodist premises, and the great majority of Irish Methodists are total abstainers, but the church does not make total abstinence a condition of membership.

In 1940, after several years of deliberation on the subject, the Conference set up the Council on Social Welfare. It defined its brief in the following terms:

> The Council shall be charged with the duty of considering the Witness of the Church in connection with such matters as the Drink Problem, Gambling, Public Health, Social Purity, Lord's Day Observance, Christian Education in Day Schools, Industrial Conditions, Christian Citizenship, International Relations and other relevant matters. In connection with any of these questions the Council or its Executive Committees are authorised to take action in harmony with existing Declarations or Resolutions of the Conference, and to communicate regarding these questions with the Governments of the country.

There are two Executives, one for Northern Ireland and the other for the Republic. The membership of the Council comprises twenty-six ministers, twenty-five lay members, and two members who may be either ministerial or lay. Some are appointed for their expertise, and others as representatives of the so-called 'man and woman in the pew'. This contributes to the balanced view which the Council so often achieves.

Language changes, and it was not long before the term 'social welfare' came to be applied in common usage almost exclusively to such state payments as old age pensions, disability and unemployment assistance, and children's allowances. It was not, however, until 1993 that the Conference followed this development by changing the name of this body to the Council on Social Responsibility.

Strictly speaking the Irish Methodist Church has no mind on any matter until the Conference has issued a statement on it. Such statements are formulated in the first instance by one or other Executive of the Council, and then endorsed by the full Council for presentation to the Conference. There they are debated, and possibly amended. Only when they are agreed by the Conference do they become the official view of the church. That does not prevent individual Methodists from holding different personal views, or from expressing personal views on subjects on which the Conference has made no pronouncement, but they must be offered as personal views only.

One of the first actions of the Council was to consider the state of the rural community, and the consequences of migration away from it. This eventually led to the foundation of Gurteen Agricultural College. Otherwise its early statements were largely addressed to the members of the church on traditional issues of morality - alcohol, gambling, sexual morality and Sunday observance. However, the Council soon began to comment on issues which were coming to the fore in public opinion, or arising from current events.

During the Second World War anti-semitism was condemned. The 1950s prompted statements on mixed marriages in Ireland, the hydrogen bomb, industrial disputes, and road safety. In the following decade there were concerns about nuclear disarmament, capital punishment, itinerants, world hunger and the treatment of animals. In a departure from the usual expressions of concern, or statements of ethical principle, the Council proposed and the Conference adopted a message of congratulation and good wishes to Radio Éireann on the commencement of its first television channel. By the 1970s drug abuse was growing, and statements were made on that subject. Housing, homelessness and child abuse were matters of concern in the 1980s. Statements in the 1990s concerned poverty in Ireland, business ethics, pluralism and the treatment of refugees and asylum seekers in this country.

Quite lengthy reports on homosexuality, abortion, euthanasia, divorce, punishment, the role of women, and leisure were approved by the Conference for circulation and study. In common with other churches Irish Methodism recognised that homosexuality was an involuntary condition, and that homosexuals should be treated with understanding. However, it declared that homosexual acts were unacceptable. It generally condemned abortion, but accepted that it was permissible in some circumstances. It defined these as when the mother's life was at risk, or there was a risk of grave injury to her physical or mental health, in cases or rape, and where there is gross abnormality of the foetus.

Believing that it is the business of the church to minister forgiveness and reconciliation, Irish Methodism has been willing to marry couples either or both of whom have been married to other living partners. However, this is not a general freedom, and each case is treated on its own merits. Ministers in such cases are required to consult with the District Superintendent, so the decision is never taken by an individual. While euthanasia is condemned, the Conference has expressed concern for the dilemmas faced by medical teams treating patients whose illness is evidently terminal, and who have to decide how far to prolong life by the use of drugs and other forms of life support.

The Northern Executive of the Council had always found time to consider a variety of ethical issues, but by far the greatest amount of its energy has been devoted to the conflict which began in 1968. At times the situation changed so rapidly that a statement prepared in March for printing in the Conference agenda was certain to be outdated by the time Conference met in June. Statements were, therefore, generally drafted only days before they were due to be debated, and were circulated as separate papers, a notable exception to the church's general practice. The debate on these drafts generally reached a very high level as in the earlier years the Conference sought the words best calculated to make a constructive contribution. In the later years the drafts tended to be so worded that there were few alterations, and the speeches at the Conference were more like illustrations of the concern which the proposals expressed.

In 1965 the Conference welcomed the initiatives of the Taoiseach, Sean Lemass and the Prime Minister, Terence O'Neill in seeking to establish greater co-operation between their two governments. That co-operation failed to achieve what had been intended, and in 1968 the campaign began for civil rights. The next Conference affirmed the conviction that peace was only possible where there was full justice for all sections of the community, and welcomed the government proposals for reform. It urged their speedy implementation.

By 1970 the worsening situation demanded a lengthy appraisal, and the Conference stated its adherence to a number of principles. Among these it declared that:

> any form of injustice, inequality or discrimination based on creed, race or colour is contrary to God's will. The Conference consequently calls on all sections of the community and in particular those in authority to work by word and deed for the removal of all injustice from our land.

It went on to urge obedience to the civil authority, and called for those organising parades and demonstrations to exercise sensitivity to the possible consequences in certain circumstances. It condemned the importation and use of illicit arms. It was in this long resolution that the first use is found of a phrase that was to recur in some later statements as the authorities were urged to act 'without fear or favour'. Separate statements in the same year condemned all killing as a means to a political end, and recognised dialogue as the only route to the settlement of disputes.

As the conflict continued there was inevitably some repetition of certain themes each year, but fresh emphases were made. In 1971 the Conference asked that the leaders of the churches should come together to make a common appeal to the population at large. This was one of the things which led to the regular meetings of the heads of the four larger churches. The same statement recognises the need to bring up children free from prejudice, the rights of all to hold and propagate, within the law, their religious and political ideals, and the justice of fair sharing by all sections of the community in the responsibility of government.

In 1974 the Conference reminded all citizens of the dangers involved in supporting movements and organisations which are not subject to the normal checks of public support and criticism, which are in defiance of the law, or use intimidation as a means to impose their will. Three years later it welcomed the publication of the Inter-Church report *Violence in Ireland,* and urged not only that it be studied, but should be the basis of action. Concern for the victims of violence, always present, became more articulate in the 1980s and lay behind an appeal to the media to give more attention to them, and less to the perpetrators.

The establishment on the New Ireland Forum was welcomed in 1983, and in the following year there was a request that its report should be the subject of public debate. Again there was the assertion that the basic right of all people was the right to life, and a strong appeal for adequate security measures.

In 1988 the Conference began to adopt a different method in dealing with the ongoing conflict. To have continued to issue brief statements would have been repetitive. In how many different ways can people say the same things about similar events? It began, instead of issuing statements, to commend detailed reports for study. The first of these took up a number of the issues contained in the Anglo-Irish Agreement and was, in effect, a restatement of principles previously affirmed, but now brought together in a form relevant to the situation as it had developed. The willingness of both parties to the Agreement to enter into meaningful dialogue was welcomed. Once again the need for a Bill of Rights was acknowledged, but for the whole of the United Kingdom. The report recognised that Roman Catholics had been the principal sufferers from discrimination in the matter of employment, and welcomed the Fair Employment legislation.

Going on to consider the role of the churches in the situation, it advocated increased co-operation between the churches in Ireland and between them and the churches in Britain in the matters of ministerial training, ministry to emigrants, and teaching. It recommended that a deeper understanding of the needs and attitudes of minorities should be sought, and suggested that light on this might be found among the ethnic minorities in Britain. In these ways it sought to place the conflict in a wider context, and help those involved to move away from enclosed thought which had so far proved unable to resolve the difficulties.

A year later two statements and a report reacted to continued paramilitary activity. Speaking from a Protestant position, and not therefore presuming to encroach on the rights and responsibilities of the Roman Catholic Church, one report deplored the fact that killing was being carried on in the name of Protestantism. It affirmed that this had no biblical, moral or theological justification. The Report was a submission to the Review of the Anglo-Irish Agreement.

In 1992 a report acknowledged the success of the churches in combating several social problems, but recognised that they had been much less successful in overcoming sectarianism. It put forward a number of suggestions regarding four ways in which this issue might be more effectively addressed – personal friendship, joint action for the disadvantaged members of the community, common Bible study, and shared ministry in areas of bereavement, education and sickness.

A lengthy report in 1994 responded to the Joint Declaration

signed by the Prime Minister John Major and the Taoiseach Albert Reynolds on 15 December 1993. It offered a detailed critique of the document, welcoming it, but also noting the ambiguities in it and asking for some clarifications. A second report in the same year gave an equally detailed response to some of the recommendations of the Opsahl Report. A report in 1995 assessed the merits and weaknesses of eight possible constitutional options for Northern Ireland, and another in 2000 reviewed the experience of victims of the conflict, interpreting the term in its widest possible sense. It pleaded that the victims should be heard, and their needs taken seriously.

As one would expect in the utterances of a church, another theme runs though many of these documents. That is the call to prayer both for those who have suffered, and for a peaceful solution. It is one thing to catalogue the things that a church has said. What effect they have had only history written much longer after the events may record. However, effect very often depends on the reactions of those who hear; whatever those reactions the statements may be judged on their inherent quality.

PART V

Irish Methodists Overseas

CHAPTER 15

Emigrants and Missionaries

There seems to have been a sort of wanderlust in the Irish psyche for many centuries. It seems to have begun in the sixth and seventh centuries with the Celtic monks who left Ireland to travel through Scotland, England and Europe, founding what came to be some of the most important religious houses in all of these places. In Latin they were termed the *Peregrini* – the wandering ones. In their wanderings there seems to have been a sense in which the journey was more important than the arrival. To travel hopefully (or faithfully) was better than to arrive. The outward journey away from Ireland was the symbol of their inward journey into spiritual reality. They were not just finding new experiences; they were finding God, and their vocation.

It is very doubtful if the early Irish Methodists would have spoken in these terms, though they are not entirely irrelevant. Whatever the immediate circumstances which led to their going elsewhere, there was a sense in which their travelling brought them to a new understanding of their vocation. However, they would certainly have talked first of the immediate circumstances.

In the eighteenth and nineteenth centuries emigration was growing as a feature of Irish life. The Great Famine of 1846-49 would swell the current to a flood, but the current had long been there to be swollen. There were several causes, in many cases inextricably intermingled. They were related to the political, religious and social divisions within the community, which caused resentment and insecurity. Prior to 1846 the great majority of the emigrants were were from the Protestant working classes and tenant farmers. The reasons for their going might be summed up in the phrase once common in this country, 'to better themselves'. It was this ambition which prompted people to rise, if opportunity afforded, from employee to tradesman or artisan, from trade to profession. When met by the glowing accounts circulated in Europe about opportunities in the new colonies along the Eastern seaboard of America, it naturally concluded in emigration.

The first well documented emigration of Irish Methodists came in 1760, but their story really begins fifty years earlier. In 1709 something like 13,000 people left the Lower Palatinate of the Rhine, an area of Germany between the Rhine and what are now the borders with France and Luxembourg. Fleeing from starvation after a succession of French invasions, and a particularly severe winter which killed their vines, they fled to England, Ireland and America.[1] Over one hundred families, nearly all originally Lutheran, but with a very few Calvinists, were settled on the Southwell Estate in central Limerick, near the town of Rathkeale, where they established three villages, Courtmatrix, Killeheen and Ballingrane. Each family was allocated between eight and twelve acres.

By the middle of the century, when Wesley encountered them, they were beginning to feel the pressure of space. Eight or ten acres might be sufficient to support one family of people as industrious as the Irish Palatines undoubtedly were, but when the children grew to manhood and womanhood, and wished to establish households of their own, where were they to go? Several families moved to the Oliver Estate in south Limerick, where they created the villages of Ballyriggan, Ballyorgan and Glenosheen. In 1746 some families moved to the Blennerhasset Estate near Castleisland. Others went to Pallaskenry, and to Adare, both in Limerick, and yet others to Kilcooley, near Urlingford in Kilkenny. Many of the Palatines responded to the Methodist preachers, and societies were formed in each of these places. With the exception of those on the Oliver estate, each built its Methodist preaching house. A young carpenter by the name of Philip Embury is believed to have worked on the building of the preaching house at Courtmatrix.

Embury was soon recognised as a local preacher, and in 1758 was placed on the list of reserve for itinerant preachers in Ireland. However, he was not called, and in 1760 he and his wife, formerly Margaret Switzer, took the decision to go to America. A number of others agreed to go with them, and the party eventually numbered forty. Among them were also Paul Heck and his wife, formerly Barbara Ruttle. Sometime in the middle of June they sailed from Limerick on the schooner *Pery*, and nine weeks later landed in New York. The Hecks were sufficiently well-to-do to bring some of their furniture with them, and when they set up house in New York to engage a servant. These were the first Methodists to arrive in America, and finding no Methodist society there, they did nothing about it for several years.

Robert Strawbridge was a native of Drumsna in Leitrim just a few miles from the source of the Shannon. He was a Catholic. It is possible that he heard Wesley preach somewhere in the vicinity, but he certainly heard some Methodist preacher, for he became a Methodist himself. When, many years later, the Rev Dr William Crook visited the area in the hope of finding something about his childhood, he found some people who remembered his family, but of Robert himself they had never heard. It would seem as though after his desertion of their faith, his family never mentioned him again.[2]

Robert spent some time in Sligo, where he worked as a builder and became a local preacher. Some years later he moved to Tandragee in Co Armagh, where he had been engaged to build some houses. It was here he met and married a young woman named Piper, whose family were Methodists in the town. He built his own house in the townland of Terryhoogan, near Scarva, possibly attracted to it by the fact that there was a small company of Methodists there. Onto the end of his house he built room to accommodate visiting Methodist preachers. Wesley used it for the first time in the May of 1758, and thus described it:

The room, built on purpose for us here, three yards long, two and a quarter broad, and six foot high. The walls, floor, and ceiling are mud; and we had a clean chaff bed.

Little Mr Wesley would have had no difficulty in standing upright in it, but some of his taller preachers would have been less convenienced. Incidentally his sense of humour comes forward in 1760 when he speaks of the construction being 'all of the same marble, vulgarly called clay'.

The date when the Strawbridges arrived in America has been debated. Some have put it as early as 1762, and others as late as 1766. All that can be said with certainty is that they arrived at some time between those dates, and settled at Sam's Creek in Frederick County, Maryland. Almost immediately he began to preach.

Also in debate is who was the first Methodist preacher in America. The story is told of Barbara Heck arriving home one day to find her husband and some others playing cards. She seized the cards from the table, threw them into the fire, and hastened to Philip Embury's house, where she told him that if he did not preach to the little group they would all go to hell, and God would require their blood at his hands. Thus challenged, Embury preached a few days later to a small company comprising Margaret his wife, Paul and Barbara Heck, another Palatine by the name of John Lawrence, and a black servant called Betsy. Some early versions of the story suggest that Embury was actually one of the card players. Most versions say that the sermon was preached in Embury's own house, but the presence of the servant would seem to suggest that of the Hecks. Upon one point all are agreed, the year was 1766.

The question, therefore, is the date on which Strawbridge commenced, and it is now unlikely that this will ever be settled to the satisfaction of all concerned. In either case the first Methodist sermon in America was preached by a man who was born in Ireland, and in a very small community in Ireland at that. To continue the Embury/Heck story, the little Methodist society in New York grew too large for a room, and a rigging loft in William Street was hired for its meetings. In 1768 a site was leased in John Street, and here the first Methodist chapel was built. Its successor still stands on the site. This was also the year in which the New York Methodists wrote to Wesley asking that they might have preachers to develop the work, and in the following year Richard Boardman and Joseph Pilmoor were sent.

As early as 1763 Philip Embury, Paul Heck and some of the other Palatines had begun to petition for land in New York Province outside the city, where they saw a greater prospect of owning their own property and businesses. With the chapel, in which Embury had personally done some of the finer carpentry, completed, and the work in the hands of experienced preachers from England, the moment seemed opportune for the move. They moved in 1769 and 1770 to the Camden Valley, to a grant of land now divided by the State Line between New York and Vermont. Here they immediately formed a Methodist Society. In 1775 Philip Embury died of an injury received while mowing a meadow.

The growth of Methodist societies in America received a tremendous impetus in 1772 when Wesley sent Francis Asbury there. New societies began to be formed, and the preachers began to assert their authority over Strawbridge's work as well. Strawbridge was a maverick, and to the end they never quite tamed him. Though a layman, and with no authorisation, he insisted on administering the sacraments, even after his action had been condemned. Attempts to appoint him to circuits under the direction of a senior preacher failed, because Strawbridge paid not the slightest heed to direction. He died in Maryland in 1781.

In 1775 the American War of Independence began, and in the following year the United States declared their independence of British government. The British preachers in America withdrew, though Strawbridge continued his work as before. During the war the property of those who remained loyal to the British was forfeited, and the Camden Valley Palatines lost their property. They were moved to Canada, where for some time they lived in Montreal. In 1785 they acquired land in Upper Canada, now the Province of Ontario. There they settled and again formed a

Methodist society. It was there in 1804 that Barbara Heck died at the age of seventy. There is evidence that Philip Embury was a somewhat shy and diffident man. Certainly Barbara Heck was the 'power behind the throne', prevented as a woman from taking a more public lead; current views of a woman's position did not permit that.

In 1866 the American Methodist Episcopal Church celebrated its Centennial, and invited an Irish delegation to attend the Centennial Conference. The Revs Dr Robinson Scott and Robert Wallace were appointed delegates, and the Rev William Arthur was invited in his own right. To mark the occasion in Ireland the Rev Dr William Crook published *Ireland and the Centenary of American Methodism*. It told the story of Embury, Heck and Strawbridge.

In 1923 the Irish Conference planned to raise a fund for evangelistic work in Northern Ireland. A church house was to be built in Belfast at a cost of £50,000, and as there had been indications that money might be forthcoming from America this was planned to include a Memorial Hall to the Irish pioneers there. The Rev William L. Northridge, later Principal of Edgehill College, was given leave of absence for twelve months in 1925 and 1926 to tour the United States. That period was later extended, and he was joined by three others. The overall target of £100,000 for the fund was not achieved, and plans had therefore to be modified.

The Irish American Memorial, therefore, took the form of a Memorial Hall behind the Donegall Square church in the centre of Belfast. The hall was opened in 1930, but only six years later was in serious trouble. The subsoil in the area was unstable, and the concrete raft on which an adjoining building had been erected began to tilt, and the building dragged the American Hall out of level. For safety reasons the city authorities banned any public meetings in the hall, thus rendering it useless. After some negotiation the owner of the adjoining building agreed to purchase the hall, and the money was used to place a Memorial Window in the church. This depicted Barbara Heck and Philip Embury with scenes and symbols of their work. The name of each family in the John Street church in New York who subscribed to the original fund was placed on one of the pews of the Donegall Square church. The church was closed in 1994.

The Bicentennial of American Methodism was celebrated in 1966 by a pilgrimage to Ballingrane, and a ceremony on the quay from which the Palatines emigrated. Barbara Ruttle, who was then living in the house in which her collateral ancestress had been born, was invited to America to share in the celebrations there.

What is now the United Methodist Church in America is the only one to have been pioneered by Irish emigrants. As the tide of emigration continued, and Irish people sought a better life in the United States, in Canada, in Australia, in New Zealand, and to a lesser extent in Africa, those of them who were Methodists contributed in large measure to the development of the church in the places to which they went.

Edward Drumgoole, born in 1751, and whom Cole claims as another native of Drumsna, became a Methodist in Sligo before emigrating to America. In 1774 he became an itinerant preacher in the Methodist Episcopal Church there, but resigned when he married as the church did not make provision at that time for married ministers. He became a very successful businessman, but continued his Methodist work as a local preacher. Thomas Dawson in 1801 settled in Prince Edward Island in Canada, and formed the first Methodist society in that province. Through the nineteenth century there was strong Irish influence in the leadership of the Methodist churches in the United States, Canada, and Australia, and the later part of the century in New Zealand.

The early colonisation of Australia was as a convict settlement. One of those sent there was Edward Eagar. He was born in Kerry of good family, his father owning an estate near Killarney. He was educated for the Irish Bar, but his career there came to an abrupt end when, in 1809, he was charged with uttering a forged bill of exchange. He was sentenced to death. The Cork Methodists visited him in the prison where he was awaiting execution, and their efforts brought about his conversion. It was because of this that the Irish bishops took an interest in the case, and had his sentence commuted to transportation for life.

On arrival in New South Wales he began conducting Bible classes with the encouragement of the local Church of England chaplain, and at Windsor formed what was probably the first Methodist society in Australia. Given a conditional pardon in 1813, he engaged in legal work and in trade. Successful in the latter, he assisted in the foundation of the Bank of New South Wales. In 1818 he received an absolute pardon, earned by his good work in New South Wales, and he appears to have been one of the first of the settlers to show a practical interest in the welfare of the aborigines. In 1919 he was appointed secretary of committee to draw up a petition to the Prince Regent seeking legal reforms.

However, there is some evidence that he was not always strictly honest, and when in 1821 he went to London to advocate the reform in the colony, he fell into disreputable, though not illegal ways. He seems to have been a curiously mixed character, and there is no question of the important role he played in the political development of New South Wales. He is the most unlikely of the Methodist pioneers.

When Wesley said, 'The world is my parish', he may have been using a hyperbole to impress the bishop whom he was addressing with the fact that his ordination as an Oxford Fellow freed him from the confines of a parish, but there are other factors in his life and work to suggest that he possessed a much wider vision. If his time in Georgia needs to be seen as a failed attempt to create the ideal Christian community among people unspoilt by the vices of city life, there was nevertheless in it the ambition to announce the saving love of God to the native American. When in 1768 the New York Methodists wrote to ask for preachers, the memory of that failure did not deter Wesley. Preachers were sent across the Atlantic.

He and his brother taught the Methodists to sing:

O for a trumpet voice
On all the world to call,
To bid their hearts rejoice
In him who died for all!
For all my Lord was crucified,
For all, for all my Saviour died.

Sooner or later somebody was bound to feel impelled to put those words into action. It was his concept of the grace of God reaching out to every man, woman and child without distinction of race, colour or condition which was the seedbed of all Methodist mission, at home and abroad.

One of the first people to feel that impulse was Laurence Coughlan, the third native of Drumsna we have met in a few pages. Coughlan was an older contemporary of Strawbridge and it is indeed to Coughlan that Crookshank attributes Strawbridge's conversion. Coughlan became an itinerant preacher in 1755, and was appointed to various circuits in Ireland and in England until 1764. In that year he fell foul of Wesley by seeking and receiving ordination at the hands of a Greek Bishop Erasmus in London without consulting or inform-ing Wesley. This Wesley saw as a serious breach of discipline in one of his preachers.

In 1765 Coughlan went to Newfoundland at his own ex-pense, and began to preach there in and about Harbour Grace. Local people asked that he might be officially appointed as a missionary to work among them, and Coughlan returned to England to make the necessary arrangements. Wesley offered some advice as to how he should go about this, and the Countess of Huntingdon used some influence to have him or-dained by the Bishop of London. He was then able to return to Newfoundland as a priest of the Church of England and a mis-sionary with the Society for the Propagation of the Gospel. He continued to think of himself as a Methodist, a fact which his congregation happily accepted. Indeed so happy were they with the arrangement that when Coughlan returned to England, his successor had some difficulty in winning the co-operation of the local people because he had no Methodist connections.

Coughlan's health was seriously affected by the difficulties of his work. On the one hand, he had to travel difficult terrain in sometimes severe weather; on the other, he met with a certain amount of fierce hostility from those who resented the changes in the lifestyle of the community which his ministry effected. At least one attempt was made to poison him, when his enemies introduced into his house as a cook a man who promised to poison his food. Before he had time to make the attempt Coughlan converted the cook. After seven years of this work Coughlan wrote to Wesley announcing his intention of returning to England, and asking whether he should accept a parish there, or return to circuit work. On his arrival in 1773 he was welcomed by Wesley, but before he could be appointed to a circuit he died quite suddenly.

It was Coughlan who first introduced Methodism into Canada, but his influence went further than there. One of those who heard him preach was a man named Pierre Le Sueur, a native of Jersey. Le Sueur had acquired an estate in Newfoundland and travelled between the two places as a trader. On his return to Jersey he tried to interest the people there, without any great success until 1775 when he was joined by a younger man, Jean Fentin, who had also been to Newfoundland and come under Coughlan's influence. Thus Methodism recrossed the Atlantic from Newfoundland to the Channel Islands. It was from there in 1784 that a local preacher called William Mahy brought it to France, when he started work in Normandy.

Between 1785 and 1837 the British Conference appointed a succession of Irish preachers to work in Newfoundland. They were John McGeary, John Remington, Samuel McDowell, and John Ellis. Quite influential work was done there by a layman, John Stretton. He was living in Waterford at one time when Elizabeth Bennis, Wesley's most influential Irish correspondent, was visiting some of her family in that city. It was through her that he came to faith in Christ, and joined the Methodist society a short while before emigrating to Newfoundland. There he greatly prospered in business, worked as a local preacher, and at his own expense built the first Methodist chapel in Harbour Grace. Indeed, it was he and Arthur Thomey, also an Irishman, who kept the Methodist work alive between Coughlan's departure in 1773, and the arrival of John McGeary in 1785.

In 1813 Thomas Coke began to realise his last and grandest dream, that of a mission to India. He propounded his ideas to the Conference which met in Dublin at the beginning of July and asked if any Irish preachers would volunteer. Three did. One of these was Gideon Ouseley, but he was far too valuable to the work in Ireland for the Conference to agree to his going. The other two were James Lynch and George Erskine. At the British Conference which met soon afterwards in Liverpool Coke was able to present seven volunteers to accompany him. Two were those commended by the Irish Conference, three were preachers from the English circuits, and the other two were English local preachers. One of the three preachers was, in fact, another Irishman, John McKenny, who did not sail with the others, but travelled on a different ship to the Cape of Good Hope, where the Conference had decided that he should work. The other seven sailed from Portsmouth at the end of December, in two ships of a small fleet bound for Bombay.

On 3 May 1814 his servant, going to Coke's cabin to awaken him, found him dead on the cabin floor. He was buried at sea on the same day. The leadership of the party now devolved on James Lynch. The loss of Coke necessitated changes of plan, and created severe financial problems as he had been funding the enterprise from his private fortune. After a month in Bombay, Lynch led the others to Ceylon, where they arrived on 29 June . Lynch himself began work in Jaffna, from where he oversaw the whole mission.

James Lynch had been born at Muff in Donegal in 1775, so that at this time he was thirty-nine years old. He only remained in Ceylon for three years, and then moved to India, where he took over the work at Madras, which had been pioneered by William Harvard. Some of the arrangements which he made in Ceylon in 1814 have stood the test of time, and the Methodist

Church in Sri Lanka continues to follow them. To some extent, however, his influence was limited by his failure to master the Tamil language. He was somewhat in advance of his time in his tolerant attitude to members of other faiths, and he was a warm advocate of the importance of education in mission. In 1824 he returned to Ireland where he served on a number of stations until his retirement in 1842. He died at Leeds in 1858.

George Erskine began work in the Sinhalese language at Matara. He was later transferred to Australia. John McKenny, a native of Coleraine, arrived in Cape Colony in August 1814, and spent two years there greatly frustrated by the refusal of the Governor to allow him to preach, largely because McKenny saw his ministry as extended to black as well as white people. McKenny was a man with a sense of diplomacy, who reckoned that he would do more harm than good if he defied the Governor, and so continued to seek an amicable settlement to the impasse. When it was evident that this was not going to happen, he followed the other members of Coke's party to Ceylon. There he joined the work among the Sinhalese. He proved to be the longest enduring of the first group of missionaries there, remaining for nineteen years. He was then transferred to New South Wales, arriving in 1836. George Erskine had not been a successful Chairman of the New South Wales District, and had been recalled. McKenny replaced him, and the District entered on a new period of growth.

The Conference which sent Coke and his companions to Ceylon and Cape Colony with its blessing, also recognised the inadequacy of the system under which it had worked since 1786. Under this preachers sent to North America and the West Indies to develop work in those places were treated in the same way as those sent to circuits in Britain or Ireland. In fact the overseas stations of ministers were simply added to the list after the British and Irish. Overseas missions needed to be treated differently; for one thing they needed funding from the home circuits.

So in 1813 the Wesleyan Methodist Missionary Society was founded. But it was not to be a society which Methodists might or might not join. By its constitution every member of the Wesleyan Methodist Church was a member of the Society. Its separate structure, however, enabled its officers to concentrate their energy on propaganda, fund raising, and the recruiting of missionaries. In 1814 the Dublin District followed the British example, forming a similar society, and in 1817 the Wesleyan Methodist Missionary Society (Ireland) came into being on exactly the same principle. The Dublin and other local societies were absorbed into it.

In 1890 an agreement was formulated with the Missionary Society by which Irish ministers working with the Society overseas retained their Irish Connexion. Its formulation suggests that previously they had to transfer to the British Conference, but this is not so. In 1890 form was given to what was happening in most if not all cases prior to that date.

There is a curious hiatus in Irish Wesleyan interest in missions from these early days until the latter half of the nineteenth century. One can only conclude that the church here was so preoccupied with internal problems – the division of 1816, the Great Famine and its aftermath, and then reunion – that it had little time to spare for the world at large. The exception is the action of the Primitive Wesleyan Methodist Conference, which operated a mission station at Goderich on Lake Huron in what was then called Canada West, now the western end of Ontario. However, this would seem to have been something in the nature of a ministry to members of the Primitive Wesleyan Methodist Connexion who had emigrated from this country as well as a mission to the original people of the area. It was not unconnected with the fact that the Primitive Wesleyans for several years drew a measure of financial support from their exiles in Canada and America.

What is interesting is that the end of the hiatus is signalled by women. That is surprising given the Victorian view of womanhood, but not surprising at all in the light of subsequent history. The first into the field were the Beauchamp sisters in 1869 when A. M. Beauchamp (whose Christian names never appear) went to Bangalore in India and her sister Charlotte to Pondo in South Africa. A. M. Beauchamp transferred to Batticaloa in Ceylon in 1876. With two short interruptions her service ended at Point Pedro in Ceylon when she retired in 1905. Charlotte did all her work in Pondo, retiring in 1896. The sisters were teachers, and it was mainly as teachers that the early women missionaries worked among women and children.

During the 1870s and 1880s ministers who went to the mission field did not have their stations there recorded in the Irish Minutes. The first to be so recognised, obviously following the 1890 agreement, were the Revs H. Guard Price, who went to Trichinoply, and Thomas J. McClelland, who went to Calcutta, both in India, and both in 1898. The number of Irish ministers in overseas appointments slowly rose through the following years, and in 1922 reached double figures. The greatest number at any one time was reached in 1940 when there were thirty-one, and the number remained near thirty for the next twenty years. In 1962 a slow decline began, and by 1978 was back to single figures.

It is too simple to relate the decline to a failure of religious commitment among Irish Methodists, though such was certainly one element in it, but of greater significance is that those who went were tending to serve overseas for shorter periods, and then return to the work at home. Where the pioneer missionaries were content to be separated from their children for long periods, their successors were not. Possibly of greatest significance was the realisation that the churches in what had been called the mission field were beginning to be strong, and their countries were beginning to be free of European rule. Churches, like people, cannot remain children for ever. It was good for them that European control should be withdrawn and that they should exercise their own authority and responsibility. To those outside the church a native born leader was better able to communicate than a foreigner. In more recent years numbers have again increased, as ministers from Ireland have gone to other countries as mission partners to work alongside and under the direction of local ministers.

At no time were there many lay men from Ireland serving in the church overseas. The number at any one time never exceeded five. Always they were greatly outnumbered by the women. Lay missionaries were not listed in the Minutes of Conference until 1917, and men and women were generally in separate lists until 1974. The curious exception to this is that the first two women to serve as doctors were placed in the list of men! Most lay missionaries were doctors, nurses or teachers, but there was at least one agriculturalist, and a couple of others who used administrative skills. The areas in which these missionaries, ministerial and lay, worked included India, China, South, West and East Africa, the West Indies, Guiana, Central America, Japan and Burma.

At least three were involved in Bible translation. Paul Kingston went to Nigeria in 1926. Working at one period among the Ogoni people, he found that their language had never been written. He invented an alphabet for it, and set to work to translate the Bible into it. For a short while he was relieved of all other responsibilities in order that he might concentrate on the translation. Ormonde McConnell was sent to Haiti in 1933. He translated into Creole, and introduced into Haiti the Laubach method of teaching people to read. He founded two colleges in Port au Prince, and received Haitian and British decorations for his work in literacy. Working under a repressive government, he was noted for his courage in opposing corruption. Valentine Silcock was appointed to Burma in 1937. Sent to the Shan Hills, he translated some of the Bible into the Lonpo dialect. His work was interrupted by the Second World War, during which he served as chaplain to the Chindits.

The work of several missionaries was similarly interrupted, as they served as chaplains to the forces of the colonies in which they were working. John Fee went to China in 1936, just a year before the Japanese invasion of that country. For some years he and his wife Deirdre remained at liberty to continue their work, but in 1941 they were placed under house arrest, and from 1943 to the end of the war were interned. Regarded as citizens of Éire they were not regarded as prisoners of war.

Quite a number of the lay missionaries, and some of the ministers, were involved in education. The Rev Richard Lockhart became principal of the college at Mfantsipim in the Gold Coast. At the time when the Gold Coast became independent and changed its name to Ghana he was working in Kenya. The Ghanaian government made special arrangements to bring him and his wife, Eileen, from Kenya for the celebrations. This was because so many of them were his former pupils. That similar honours were not accorded to other teachers does not mean that none of them deserved it. It was just that the circumstances did not arise.

Several of the lay missionaries were doctors and nurses. The Rev Robert Booth of Hankow was unusual in being both a minister and a fully qualified doctor. He worked at the Men's Hospital in Hankow, and was involved in the establishment of the Red Cross in China. His death at the age of thirty-nine from complications arising out of what had been expected to be a minor operation was a great loss. Some years later Dr Sally Wolfe gave outstanding service in the same city, and only left when the political situation made it imperative. From her correspondence her niece wrote her biography under the title *She Left Her Heart in China*. That very well summed up her approach to the people among whom she worked, and from among whom she adopted three children. With a change of programme and location it could have served as a title for accounts of more than her.

In 1948 Maureen Neill-Watson went to Eastern Nigeria, and gave her heart to the Ibo people in and about Port Harcourt with whom she worked. When the Eastern Region declared its independence as Biafra it stood little chance of success, and she did not spare herself in her efforts to relieve the suffering of the people. Eventually persuaded to take a furlough in order to recruit her strength, she died of exhaustion at the airport on her way home. 'Greater love has no-one than this, that one lay down her life for her friends.'

In 1923 some Irish Methodists attended a missionary conference at Swanwick in Derbyshire. It gave them the idea for something similar in Ireland, and in the following year the first Irish Methodist Missionary Summer School was held at 'Excelsior', Portrush. Thirty-two people attended. The numbers soon outgrew the accommodation a holiday home provided, and it became the practice to take a boarding school for a week before the August Bank Holiday. The employment of trainee cooks reduced the cost. Conditions were sometimes spartan, but the young people who came did not mind that.

The programme never varied. In the early part of the morning the main speaker gave an address on a theme, usually biblical, and in the later morning the school was divided into groups to discuss the points raised. The afternoon was free for recreation, making use of the school sports facilities, and, if the sea were close enough, the beach. At least one excursion by coach was included in the programme. Every missionary on furlough was invited, and in the evenings they presented programmes on the work in the particular country where they were serving. One evening near the end of the time was reserved for a 'frivol' – an impromptu light-hearted concert. The climax of the programme came with the Holy Communion on the Sunday, and the Monday was the day for travelling home.

Young people from all parts of Ireland went to the school. It earned a reputation for good fun, and it was cheap. Many met their future spouses at it. The list of speakers reads like a roll call of distinguished Irish and British ministers. It certainly increased missionary interest among many young people, and it was said, with only slight exaggeration, that there was never a Summer School at which somebody did not make a commitment to mission at home or abroad.

John Fee marked the 50th School in 1973 by publishing a brief history of the enterprise. However, times were changing, and young people at college or university were looking for summer jobs, and those who were at work were better paid and could afford more expensive holidays. The 52nd Summer School, which met at Gurteen College in Tipperary in 1975 was to be the last.

PART VI

Conclusion

CHAPTER 16

And So On …

Irish Methodists, with a little more than two and a half centuries of history behind them, enter the twenty-first century with four major challenges, some of which have confronted them for quite a long time.

One is the growing secularisation of Irish life. Very much a feature of Europe and America in the latter half of the twentieth century, this came to Ireland somewhat later than it did to other countries, but it has grown with considerable rapidity. Its roots are varied, some being found in the aftermath of global conflict, or the fear of nuclear destruction; some in the growth of consumerism, and the pursuit of pleasure; some in the failure of the Christian churches to be true to the message they preached. Whatever the causes, no church in Ireland can expect anyone to listen to it simply because it is a church. People will only listen to those whom they recognise as relevant, realistic and sincere.

A second is the aftermath of the conflict focused on Northern Ireland. It is not a problem within Northern Ireland, for its effects have been felt throughout Ireland, Britain and beyond. Basically a problem of power, the religious element in it has embroiled all of the churches, none of whom have a stainless record in the matter. If the fragile peace established at the end of the last century is to grow, it will require the imaginative participation of the churches no less than of any other group.

Revelations in the political life of the Republic and of the United Kingdom in recent years have shown the degree of corruption among the politicians in both, but this is not a peculiarity of national politics. Dishonesty and corruption are found at every level in society. They infect our commerce, industry, social life and leisure. It is not a matter of size, for dishonesty is dishonesty whether it is written in millions or in the smaller figures of what manufacturers and shopkeepers have sometimes called 'an acceptable level of pilferage'.

The fourth challenge is of more recent origin. For many years the foreigners in our midst have been few, and observable only in the major urban areas. They came to Ireland to study, and most of them then went elsewhere to work. Only a few went into business and stayed. Accustomed to exporting people, because there was too little work here, we have found ourselves in a situation where people are coming here for work. We have witnessed a large influx of people from the poorer countries of Europe and from Africa. Some are fleeing from life threatening situations; more are refugees from poverty. These people have challenged our attitudes to ethnic difference. It is easy to condemn racism thousands of miles away – but now it has come home to us.

Of course, these challenges are not peculiar to Methodism; they confront the whole community, Christian or not. Nonetheless it is by their responses to these issues that Methodists no less than the others will be judged. The fact that Methodists face them alongside all the other members of the community is in itself a source of strength. It is many years since Methodism thought of itself in isolation.

The Irish Methodist Church is in membership with the World Methodist Council, which brings it into relationship with Methodists throughout the world. Its membership of the Irish Council of Churches, of Churches Together in Britain and Ireland, of the Conference of European Churches, and of the World Council of Churches opens doors for consultation with many Christian denominations. It is through these bodies that the Irish Methodist Church interacts with the world wide Christian community. Two ministers and one lay woman have given distinguished service to international and interdenominational church organisations.

The first of the ministers was Alan R. Booth, whose family

had given prominent lay leadership in the Methodist Centenary Church in Dublin. During his student years in Trinity College in that city he became involved in the work of the Student Christian Movement. Accepted for the ministry in 1935, he was released from circuit work five years later to spend three years with International Student Service. In 1956 he was again released, this time to serve as Secretary of the Churches' Commission on International Affairs. From that appointment he moved in 1970 to become Director of Christian Aid. Working there he saw the income of the agency doubled, and introduced a more effective method of selecting projects for grant aid. Both appointments were in London, and after his retirement in 1976 he continued to live in England. He died in 1990

Charles W. Ranson was the second minister though he entered the ministry eleven years before Booth, in 1924. His father was also a minister, and he had been born at Ballyclare in Co Antrim. On completing his training, he went to India where he served until 1946. In that year he became Research Secretary of the International Missionary Council, later becoming its General Secretary. Both offices were in New York. He served with the Council until 1958. In 1964 he was appointed Professor of Ecumenical Theology at Drew University in New Jersey. On retirement he went to live in Florida, where he died in 1988.

In 1971 Dr Edith Loane went to Denver, Colorado to attend the World Federation of Methodist Women, now the World Federation of Methodist and Uniting Church Women. Over the next twenty years she served the federation in various capacities, including that of treasurer. In 1991 she was elected president for a six year term. She was the first Irish Methodist to serve as president of a World Methodist organisation.

Locally the latter half of the twentieth century has seen a growth in co-operation between churches. Reference has been made the shared training of Presbyterian and Methodist ministers. In various locations Methodists are sharing buildings with Presbyterian or Church of Ireland congregations, or with both. From 1964 to 1988 conversations were held with these two churches and at one stage a scheme of union for the three was proposed. It did not not meet with acceptance, and the Tripartite Conversations as they were called, reached an inconclusive end in 1988. In that year a Joint Theological Working Party was established with the Church of Ireland, and this continues to work on the relationship between the two churches. At parochial level there is a great deal of practical co-operation in many places.

Co-operation with the Roman Catholic churches varies from place to place. There is a great deal in some areas relating to matters of social and community concern. Shared worship is less common, and tends in most places to be limited to the Week of Prayer for Christian Unity in January, and the Women's World Day of Prayer in March. Shared Bible study groups of an unofficial character are widespread.

In facing the challenges presented by the community, the Methodist Church has a certain advantage in never having been an established church anywhere. We have noted instances of political favour, as when the Conference was licensed to meet in 1798, but these have been the exception rather than the rule. If in Britain the Methodists were largely the custodians of the 'Non-Conformist Conscience' of which late Victorian and Edwardian politicians were well advised to take notice, in Ireland they had no such political opportunity. They suffered certain disadvantages in relation to marriage and burial for forty years after their separation from the Church of Ireland, and if Methodists went into one or other parliament, they did so as individuals.

We have seen that, although overwhelmingly unionist in the years of the successive Home Rule Bills, they were not uniformly so, and a variety of opinion on such matters has been demonstrated by the diversity in party allegiance of Methodist Members of Parliament and Teachtaí Dála. As a church Irish Methodism has therefore been less politicised than some of its sister churches.

Possibly its greatest advantage, however, is its flexibility around a central core. Committed to the doctrinal emphases of which we have taken note, the Irish Methodist Church has shown a great willingness to adapt its forms and expressions to the changing demands of the community. One hears older Methodists complain that 'Things are not done the way they used to be!' But in fact they never were! Forms of service, fellowship meetings, and other structures have been changed quite regularly in order to express the faith with relevance. Today it is, not surprisingly, where the church has been willing to vary its worship pattern, adapt its premises, and reorganise its weekly programme that there are signs of vibrant life, and growth at present.

It is not the business of historians to forecast the future, but of one thing there can be no doubt. Whatever Irish Methodists may say or do in the future will be received, not because it has come from them, but on whatever may be its intrinsic worth. That is the ultimate challenge in this world.

APPENDIX

1. Irish Methodist Conferences and Presidents

The locations of the Conferences are abbreviated as follows:
(L) Limerick, (D) Dublin, (C) Cork, (B) Belfast, (P) Portadown, (Ba) Bangor,
(E) Enniskillen, (Lo) Londonderry

Year	President	Year	President
1752 (L)	John Wesley	1807 (D)	Thomas Coke
1756 (D)	John Wesley	1808 (D)	Thomas Coke
1758 (L)	John Wesley	1809 (D)	Thomas Coke
1760 (L)	John Wesley	1810 (D)	Adam Averell
1762 (D)	John Wesley	1811 (D)	Adam Clarke
1765 (D)	John Wesley	1812 (D)	Adam Clarke
1767 (D)	John Wesley	1813 (D)	Thomas Coke
1769 (D)	John Wesley	1814 (D)	Adam Averell
1771 (D)	John Wesley	1815 (D)	Walter Griffith
1773 (D)	John Wesley	1816 (D)	Adam Clarke
1775 (D)	John Wesley	1817 (D)	Richard Reece
1778 (D)	John Wesley	1818 (D)	John Gaulter
1782 (D)	Thomas Coke	1819 (D)	Jonathan Edmundson
1783 (D)	John Wesley	1820 (D)	Jonathan Crowther
1784 (D)	Thomas Coke	1821 (D)	Jabez Bunting
1785 (D)	John Wesley	1822 (D)	George Marsden
1786 (D)	Thomas Coke	1823 (D)	Adam Clarke
1787 (D)	John Wesley	1824 (D)	Henry Moore
1788 (D)	Thomas Coke	1825 (C)	Robert Newton
1789 (D)	John Wesley	1826 (D)	Joseph Entwistle
1790 (D)	Thomas Coke	1827 (B)	Richard Watson
1791 (D)	*John Crook This was officially*	1828 (D)	John Stephens
not a Conference, but a meeting of the		1829 (C)	Jabez Bunting
Preachers in Ireland.		1830 (D)	James Townley
1792 (D)	Thomas Coke	1831 (B)	George Morley
1793 (D)	John Crook	1832 (D)	George Marsden
1794 (D)	Thomas Coke	1833 (C)	Robert Newton
1795 (D)	Thomas Coke	1834 (D)	Richard Treffry
1796 (D)	Thomas Coke	1835 (B)	Joseph Taylor
1797 (D)	Thomas Coke	1836 (D)	Richard Reece
1798 (D)	Thomas Coke	1837 (C)	Jabez Bunting
1799 (D)	Thomas Coke	1838 (D)	Edmund Grindol
1800 (D)	Thomas Coke	1839 (B)	Thomas Jackson
1801 (D)	Thomas Coke	1840 (D)	Theophilus Lessey
1802 (D)	Thomas Coke	1841 (C)	Robert Newton
1803 (D)	Thomas Coke	1842 (D)	James Dixon
1804 (D)	Thomas Coke	1843 (B)	John Hannah
1805 (D)	Thomas Coke	1844 (D)	John Scott
1806 (D)	Thomas Coke	1845 (C)	John Scott

Year	President	Year	President
1846 (D)	Jacob Stanley	1857 (C)	Robert Young
1847 (B)	William Atherton	1858 (D)	Francis A. West
1848 (D)	Samuel Jackson	1859 (B)	John Bowers
1849 (C)	Robert Newton	1860 (D)	Samuel D. Waddy
1850 (D)	Thomas Jackson	1861 (C)	William W. Stamp
1851 (B)	John Beecham	1862 (D)	John Rattenbury
1852 (D)	John Hannah	1863 (B)	Charles Prest
1853 (C)	John Scott	1864 (D)	George Osborn
1854 (D)	John Lomas	1865 (C)	William L. Thornton
1855 (B)	John Farrar	1866 (D)	William Shaw
1856 (D)	Isaac Keeling	1867 (B)	William Arthur

2. Irish Methodist Conferences, Presidents and Vice-Presidents

The locations of the Conferences are abbreviated as follows:
(L) Limerick, (D) Dublin, (C) Cork, (B) Belfast, (P) Portadown, (Ba) Bangor,
(E) Enniskillen, (Lo) Londonderry

Year	President	Vice-President
1868 (D)	John Bedford	Henry Price
1869 (C)	Samuel Romilly Hall	James Tobias
1870 (D)	Frederick J. Jobson	Joseph W. McKay
1871 (B)	John Farrar	Robinson Scott
1872 (D)	John H. James	Wm Parker Appelbe
1873 (C)	Luke H. Wiseman	George Vance
1874 (D)	George T. Perks	Wallace McMullen
1875 (B)	W. Morley Punshon	Gibson McMillan
1876 (D)	Gervase Smith	Joseph W. McKay
1877 (C)	Alexander McAuley	James Tobias
1878 (D)	William Burt Pope	Wallace McMullen
1879 (B)	James H. Rigg	Wm Guard Price
1880 (D)	Benjamin Gregory	Wm Parker Applebe
1881 (C)	Ebenezer E. Jenkins	James Tobias
1882 (B)	George Osborn	Oliver McCutcheon
1883 (D)	Charles Garrett	William Crook
1884 (B)	Thomas McCullagh	James Donnelly
1885 (C)	Frederic Greeves	Thomas A. M. McKee
1886 (D)	Richard Roberts	Joseph W. McKay
1887 (B)	Robert N. Young	John Donor Powell
1888 (D)	John Walton	Wallace McMullen
1889 (C)	Joseph Bush	Wm. Guard Price
1890 (B)	Charles H. Kelly	Oliver McCutcheon
1891 (D)	William F. Moulton	John Woods Ballard
1892 (B)	T. Bowman Stephenson	William Gorman
1893 (C)	James H. Rigg	Wesley Guard
1894 (D)	Henry J. Pope	William Nicholas
1895 (B)	Walford Green	Wallace McMullen
Year	President	Vice-President
1896 (D)	David J. Walker	William Crook
1897 (C)	Marshall Randles	James Robertson
1898 (B)	William L. Watkinson	R. Crawford Johnson
1899 (D)	Hugh Price Hughes	Charles H Crookshank
1900 (B)	Frederic W. MacDonald	William Crawford
1901 (C)	Thomas Allen	John Oliver Park
1902 (D)	W. Theophilus Davison	Wesley Guard
1903 (B)	John Shaw Banks	William Nicholas
1904 (D)	Marshall Hartley	Thomas Knox
1905 (C)	Silvester Whitehead	George R. Wedgwood
1906 (B)	Charles H. Kelly	James Robertson
1907 (D)	Albert Clayton	William Crawford
1908 (B)	John S. Simon	James D. Lamont
1909 (C)	John Scott Lidgett	Joseph W. R. Campbell

Year	President	Vice-President
1910 (D)	William Perkins	John Oliver Park
1911 (B)	John Hornabrook	Wesley Guard
1912 (D)	Henry Haigh	George R. Wedgwood
1913 (C)	Frederick L. Wiseman	Samuel T. Boyd
1914 (B)	Samuel F. Collier	William R. Budd
1915 (D)	Dinsdale T. Young	John Oliver Park
1916 (B)	Richard Waddy Moss	Pierce Martin
1917 (C)	John G. Tasker	William Maguire
1918 (D)	Simpson Johnson	Hugh McKeag
1919 (B)	Samuel Chadwick	James Kirkwood
1920 (D)	William T. A. Barber	Henry Shire
1921 (B)	J. T. Wardle Stafford	William H. Smyth*
1922 (D)	J. Alfred Sharp	James M. Alley
1923 (B)	John E Wakerley	James W. Parkhill
1924 (C)	T. Ferrier Hulme	William Corrigan
1925 (D)	Amos Burnet	Edward B. Cullen
1926 (B)	John R. Ritson	Robert M. Ker.
1927 (D)	W. Russell Maltby	William H. Smyth
1928 (B)	W. Hodson Smith	Randall C. Phillips
1929 (C)	John W. Lightly	John C. Robertson
1930 (D)	William F. Lofthouse	William Moore
1931 (B)	Herbert B. Workman	Frederick E. Harte
1932 (D)	C. Ryder Smith	John A. Duke
1933 (B)	J. Scott Lidgett	R. Lee Cole
1934 (C)	F. Luke Wiseman	John A. Walton
1935 (D)	William Younger	Thomas J. Irwin
1936 (B)	William C. Jackson	William H. Massey
1937 (D)	C. Ensor Walters	C. Henry Crookshank
1938 (B)	Robert Bond	Thomas J. Allen
1939 (C)	William L. Wardle	Alexander McCrea
1940 (B)	Richard Pyke	Hugh M. Watson
1941 (D)	Henry Bett	John N. Spence
1942 (B)	Walter H. Armstrong	Beresford Lyons
1943 (D)	Walter J. Noble	George A. Joynt
1944 (B)	George A. Joynt	William L. Northridge
1945 (B)	Wilbert F. Howard	Edward Whittaker
1946 (D)	Archibald W. Harrison	Robert H. Gallagher
1947 (P)	R. Newton Flew	John England
1948 (C)	William E. Farndale	W. E. Morley Thompson
1949 (B)	E. Benson Perkins	John W. Stutt
1950 (D)	Harold B. Rattenbury	J. R. Wesley Roddie
1951 (B)	W. Edwin Sangster	Henry N. Medd
1952 (C)	Howard Watkin-Jones	John Montgomery
1953 (P)	Colin A. Roberts	Richard M. L. Waugh
1954 (D)	Donald O. Soper	Ernest Shaw
1955 (B)	W. Russell Shearer	Albert Holland
1956 (C)	Leslie D. Weatherhead	Samuel E. McCaffrey
1957 (D)	H. Crawford Walters	J. Wesley McKinney
1958 (B)	Harold Roberts	Robert J. Good
1959 (P)	Norman H. Snaith	R. Ernest Ker

Year	President	Vice-President
1960 (D)	Eric W. Baker	Robert W. McVeigh
1961 (B)	Edward Rogers	Charles W. Ranson
1962 (C)	Maldwyn L. Edwards	James Wisheart
1963 (D)	Leslie Davison	Frederick E. Hill
1964 (B)	Frederic Greeves	Samuel H. Baxter
1965 (P)	A. Kingsley Lloyd	Robert A. Nelson
1966 (D)	W. Walker Lee	Samuel J. Johnston
1967 (B)	Douglas W. Thompson	R. D. Eric Gallagher
1968 (C)	Irvonwy Morgan	Gerald G. Myles
1969 (D)	E. Gordon Rupp	George E. Good
1970 (B)	Brian S. O'Gorman	James Davison
1971 (P)	Rupert E. Davies	Charles H. Bain
1972 (D)	Kenneth L. Waights	Edward R. Lindsay
1973 (Ba)	Harry O. Morton	Harold Sloan
1974 (C)	Donald R. Lee	R. Desmond Morris
1975 (B)	J. Russell Pope	Hedley W. Plunkett
1976 (D)	A. Raymond George	Richard Greenwood
1977 (P)	Colin M. Morris	Robert G. Livingstone
1978 (B)	B. Arthur Shaw	John Turner
1979 (D)	Donald English	Vincent Parkin
1980 (Ba)	William Gowland	W. Sydney Callaghan
1981 (C)	Kenneth Greet	Ernest W. Gallagher
1982 (B)	John A. Newton	Charles G. Eyre
1983 (E)	Norwyn E. Denny	Cecil A. Newell
1984 (D)	Amos S. Cresswell	Paul Kingston
1985 (P)	Gordon E. Barritt	Hamilton Skillen
1986 (B)	Chris. Hughes Smith	Sydney Frame
1987 (Ba)	Nigel L. Gilson	William I. Hamilton
1988 (D)	William R. Davies	T. Stanley Whittington
1989 (Lo)	Richard G. Jones	George R. Morrison
1990 (B)	John J. Vincent	William T. Buchanan
1991 (C)	Donald English	J. Winston Good
1992(E)	Ronald W. C. Hoar	J. Derek H. Ritchie
1993 (D)	Kathleen M. Richardson	Richard H. Taylor
1994 (P)	Brian E. Beck	E. T. I. Mawhinney
1995 (B)	Leslie J. Griffiths	Christopher G. Walpole
1996 (Ba)	Brian R. Hoare	Kenneth Best
1997 (Lo)	Nigel T. Collinson	Norman W. Taggart
1998 (D)	John B. Taylor	David J. Kerr
1999 (C)	W. Peter Stephens	Kenneth A. Wilson
2000 (B)	Stuart J. Burgess	S. Kenneth Todd

* William H. Smyth, in 1921, was the first to be titled President of the Methodist Church in Ireland and Vice-president of the Conference, as were all of his successors to date.

2. Secretaries of the Conference

1792	John Crook	1826	Andrew Hamilton
1793	Walter Griffith	1827	Samuel Wood
1794	John Crook	1828	Samuel Wood
1795	John Crook	1829	William Stewart
1796	William Smith	1830	William Stewart
1797	John Crook	1831-1840	Thomas W. Doolittle
1798	Andrew Hamilton, Jun.	1840-1848	William Stewart
1799	John Kerr	1848-1861	John F. Matthews
1800	John Duncan	1861-1870	James Tobias
1801	Adam Averell	1870-1881	Joseph W. McKay
1802	John Kerr	1881-1893	James Donnelly
1803	Andrew Hamilton, Jun.	1893-1898	R. Crawford Johnson
1804	William Smith	1898-1901	John Oliver Park
1805	Samuel Steele	1901-1905	Caleb Shera Laird
1806	John Grace	1905-1908	James D. Lamont
1807	Matthew Tobias	1908-1913	Samuel T. Boyd
1808	William Ferguson	1913-1922	James M. Alley
1809	Charles Mayne	1922-1926	Robert M. Ker
1810	Samuel Wood	1926-1933	R. Lee Cole
1811	Matthew Lanktree	1933-1937	C. Henry Crookshank
1812	James McKeown	1937-1941	John N. Spence
1813	Robert Banks	1941-1948	W. E. Morley Thompson
1814	William Stewart	1948-1956	Joseph B. Jameson
1815	Robert Crozier	1956-1958	Richard S. Morris
1816	Samuel Wood	1958-1967	R. D. Eric Gallagher
1817	Samuel Wood	1967-1978	Harold Sloan*
1818	William Smith	1978-1991	Charles G. Eyre
1819	William Smith	1991-	Edmund T. I.
1820	Samuel Wood		Mawhinney
1821	Andrew Hamilton, Jun.		
1822	Andrew Hamilton, Jun.		* In 1970 the Secretary of the
1823	Samuel Wood		Conference was relieved of all circuit
1824	Andrew Hamilton		responsibilities to concentrate on
1825	Samuel Wood		administration.

SOURCES AND NOTES

The primary sources of the history of Irish Methodists are to be found in the writings of John Wesley, the biographies of the Methodist preachers and missionaries, the magazines published by the Methodist churches through the years, and the Minutes of their Conferences.

The editions of Wesley's writings which I have used are:
> *The Journal of John Wesley*, Standard Edition, edited by Nehemiah Curnock, in 8 volumes, London 1909-1916
> *The Letters of the Rev. John Wesley, A.M.*, edited by John Telford in 8 Volumes, London 1931
> *The Works of John Wesley*, Third Edition, in 14 Volumes, London 1872, Reprinted Grand Rapids 1986
> *The Works of John Wesley*, Bicentennial Edition, in 30 volumes, Oxford and Nashville 1975 – in process.

The magazines are:
> *The Methodist Magazine*
> *The Wesleyan Methodist Magazine*
> *The Primitive Wesleyan Methodist Magazine*
> *The Irish Evangelist*
> *The Christian Advocate*
> *The Irish Christian Advocate*
> *The Methodist Newsletter*

The most important of the biographies are listed in the bibliography which follows. I have also found fresh light thrown on certain events by documents recorded in the Registry of Deeds in Dublin.

Between 1885 and 1888 Charles H. Crookshank published his *History of Methodism in Ireland* in three volumes. In this comprehensive work he devoted a chapter to each year, and the abundance of detail makes it, when read through the index, a useful source of local Methodist history. He brought the story up to 1860. In 1960 R. Lee Cole published a *History of Methodism in Ireland 1860-1960*. Designed as a sequel to Crookshank's work, it devoted a chapter to each decade. In 1964 Frederick Jeffery published *Irish Methodism: An Historical Account of its Traditions, Theology and Influence*. In 1998 Risteard Ó Glaisne published *Modhaigh*, a history of Irish Methodism in Ireland written in the Irish language.

NOTES

Chapter 1. The Historic Background

1. Statistic quoted from World Methodist Council Directory, Millennium Edition, 2000

Chapter 2. The Wesleys

1. Of the making of books about John Wesley there is no end. The best account of his life and the development of the early Methodist societies is Henry Rack's *Reasonable Enthusiast*. A good critical biography of him is Stanley Ayling's *John Wesley*. Other valuable studies tend to deal with particular aspects of his his life and work

2. Wesley spoke of the societies connected with him, and the title page of the Minutes of the Irish Methodist Conference still preserves the traditional formula, Conference of the People called Methodists in the Connexion Established by the late Rev. John Wesley A.M. It has become customary to refer to an autonomous Methodist Church as a Connexion, using the eighteenth-century spelling.

3. The Joural entry for 24 May 1738 includes a short account of Wesley's religious experience throughout his life up to that point – as he saw it then

Chapter 3. The Methodist Contribution

1. From the hymn 'Let earth and heaven agree', in *Hymns and Psalms* (1983) No 226

2. *Hymns and Psalms*, No 563

3. *Hymns and Psalms*, No 749

4. *Methodist Hymn Book* (1933), No 717

5. Towards the end of the twentiethth century some American theologians, believing that speculative theology had begun to be unrelated to everyday life, started to reappraise Wesley's theology, seeing in his teaching a way to re-establish the relationship

Chapter 4. In Wesley's Time

1. Benjamin La Trobe later moved to the Moravian settlement at Fulneck, near Pudsey in Yorkshire. There his son, Benjamin H. La Trobe was born. The younger La Trobe qualified as an architect, and in 1795 emigrated to America, where he is considered to be the first professional architect in the United States. Among his work are the chambers for the House of Representatives and the Senate in the Capitol at Washington.

2. For a fuller account of this society see Cooney, 'Skinners' Alley

Meeting House, Dublin' in the *Bulletin of the Wesley Historical Society (Irish Branch)*, Vol. 2, Part 7, Summer 1994.

3. Anne Lunell was born Anne Grattan, a close relation of Henry Grattan the Irish Parlaimentarian; her niece Olivia Whitmore married Arthur Guinness who founded the brewery.

4. Cooney, op.cit.

5. Recently reported by the author by a friend who heard the term used there in 2000.

6. *Letters of John Wesley*, Vol 6 p.29 Emphasis is Wesley's. The Latin means 'Whilst we live, let us live.'

7. Robert H. Gallagher, *Pioneer Preachers of Irish Methodism*. C. H. Crookshank, *History of Methodism in Ireland*, Vol 1.

8. David Hempton & Myrtle Hill, *Evangelical Protestants in Ulster Society*, p 30.

9. Thomas Jackson, Editor, *Lives of the Early Methodist Preachers*, Vol 2.

10. Robert H. Gallagher, *Robert Bredin.*

11. *Journal of John Wesley*, 25 July 1726.

12. Ibid, 28 April 1760.

13. Ibid, 6 April 1748.

14. Cooney, 'The Entry of the Methodists' in the *Bulletin of the Wesley Historical Society (Irish Branch)*, Vol 6, Autumn 2001.

Chapter 5. After Wesley

1. C. H. Crookshank, op.cit., Vol 2, p 132.

2. For a fuller account of the Methodists in the 1798 Rising, see Cooney, 'Methodists and the Year of Liberty' in the *Bulletin of the Wesley Historical Society (Irish Branch)*, Vol 5, Autumn 1999.

3. William G. Campbell, *Charles Graham: The Apostle of Kerry.*

4. Robert H. Gallagher, *Pioneer Preachers*, pp 61ff.

5. William Arthur, *The Life of Gideon Ouseley.*

6. Lecture at Edgehill College, 1994.

7. Frederick Jeffery, *Irish Methodism*, p 57.

8. Hempton & Hill, op. cit., pp 60, 61.

9. Alexander Stewart & George Revington, *Memoir of the Life and Labours of the Rev Adam Averell.*

Chapter 6. Methodism Divided

1. Cooney, 'They Met in South Great George's Street' in the *Bulletin of the Wesley Historical Society (Irish Branch)*, Vol 6, Autumn 2001.

2. Cooney, 'A Wedding in St Bride's' in the *Dublin Historical Record*, Vol XLVIII, No 1, Spring 1995.

3. Cooney, 'A Pious Dublin Printer' in the *Dublin Historical Record*, Vol XLVI, No 2, Autumn 1993.

4. Cooney, *Methodism in Galway*.

5. Cooney, 'Methodists in the Great Irish Famine' in the Bulletin of the Wesley Historical Society (Irish Branch), Vol 3, No 1, Autumn 1996 and Vol 4, No 1, Summer 1998.

6. Hempton & Hill, op. cit., pp 145-160.

Chapter 7. The Methodist Church in Ireland

1. Samuel Madden, *Memoir of the Life of the late Rev Peter Roe, AM.* Cooney, 'An Irish Evangelical' in the *Bulletin of the Wesley Historical Society (Irish Branch)*, Vol 2, No 3, Summer 1992.

2. John Moulden, *A History of Methodism in Portrush*.

3. R. P. Roddie, 'Reflecting and Recording' in the *Methodist Newsletter*, January 1998.

4. C. H. Crookshank, op. cit., Vol 2, p 178.

5. John Kent, *Holding the Fort*.

6. R. Lee Cole, *History of Methodism in Ireland 1860-1960*, p 69.

7. Davis, George and Rupp, *A History of the Methodist Church in Great Britain*, Vol 3, pp 135-138.

8. Eric Gallagher, *At Points of Need*.

9. Lionel Booth, *Dublin Central Mission 1893-1993*.

10. Cole, op. cit., p 64.

11. Duncan Alderdice, *Need Not Creed*.

12. Hempton and Hill, op. cit., pp 174-180. David McConnell, 'Irish Methodism and Home Rule' in the *Bulletin of the Wesley Historical Society (Irish Branch)*, Vol 5, Autumn 1999. Risteard Ó Glaisne, *Modhaigh*, pp 135-140.

13. Cooney, 'Medical and Musical' in the *Dublin Historical Record*, Vol XLIX, No 1, Spring 1996.

Chapter 8. Under Two Jurisdictions

1. 'Layman', *Irish Methodist Chaplains to His Majesty's Forces, 1939-1946*.

2. Minutes of Conference.

3. Cooney, 'An Englishman in Ireland: Arthur Dean Codling' in the *Dublin Historical Record*, Vol XLVII, No 1, Spring 1994.

4. Cooney, 'The People called Methodists from the Free State to the Irish Republic' in the *Bulletin of the Wesley Historical Society (Irish Branch)*, Vol 6, Autumn 2001.

5. Dermot Keogh, *Twentieth Century Ireland: Nation and State*, pp 55-58

6. *Methodist Newsletter*, January 2000.

7. *Methodist Newsletter*, November 1998. Anonymous article by a minister of the Fellowship.

8. Henry D. Rack, *Reasonable Enthusiast*, p 244.

9. C. H. Crookshank, *Memorable Women of Irish Methodism*, pp 191-203.

10. 'JHW', *Memorials of a Consecrated Life.*

Chapter 9. The Smaller Connexions

1. Boyd Stanley Schlenther, *Queen of the Methodists* is an account of Lady Huntingdon and her Methodist interests.

2. Crookshank, *History*, Vol 2. Robert P. Roddie, Article in the *Dictionary of Methodism in Britain and Ireland.*

3. Robert P. Roddie, 'The Wesleyan Methodist Association in Ireland 1834-72' in the *Bulletin of the Wesley Historical Society (Irish Branch)*, Vol 5, Autumn 1999.

4. Ernan P. Blythe, 'The Welsh Chapel in Dublin' in the *Dublin Historical Record*, Vol XIV, No 3, July 1957.

III PREACHERS AND PEOPLE

Chapter 11. The Life of the Preachers

1. C. H. Crookshank, *History*, Vol 1, p 117.

2. *The Story of Edgehill*, published anonymously and undated, but actually by W. L. Northridge.

3. *Letters of John Wesley*, Vol 5, pp 132-134.

4. Large Minutes, Question 36.

5. Ibid.

6. George J. Coalter, *My Memories, 1890-1950.*

Chapter 12. Circuit Life

1. J. Ernest Rattenbury, *The Eucharistic Hymns of John and Charles Wesley*, p 149.

2. Charles Wesley actually wrote the first two lines of the hymn thus:
   Hark! how all the welkin rings,
   Glory to the King of kings!
   The lines were altered to their present form when the word 'welkin' went out of use, and therefore out of understanding. The *Concise Oxford Dictionary* defines it as 'sky'.

IV SOCIAL CONCERNS

Chapter 13. Education

1. Anonymous, *Methodist Centenary Church, Dublin: A Commemorative Record* 1843-1943, pp 42ff.

2. Ibid, p 75. R. Lee Cole, op. cit., pp 30, 31. Douglas Bennett, *Encyclopaedia of Dublin*, p 94. Henry Boylan, *Dictionary of Irish Biography*, Third Edition, p 274. William J. Feeney, *Drama in Hardwicke Street.*

3. Thomas Parnell was a great-uncle of Charles Stewart Parnell.

4. Ernest Armitage, *Wesley College Dublin, 1845-1995: An Illustrated History*.
5. Ronald Marshall, *Methodist College, Belfast: The First Hundred Years*. Frederick Jeffery, *A Brief History of Methodist College, Belfast*.
6. J. Wesley McKinney and Salters Sterling, *Gurteen College: A Venture in Faith*. Hugo Perdue, *Gurteen Agricultural College 1947-1997*.

Chapter 14. Poverty and Suffering
1. Cooney, 'Twenty Reduced Widows' in the *Dublin Historical Record*, Vol L, No 1, Spring 1997.
2. R. Lee Cole, *A History of Methodism in Dublin*, p 96.
3. R. Lee Cole and J. Wesley Ludlow, *A Short History of the Stranger's Friend Society in Dublin*.
4. Cooney, *Asses Colts and Loving People*, pp 116, 117.
5. Eric Gallagher, op. cit., pp 129-143.

Chapter 15. Manners and Morals
1. Cooney, 'Irish Methodists and the Demon Drink' in the *Bulletin of the Wesley Historical Society (Irish Branch)*, Vol 3, Part 4, Winter 1992.
2. John Kent, *Holding the Fort*, p 90.

V IRISH METHODISTS OVERSEAS

Chapter 16. Irish Methodists Overseas
1. Eula Lapp, *To Their Heirs for Ever*. Patrick O'Connor, *People Make Places*.
2. William Crook, *Ireland and the Centenary of American Methodism*.

Aldersice, Duncan, *Need Not Creed*, Belfast (1998)

Armitage, Ernest, *Wesley College, Dublin 1845-1995: An Illustrated History*, Dublin (1995)

Arthur, William, *The Life of Gideon Ouseley*, London (1876)

Ayling, Stanley, *John Wesley*, London (1979)

Berger, Teresa, *Theology in Hymns?*, Nashville (1995)

Booth, Lionel, *Dublin Central Mission 1893-1993*, Dublin (1993)

Bradshaw, David B. (Editor), *Methodist Centenary Church, Dublin : A Commemorative Record, 1843-1943*, Dublin (1943)

Campbell, William G., *Charles Graham: The Apostle of Kerry*, Dublin (1868), Reprinted Clonmel (1995)

Coalter, George J., *My Memories 1890-1950*, Enniskillen (1950)

Cole, F. J., *The Cavalry Preachers*, Belfast (1945)

Cole, R. Lee, *A History of Methodism in Dublin*, Dublin (1932)

— *History of Methodism in Ireland 1860-1960*, Belfast (1960)

Cole, R. Lee and Ludlow, J. Wesley, *A Short History of the Stranger's Friend Society in Dublin*, Dublin (1990)

Collins, Kenneth J., *The Scripture Way of Salvation*, Nashville (1997)

Crook, William, *Ireland and the Centenary of American Methodism*, London & Dublin (1866)

Crookshank, Charles H., *History of Methodism in Ireland*, Belfast & London (1885-1888)

— *Memorable Women of Irish Methodism*, London (1882)

Davey, Cyril, *Mad About Mission*, London (1985)

Davies, Rupert, George, A. Raymond & Rupp, Gordon (Editors), *A History of the Methodist Church in Great Britain*, 3 Vols, London (1965-1983)

Edwards, Maldwyn, *Family Circle*, London (1949)

Etheridge, J. W., *The Life of the Rev Thomas Coke*, DCL, London (1860)

Fee, John and Deirdre, *Happy Landings*, Belfast (1988)

Feeney, William J., *Drama in Hardwicke Street*, London and Toronto (1984)

Gallagher, Eric, *At Points of Need*, Belfast (1989)

Gallagher, Robert H., *Adam Clarke: Saint & Scholar*, Belfast (1963)

— *John Bredin*, Belfast (1960)

— *Pioneer Preachers of Irish Methodism*, Belfast (1965)

Good, George E., *God's Man for Ogoni*.

Heitzenrater, Richard P., *Wesley and the People Called Methodists*,
          Nashville (1995)

Hempton, David, *Methodism and Politics in British Society 1750-1850*,
          London (1984)

Hempton, David and Hill, Myrtle, *Evangelical Protestants in Ulster
          Society 1740-1890*, London (1992)

Jackson, Thomas (Editor), *Lives of the Early Methodist Preachers*, Fourth
          Edition, London (1871), reprinted in 3 volumes, Stoke-on-
          Trent (1998)

Jeffery, F., *Irish Methodism*, Belfast (1964)

— *A Brief History of Methodist College, Belfast*, Belfast (1997)

Jennings, Theodore W. Jr., *Good News to the Poor*, Nashville (1990)

JHW, *Memorials of a Consecrated Life*, London (1882)

Kent, John, *Holding the Fort*, London (1978)

Keogh, Dermot, *Twentieth Century Ireland: Nation and State*, New Gill
          History of Ireland, Dublin (1994)

Langford, Thomas A., *Practical Divinity*, 2 volumes Nashville (1998,
          1999)

Lapp, Eula, *To Their Heirs for Ever*, Belleville, Ontario (1977)

'Layman', *Irish Methodist Chaplains to His Majesty's Forces 1939-1946*,
          Dublin (1946)

McKenney, J. Wesley and Stirling, Salters, *Gurteen College: A Venture in
          Faith*, Omagh (1972)

Madden, Samuel, *Memoir of the Life of the Late Rev Peter Roe AM.*

Maddox, Randy L., *Responsible Grace*, Nashville (1994)

Maddox, Randy L. (Editor), *Rethinking Wesley's Theology*, Nashville
          (1998)

Marshall, Ronald, *Methodist College, Belfast: The First Hundred Years*,
          Belfast (1968)

Moulden, John, *A History of Methodism in Portrush*, Portrush (1987)

Northridge, W. L., *The Story of Edgehill Belfast.*

O'Connor, Patrick, *People Make Places*, Limerick (1989)

Ó Glaisne, Risteárd, *Modhaigh,* Baile ·Átha Claith (1998)

Perdue, Hugo, *Gurteen Agricultural College 1947-1997*, Tipperary 1997

Rack, Henry D., *Reasonable Enthusiast*, London (1989)

Rattenbury, J. Ernest, *The Eucharistic Hymns of John and Charles Wesley*,
          London (1948)

Schlenther, Boyd Stanley, *Queen of the Methodists*, Durham (1997)

Stacey, John (Editor), *John Wesley: Contemporary Perspectives*, London
          (1988)

Stewart, Alexander and Revington, George, *Memoir of the Life and
          Labours of the Rev Adam Averell*, Dublin (1848)

Vickers, John A., *A Dictionary of Methodism in Britain and Ireland*, London (2000)

Wesley, John, *The Journal*, Standard Edition, 8 volumes, London (1909-1916)

— *The Letters*, 8 volumes, London (1931)

— *Primitive Physic*, Introduction by A. Wesley Hill, London (1960)

— *Works*, Third Edition, 14 volumes, reprinted Grand Rapids (1986)

— *Works: Bicentennial Edition*, Oxford & Nashville (1975 – in progress)

Yrigoyen, Charles Jr., *John Wesley: Holiness of Heart and Life*, Nashville (1996)

Index

Abbey Street, Dublin 92
Abbey Theatre 188
Abortion 224
Act of Uniformity 16
Adare 207
Agnes St Belfast 109
Agricultural Revolution 14
Alcohol 88 218–222
Aldersgate House, Belfast 199
Aldersgate Street, London 19 20
Alexander I, Tzar 84
Alexander, Robert B. 108
Allan, Frederick J. 98
Allen, I. S. 85
Alley, James M. 96 160
America 46 48 105–108
American evangelists 86–88
American Memorial Hall 235 236
American Memorial Window 236
American War of Independence
    183 207 234
Anderson, Robert N. 97
Andrews, Francis 60
Annesley, Dr. Samuel 16
Antrim 43
'Apostle of Kerry' 53
Apostolic Fathers 147
Aran Islands 137
Architecture 82 83
Ardill, Capt. R. Austin 108
Arkwright, Sir Richard 14
Armagh 43 61
Armitage, Gerald C. 116
Armitage, Ted 196
Army – influence on Methodism
    28 36 54
Arthur, William 149
    & American Methodism 235
    & Methodist College 193
Asbury, Francis 46 48 234
Association of Friends of the Sick
    Poor 210
Athlone 21 64

Aughentain 36
Aughrim, Co Galway 32 33 43 44
    64 68
Australia 236 237 241
Averell, Rev Adam 35 50 128 189
    205
    & Primitive Wesleyan
        Methodists 64 65
    & sacraments 59 60
    career 60
Averell, John, Bishop of Limerick
    60
Ayckbaum, John Dedrich 206

Ballinamallard 103
Ballineen 112
Ballingrane 40 231 236
Ballyclare 137
Ballynmacarrett 106
Ballymena 43
Ballymoney 44
Ballyorgan 231
Ballyriggan 231
Banbridge 138
Bandon 32 83
Bands 163–165
Bangor, Co Down 117 137.
Bantry 102
Baptists 31
Barber, Thomas 83
Barrett, John 'Jacky' 184
Beauchamp, A. M. 242 243
Beauchamp, Charlotte 242 243
Beckett, George F. 191
Belfast 33 43 61 63 65 138
    blitz 106
    MNC 136
Belfast Central Mission 91 207 211
    212
Belfast Methodist Council 89
Bennis, Elizabeth 156 239
Berehaven 101
Berkeley, George, Bishop of
    Cloyne 45

Best, Edward 173
Bethel Bible College 120
Bethel Chapel, Dublin 141
Bethesda Chapel, Dublin 52
Betsy 233
Bible Christians 137
Bible translation 56 244
Bitter Cry of Outcast London, The 91
'Black Cap Preachers' 57
Blackwell, Ebenezer 39 40
Blayney, Neil 197
Board of National Education 186
    transfer of schools 186
Boardman, Richard 234
Bombay 240
Bonsall, John Ouseley 209
Book of Offices 174
Booker, Rev Moore 44 45
Bookrooms 181
Booth, Alan R. 249 250
Booth family 185 210
Booth, Lionel O. 113
Booth, Richard W. 97 172
Booth, Dr. Robert 245
Booth, Robert 94
Booth, William 137
Borrisokane 40
Bosanquet, Mary 121
Boswell, James 41
Bourne, Hugh 138
Boy Scouts 177
Boyd, Samuel T. 96
Boyd, Willliam R. 107
Boyle 55
Boyle, Alexander 189
Boyles of Kirlish Lodge 38
Boys' Brigade 177
Bradburn, Samuel 153 183 184
Bradney, Mark 140
Bradshaw, David B. 199
Bredin, John 42
Brine, James of Tolpuddle 212
Bristol 20
British Home Mission Fund 94
Brookeborough 36 83
Browne, A. Crawford 97

Budd, William R. 93 96
Building style 82 83
Bunting, Dr. Jabez 139 148
Burgoyne, General 183
Burial 172–174
Butler, Nicholas 36 37

Callaghan, W. Sydney 116
Calvinist controversy 144
Cambridge, Alice 121 122
Cambridge Platonists 147
Camp meetings 137
Campbell, Joseph W. R. 93 96
Campbell, William G. 73
Canada 234 236
Cape of Good Hope 240
'Capt. Moonlight' 97
Carlisle, James 192
Carlisle Memorial church, Belfast
    83 109
Carrickfergus 42 61 138 139 140
Castlebar 32 115 155
Castlecomer 50
Castlepollard 109
Castlereagh, Robert, Viscount 52
Cather, Robert G. 189
Catholic emancipation 66 97
Caughey, Charles 221
'Cavalry Preachers' 57 73
Cavan 64
Celbridge 64
Cemeteries 174
Cennick, John 29 31
Censorship 107
Centenary Church, Dublin 172
Centenary Fund 148
Ceylon 240 241 243
Chambers, John 160
Chaplains to the Forces 101 106
    244
Charity 217
Charlemont 36
Charlotte, Princess 202
Charterhouse School 17 38
Checks to Antinomianism 135
Childhaven 212

China 244 245
Christian Advocate 86 98 99 100
Christian Endeavour 176 177
Christian Library 147 180
Christian Stewardship 118 119
Christians in Ulster 1968–1980 110
Church, Dr. Leslie 107
Church of England in 18th century
    12 13
Church of Ireland 34 44
    bishoprics 'suppressed' 75
    disestablishment 76 77
    evangelical revival 81
    separation from 48 49 62 169
Circuits 131
City missions 90–93
Civil rights 109
Civil War 102
Clarke, Dr. Adam 83 84 128 208
    scholarship 148
Classes 163
    leaders 163
    tickets 165
Clones 62 63
Clones Conference 63
Clonliffe church, Dublin 98
Clontarf church, Dublin 83
Clooney Hall 92
Cloughjordan 35 40 116
Clowes, William 138
Coade, J. Robertson 97
Coade, W. Loftus 160
Cobain, Edward 61
Cobbe, Charles, Archbishop of
    Dublin 29 30 34
Cockroft, John 198
Codling, Arthur Dean 112 209
Co–education 191 194 197
Coke, Rev Dr. Thomas 46 47 48 59
    & Irish Conference3 126–128
    death 240
    in 1798 52
    missions 240
Cole, Francis J. 199
Cole, Richard 86
    R. Lee 96

Coleraine 43 50 51 62
    sacraments 61
Condy, Richard 182
Conference 107 125–128 137
    Cork 1877 129
    first in Ireland 125
    in 1798 51 52
    lay membership 130 136
    presidency 127–129
    venues 129
Conference of European Churches
    249
Connexion 130 131 145
Consecutive History 126
Cooke, William 137
Cooney, Dudley Levistone 118 119
    174
Cooper, Mr. 81
Cootehill 42 43
Cork 32 33 58 135 201 207
    harbour 101
    persecution 36 37
Cornwallis, Charles, Marquess 52
    183
Corrigan, William 96
Cottage meetings 157 158
Coughlan, Laurence 238 239
Countess of Huntingdon's
    Connexion 19 135 136
Courtmatrix 40 231
Covenant Service 167 168
Cownley, Joseph 125
Cradock, William, Dean of St.
    Patrick's 30
Craigmore Home 94 211 212
Cranston, Robert 61
Crawford family 210
Crawford, R. C. Plaice 113
Crawford, William 92 96 99
Creighton, Rev James 45 46
Crompton, Samuel 14
Cromwellian Wars 112 26
Cronhelm, Theodore 85
Crook, John 128
Crook, Dr. Robert 193
Crook, Dr. William 85 232 235

Crookshank, Charles H. 49 73 74
    81 122 221 222
Crosby, Sarah 121 153
Crumlin Road church, Belfast 109
Currin, John 50
Curry, John 65
Curtis, John 44

Dáil Éireann 113
Dawson, Thomas 236
Debtors 202
Delamotte, Charles 19
'Delegate, The' 128 129
Delvin 44
Dempster, James 153
Derriaghy 38 39
De Valera, Eamonn 197
Didsbury College, Manchester 149
Dinnen, John 63 64
Discipline 150–154
Disestablishment 76 77 97
Districts 104 105 132 133
Divorce 224
D'Olier, Dr. Isaac 81 189 209
Donald, Dr. John 85
Donegall Square church, Belfast 87
    109
Donovan, P. Ernest 92 160
Dooley, Thomas 103
Doolittle, Thomas Wade 181
Doran, Wilson 119
Dow, Lorenzo 86 87
Downey House School 194
Downey, John 194
Drew, Samuel 126
Dromore 137 138
Drumgoole, Edward 236
Drumsna 232 236 238
Dublin 28–32 90 138 140
    Marlborough St. 30–32
    meeting time 169
    riot 30
    Wesley Chapel 67
Dublin Central Mission 90–92 207
Dublin Methodist Council 89–91
    Year Book 90

Dugdale, Bennett 67 81 209
Dunbar–Harrison, Letitia 113 114
Duncairn Gardens church 106
Dundalk 71
Dun Emer Guild 188
Dungannon 63
Dungannon Committee 63 64
Dún Laoghaire church 83
Dunmore, Co Galway 54

Eager, Edward 236 237
Easter Rising 1916 102
Eastwell 206
Edenderry 44
Edgar, John 220
Edgehill College 150 194
Edwards, Samuel 31
Ejectment, Great 16
Elderly 207
Ellis, John 126 239
Embury, Margaret Switzer 232 233
Embury, Philip 231–235
    first sermon in New York 233
Emigration 57 98 230 231
Enniscorthy 44 205
Enniskillen 63 64 83 103 110
    riot 35
Enthusiasm 12 34
Epworth 16 17
Epworth Club, Dublin 90 191
Epworth House, Belfast 86 181
Erasmus, Bishop 238
Erskine, George 240 241
Euthanasia 224
Evangelical Alliance 76
Evangelical Revival 13
Evangelism, Superintendent of
    116
Evans, Henry 86 96

Falls Road church 109
Famine 69 70 209 230
Fannin, Dr. Eustace 206
Fannin family 102 210
Fee, Dierdre 244
    John A. T. 244 246

Feely, John 73
Felster, Agnes 31 32
Fentin, Jean 239
Ferguson, William 189
Fermoy 102 103
Field meetings 175
Field preaching 14 20
First World War 101 102
Fisher, John 125 156
Fisher, William 44
Fletcher, John of Madeley 121
    & Calvinist controversy 135
Fleury, Rev George L. 34
Fly boat 37 38
Fogarty, William 193
Foreign Missions 95
Foster, James D. 103
Foster, Mrs. 103
Fox, Charlotte Milligan 98
Fox, Patrick 182 209
France 239
Free Methodist Church 120
Free School for Boys 182 183
Friends, Society of see Quakers
Frugality 216 220
Fuller, Deborah 201
Fullerton, Alexander 161
Fullerton, Alexander M. 93 97
Fulton, George H. 97

Gaelic League 98
Gallagher, Dr. R. D. Eric 110
Galt, John 50 51
Galway 32 127
Gambling 218
Gambold, John 18
Gardner, John 207 208
Gaskell, William 205
Gayer, Henrietta 38
Gayers of Derriaghy 38
General Mission 52–57 73 116
Geoghegan, Patrick 205
George IV 202
Georgia 19
German refugees see Irish
    Palatines

Ghana 245
Gillman, James B. 189
Girl Guides 177
Girls' Brigade 177
Girls' League 123
Gladstone, William Ewart 76 99
Glass, Basil 109
Glenosheen 231
Gloster, near Birr 45
Goderich 242
Gold Triangle 178
Gordon, David 58 136
Graham, Dr. Billy 89
Graham, Charles 53 73
Grand Canal 37 38
Graveyards 174
Gray, W. J. Wesley 116
Great Ejectment 16
Greystones 117
Griffith, Walter 60
Grosvenor Hall, Belfast 91
Guard, Wesley 99
Guides 177
Guier, Philip 126 144
Guiness, Arthur 216
Guinness family 191
Guinness, Michelle 216
Gunne, William 71
Gurley, William 50
Gurteen College 85 117 196–198
    246

Hadden, George 97
Hall, Newman 176
Hall, William 205
Hamilton, William 61
Hammett, James 212
Hampson, John 184
Handy, John 64 68
Handys of Coolalough 38 65
Harbour Grace 238 240
Hardwicke Street, Dublin 187 188
Hargreaves, Josiah 14
Harmoniums 172
Harris, Howell 19 134 140
Hart, Sir Robert 190

Harte, Frederick E. 96
Harvard, William 240
Haskins. Nathaniel R. 160
Haslam, William 138
Haughton, John 125
Hay, Samuel 139 140
Heck, Barbara Ruttle 232–235
   Paul 232–234
Hempton, David 40 58
Henderson, James W. 194
Hepburn, Tommy 214
Herbert, George 147
Herrnhut 20
Hibernian Sunday School Society
   189
Hill, Myrtle 40
Hinds, Griffith 113
Hobart, Samuel 126
Holiness 23
Hollingsworth, Dr. Samuel 188
   191
Holmes Miss P. 123
Holy Club 18 19 201
Home Mission Fund, British 94
Home Mission Fund, Irish 94
Home Rule 97–100
Homosexuality 224
Hughes, Hugh Price 99
Huntingdon, Selina, Countess of
   134 135 140 238
   Connexion 19 135 136
Hymn singing 32 56 88 166
   170–172
Hymns 22 32 147
Hymns & Psalms 89

Increase of the Wesleyan Agency
   187
Independent Methodist Churches
   120
India 240 243
Industrial Revolution 14
Ingham, Benjamin 18 19
Inter–church relations 251
*Ireland and the Centenary of
   American Methodism* 235

Ireland in the 18th century 26 27
Irish American Memorial 235 236
Irish bishoprics 'suppressed' 75
Irish Christian Advocate 86 110 181
Irish Council of Churches 249
Irish Evangelist 85
Irish Folk Song Society 98
Irish Free State 103 104 111 112
Irish Home Mission Fund 94
Irish Ladies Committee 122
Irish language 53 54 56
Irish Literary Revival 98
Irish Methodist Publishing Co 110
   181
Irish Methodist Revival
   Movement 120
Irish Palatines 40 126 231
Irish Republican Brotherhood 98
   100
Itinerancy 144 145

Jebb, Henry, Bishop of Limerick 60
Jefferson, William J. 97
Jeffery, Frederick 58
Jersey 239
Jersey, Francis N. 138
Johnson, Dr. Crawford 91 211
Johnson, John 153
Johnston, James 61
Johnston, John Kerr 189
Johnston, John W. 160
Johnston, Thomas 61
Jones, Alfred Gresham 191
Jones, Edward 141
Jordon, Jeremiah 98
Joyce, Matthias 181
Joynt, George A. 107
Judge, Mrs. 123
Junior Ministers' Convention 159

Kead, Thomas 125
Keble, John 75
Keene, Arthur 67 81 182 184 206
   209
Keene, Isabella 67
Keene, James 67

Keene, Martin 67 189 209
Kells, Co Antrim 73 74
Kelly, Marion 199
Kent, John 221
Ker, John 80
Ker, Robert M. 96
Kerr, John 181
Kerr, Thomas 61
Kerry 53
Kilcooly 231
Kilham, Alexander 136
Killeheen 40 231
Kilkenny 81
Kilrea 43
Kingston, Paul 244
Kirkwood, James 96
Knox, Alexander, Junior 52 60
Knox, Alexander, Senior 52
Kylemore Clinic 159

La Trobe, Benjamin 29
Lay members in Conference 130
   136
Lay missionaries 244
Lamb, Roger 182 183
Lamont, James D. 93 176
Land League 97
Land reform 97
Lanktree, Matthew 61 137
Larne 99
Larwood, Samuel 125
La Trobe, Benjamin 29
Lawrence, John 233
Laymen's Fellowship 116–118
Lay Witness Movement 119–120
Leaders' Meeting 132
'Legal Hundred' 115 127 128
Lending stock 202
Le Sueur, Pierre 239
Letter to a Roman Catholic 41
Levick, George 126
Ligoniel 109 140
Limerick 32 40 135 137
   first Conference 57
Lindsay, David J. 97
Lindsay, Edward R. 110

'Linen Triangle' 40
Lisburn 33 43
   & sacraments 58 59 136
Literacy 186
Lloyd, Richard 45
Lloyds of Gloster 45
Loane, Edith 251
Local Preachers 144 145 163
Lockhart, Eileen 245
Lockhart, Richard A. 246
London Wesleyan Methodist
   Mission 91
Londonderry – property test case
   63 64
Londonderry City Mission 92
Londonderry, Lord 204
Loughbrickland 138
'Lough Erne Rectangle' 40
Loughrea 134 135
Love feast 170
Loveless, George of Tolpuddle 212
Loveless, James of Tolpuddle 212
Lusitania 101
Lumley, William B. 96
Lunell, Anne 29 216
Lunell, William 29 216
Lurgan 137
Lutton, Anne 122
Lynch, James 240 241
Lynn Memorial church, Belfast
   109

McArthur, Sir William 193 194 195
McArthur Halls 194 195
McAulay, Alexander 129
McBurney, John martyred 36
McClelland, Thomas J. 243
McClure, John 136
McClure, William 137
McConnell, Ormonde 244
McCormick, Albert V. 97
McCormick, Nial 113
McCracken, Dr. Thomas M. 158
   159
McCrea, Dr. Alexander 150
McCutcheon, John B. 93

McCutcheon, Dr. Oliver 99
MacDonagh, Thomas 188
McDowell, Samuel 239
McElwaine, Archibald 193
McFarland, John 58
McGeary, John 239
McIntosh, Dr. Maxwell 191
McIvor, W. Basil 108
McKay, Dr. Joseph 222
McKee, Dr. Thomas A. 191
McKenny, John 240 241
McKinney, J. Wesley 197
McKnight, Gordon 195
McLoughlin, Hugh 205
    Widow 205 206
McMullen, Robert B. 97
McQuigg, James 53 55
    Bible translation 55
McQuilkin, James 74

Mackee, Robert 210
Magistrates 34 35 51
Maguire, William 92
Maguire, William E. 160
Maguire, William J. F. 96
Mahy, William 239
Major, John 228
Marlborough Street, Dublin 30 31
    32
Marriage 172–174
Martin, James 184 205
Martyn, Edward 188
Maryborough (Portlaoise) 189
Mason, Abraham 139 148
Mather, Alexander 47 128
Mathew, Theobald 88 221
Maule, Henry, Bishop of Meath 45
Maynooth Grant 76 97
Mayo librarian 114
Megarry, Frank 94
Membership 39 57 68 69 72 104
    111-114
    Primitive Wesleyan 68 69 70 76
Memorable Women 122
Merchant Tailors' Hall, Dublin 135
    136

Mercier, Claude C. 97
Mercier, Samuel T. 97 123
Mercier Mrs S. T. 123
Methodism and the Trade Unions 213
Methodist Child Care Society 211
Methodist Church in Ireland 80
    138
    Acts 96 115
Methodist College 85 98 149 191
    193-195
    Theological Hall 149 150 193
Methodist Episcopal Church in
    America 48 235
Methodist Female Orphan School
    184 204
Methodist Hymn Book 89
Methodist Magazine 180 181
Methodist Missionary Summer
    School 246
Methodist New Connexion 59 136
    137
Methodist Newsletter 110
Methodist Orphan Education
    Trust 185
Methodist Orphan Society 185 211
Methodist Service Book 174
Methodist Stewardship
    Organisation 118 119
Methodist Times 99
Methodist Women's Association
    123
Methodists
    faith 22–24
    first Irish society 28
    origin of name 18
    origins 12 18 20
    sacraments 48 58–61
    separation from Church of
        Ireland 48 49
Mfantsipim 245
Milligan, Alice 98
Millisle 212
Ministerial candidates 105 106
Ministerial development 84 85
Ministers, adoption of title 154 157
Mission partners 243

Mission Praise 89
Monasterevan 64
Moody, Dwight L. 87 88
Moore, Henry 47
Moore, Hugh 153
Moran, Francis 160
Moran, John Hickey 159
Moran, Thomas 101
Moravians 18 19 20 29 31
Morgan, James 153 156
Morgan, Robert 199
Morgan, William 18
Morris, James 125 146
Musical instruments 172
Myles, Gerald G. 192

National Education Board 97 186
Nationalism 98
Neill–Watson, Maureen 245
Newcastle, Duke of 84
Newfoundland 238 239
Newman, John Henry 75 166
Newry 32 43 61 63 64 138
New South Wales 237
Newtownabbey Mission 92
Newtownards 43 136
New York 232–234
Nicholas, Dr. William 93
Nicholson, W. P. 105
Nigeria 245
Normanby, Marquess of 16 17
North Belfast Mission 92 207
North Tipperary 40
Northern Ireland 104 224–228 248
Northridge, Dr. William L. 86 150
    158 159 196 235
Notes on the New Testament 147
Notes on the Old Testament 147

O'Connell, Daniel 66
Oddie, James 156
O'Donovan, Daniel 71
Oglethorpe, General James 19
Old Men's Asylum 207
Oldcastle 64
O'Leary, Arthur 41

O'Leary, John 98
Omagh 98
Ontario 234
Opposition 29 30 34 35
Ormeau Road, Belfast 109
Osborne Park, Balfast 109
O'Sullivan, Seamus *see* Starkey, J. S.
Ouseley, Gideon 54 209 240
    methods 56
Oxford 17 18
    Christ Church College 17 18
    Lincoln College 18

Palatines *see* Irish Palatines
Pallaskenry 42, 231
Palmer, Phoebe 87 221
Palmer, Walter 87
Park, John Oliver 96
Parkhill, James W. 96
Parnell, Thomas 189
Partition 102
Pawnbrokers 218
Pearse, Patrick 98
People's Hall, Belfast 92
Peregrini 230
Pery schooner 232
Pettigo 159
Pilgrimage 230
Pilmoor, Joseph 234
Pim, Susanna 201
Pipe organs 172
Pirrie Park 194
Plan of Pacification 48 49
Plunkett, Countess 188
Plunkett, Hedley W. 116
Plunkett, Joseph M. 188
Politicians 107–109 113
Pope, Dr. W. Burt 80
Portadown 71 83 189
Portaferry 43
Portlaoise 189
Portrush 83 84
Portstewart 83 84
Poverty 204
Preachers 144
    admission 144

discipline 150–154
education 146–150
health 152
length of appointment 156
ordination 157
role 155–159
stipends 160–162
strains 155 156
Presbyterian Assembly's College 150
Presbyterians 42 43
President of the Methodist Church 129
Price, Henry 129
Price, H. Guard 243
Price, Nehemiah 64
Primitive Methodists 65 138 139
    Preston Brooks circuit 138
    Shrewsbury circuit 138
Primitive Physic 203 204
Primitive Street, Belfast 109
Primitive Wesleyan Methodist Society 64 139
    & Disestablishment 76 77
    & Tractarians 75 76
    bookroom 181
    constitution 64 65
    education of ministers 149
    in Canada 242
    membership 68 69 70 76
    reasons for secession 65–67
    reunion 77–80
Primitive Wesleyan Methodist Magazine 181
Prince Edward Island 236
Prosperous 37 38
Psychiatry 158
Psychology 158
Public Advertiser 41
Puritan Divines 147
Pusey, Edward 75

Quakers 43 44
Quarterly Meeting 131 132
'Queen of the Methodists' 134
Queen's University, Belfast 150

Raikes, Robert 188
Rank, Joseph 217
Rank Trust 217
Ranson, Dr. Charles W. 251
Rathcormac 45
Rathgar National School 187
Rathfriland 43
Rathkeale 231
Rattenbury, J. Ernest 166
Rea, James 153
Rectory fire 17
Reece, Richard 128
Reilly, Alfred C. 97
Religious societies 13
Remington, John 239
Repeal 97
Reunion 77–80
Revival 73 74 81
Reynolds, Albert 111
Richey, William 71 72
Richhill 173
Richmond College, London 149
Riots 30 35
Rising in 1798 49–51
Robertson, Dr. John C. 96 150
Robinet, Quartermaster Sergeant 54 55
Robinson, Philip B. 97
Roe, Rev Peter 81
Roquier, Rev Moses 29
Roscrea 103
Ross 64
Rowell, Jacob 125
Royal Irish Constabulary 103
Roycroft, Trevor 86
Rules of a Helper 151 152
Rupp, Gordon 147
Russell, William J. 160
Russian Bell 84
Rutherford, Thomas 153
Ruttle, Barbara 236

Sacraments 48 58–61 136 166 167
    Lisburn 58 59
Sacred Songs & Solos 88 89
Salvation Army 137 196

Sam's Creek, Maryland 233
Sankey, Ira D. 87 88 89
Saratoga 183
Scarva 232
Scotland 47
Scott, Dr. Robinson 190 193 235
Scouts 177
Seale, William 68
Second World War 106 107
Self–confidence 81
Separation from Church of Ireland
    48 49 62 169
Shaw, George Bernard 190 191
She Left her Heart in China 245
Shillington, Thomas 63
Shillington, Thomas Averell 189
Shillington, T. Foulkes 211
Shirley, Walter 134 136
Silcock, Valentine 244
Simmonds ship 19
Simpson, F. Vivian 107 108
Skerries 185
Skibbereen 71
Slackes of Annadale 38
Sligo 61 72 135 232
Sloan, Harold 110
Smiley, William 149
Smith, John 35 36 42
Smith, Patrick 97
Smith, William 126
Smylie, Dr. James 110
Social Responsibility, Council on
    223
Social Welfare, Council on 196 197
    198 222–228
Society for the Promotion of
    Christian Knowledge 13
Society for the Propagation of the
    Gospel 13 238
Society of Friends see Quakers
South Africa 240 241
Special Evangelistic Agency 181
Stanfield, John of Tolpuddle 212
Stanfield, Thomas of Tolpuddle
    212
Starkey, James Sullivan 98

Starkey, William 72 98
'Statutory Trustees' 96
Steele, Samuel 61
Stephenson, George 61
Stewart, James 160
Stewart, William 189
Stillingfleet, Edward 46
Stirling, Mr. 97
Stopford, Joseph 207
Stormont 107–109
Strabane 61
Stranger's Friend Society 207–210
Strawbridge, Robert 232–235 238
Stretton, John 239 240
Sturgeon, Alexander 61
Sullivan, James 98
Sunday Schools 188 189
Sunday School Society of Ireland
    189
Sutcliffe, Joseph 58 59
'Swaddlers' 31 36
Swanlinbar 45
Swanton, James H. 71
Swindells, Robert 41 125
Synods 133

Tackaberry, Fossey 72
Tailors' Hall, Dublin 135 136
Tandragee 61 232
Tayler, Antisel 29
Taylor, George 50
Taylor, Jeremy 147
Tea drinking 219 220
Teacher training 187 188
Temperance 218–221
Templemore 103
Terryhoogan 232 233
Theological Institution 139 148
Thomey, Arthur 240
Thompson, Frederick 108
Thompson, George W. 96
Thompson, John H. 94 97
Thompson, Joseph 140
Thompsopn, Mrs J. H. 122
Thompson, William 127
Thompson, Sir William J. 97

Tidd, Christopher 145
Tighes of Rosanna 38
Tillotson, John, Archbishop of
    Canterbury 16
Tobias, Matthew 221
Tolpuddle Martyrs 212 213
Tone, Theobald Wolfe 49
Toplady, Augustus Montague 146
Torrey, Reuben 87
Total Abstinence 88 218 221 222
Tractarian Movement 75 166 167
Trade Unions 138 212–214
Trembath, John 30
Trench, Julia 198
Trench, Patrick 197
Trevecca College 134 140
Trustees 95 96
Tuam 32
Tullamore 122
Turtle, Dr. Hugh 150 212
Turtle, Mrs. 212
Twentieth Century Fund 93 94
Tyrrellspass 33

Ulster Unionist Convention 99
Ulster Volunteer Force 99
Uniformity, Act of 16
United Irishmen 49
United Methodist Church 137
United Methodist Church,
    America 236
United Methodist Free Churches
    137 140
University Road, Belfast 83

van Alstyne, Fanny Crosby 89

Wades of Aughrim 38 68
Walker, John 52
Walker, Robin 192
Walker, Solomon 183
Wallace, Robert 235
Walpole, Horace 134
Walsh, Thomas 35 125 126
    career 41 42
    scholarship 148
    strain 156

Walton, Ernest T. S. 192 198
Warburton, Whitelaw & Walsh
    205
Warren, Dr. Samuel 139 140
Waterford 64 135 137 210 211
    riot 35
Waterford Fever Hospital 210
Waugh, Thomas 189
Wearmouth, Robert F. 213
Weavers' Hall, Dublin 136
Webster, George R. 160
Wedgwood, George R. 93 96
Wedgwood, Josiah 14
Welsh Calvinistic Methodist
    Church 19 140
'Welsh Chapel', Dublin 141
Wesley Chapel, Cork 102
Wesley Chapel, Dublin 67
Wesley, Charles 17 18 20
    bicentenary 90
    hymns 22 23 32 89 170
    in Georgia 19
    in Ireland 31 32
Wesley, John 12 13 37
    & Calvinist controversy 134 135
    & Charles Cobbe 29 30
    & Church of Ireland 29 30
    & Irish Catholics 40 41
    & Irish language 40 41
    & Moravians 20 29 31
    & Presbyterians 42 43
    & Quakers 43 44
    & Skinners' Alley 31
    at Aldersgate Street 19 20
    at Bristol 20
    at Oxford 17 18
    character 21
    childhood 17
    compassion 153 154
    death 46
    discipline 150-153
    education 17 18
    electricity 203
    encourages women preachers
        120 121
    fever 38 39

first field sermon 20
first Irish visit 29
foundation stone 32
Georgia 19
Grand Canal journey 37 38
Letter to a Roman Catholic 41
Notes on the New Testament 147
Notes on the Old Testament 147
ordination 18
Primitive Physic 203 204
singing 171
stamina 30
World parish 237 238
Wesley, John of Winterbourne
    Whitechurch 16
Wesley, Samuel of Epworth 16 17
Wesley, Susanna 16 17
Wesley College 85 185 188 191 192
Wesley Historical Society 199 200
Wesleyan Connexional School 190
    191
Wesleyan Methodist Association
    140 148
Wesleyan Methodist Collegiate
    Institution 193
Wesleyan Methodist Missionary
    Society 95 149 241 242
Wesleyan Methodist School
    Society 186
Wesleyan Methodists 65
West Cork 40
West, George M. 64 65
Wexford 50
Whalley, Ellen 123 124
White family 210
White, James 160
Whitefield, George 18 20 134 140
Whitefriar Street, Dublin 32 181
    182
Whitford, John 125
Whither Methodism? 120
Whitla Halls 194
Whitla, Jones 103
Whitla, Sir William 97 99 150 194
    195 196

Widows' Almshouse 184 204 205
    206
Wild, James 126
Wilkinson, Alexander 63
Williamite Wars 27
Williams, Robert 140 141 153
Williams, Thomas 29 30 31 41
Willoughby, Charles 113
Wilson, Dist. Insp. 103
Wilson, Gordon 110 111
    Marie 110
Wiseman, Caroline 123
Wisheart, James 116
Wolfe, Jasper 113
Wolfe, Dr. Sally 245
Women 121 123 242 245
Women's Auxiliary 123
Women's Department 123 175 176
Wolrd Council of Churches 249
'World is my Parish, The' 237
World Methodist Council 249
World poverty 215
Worrall, Dr. Stanley 110 195
Worship 82 166–169
Wright, Stanley F. 190

Youghal 72
Young Men's Christian
    Association 196
Young Women's Association 123
Youth Clubs 178

Zinzendorf, Nikolaus, Count von
    20